SLAVE SITES ON DISPLAY

**AFRICAN
DIASPORA
MATERIAL
CULTURE**

Jessica B. Harris, General Editor

SLAVE SITES ON DISPLAY

Reflecting Slavery's Legacy through Contemporary "Flash" Moments

HELENA WOODARD

University Press of Mississippi / Jackson

Publication of this book was made possible in part by a generous donation
from the President's Office of the University of Texas at Austin.

The University Press of Mississippi is the scholarly publishing agency of
the Mississippi Institutions of Higher Learning: Alcorn State University,
Delta State University, Jackson State University, Mississippi State University,
Mississippi University for Women, Mississippi Valley State University,
University of Mississippi, and University of Southern Mississippi.

www.upress.state.ms.us

The University Press of Mississippi is a
member of the Association of University Presses.

First printing 2019

∞

All photographs were taken by the author unless otherwise indicated.

Library of Congress Cataloging-in-Publication Data

Names: Woodard, Helena, 1953– author.
Title: Slave sites on display : reflecting slavery's legacy through
contemporary flash moments / Helena Woodard.
Description: Jackson : University Press of Mississippi, [2019] | Series:
African diaspora material culture series | "First printing 2019." |
Includes bibliographical references and index.
Identifiers: LCCN 2019006709 (print) | LCCN 2019022332 (ebook) | ISBN
9781496824165 (hardcover : alk. paper) | ISBN 9781496824172 (pbk. : alk. paper)
Subjects: LCSH: Slavery—United States—History. | African diaspora.
Classification: LCC E441 .W874 2019 (print) | LCC E441 (ebook) | DDC
306.3/620973—dc23
LC record available at https://lccn.loc.gov/2019006709
LC ebook record available at https://lccn.loc.gov/2019022332

British Library Cataloging-in-Publication Data available

CONTENTS

SLAVE SITES ON DISPLAY

The Abolition of the Slave Trade by Isaac Cruikshank. Library of Congress, Prints and Photographs Division, LC-USZC4-6204.

INTRODUCTION

The temporal status of any act of memory is always the present and not, as
some naïve epistemology might have it, the past itself, even though all memory
in some ineradicable sense is dependent on some past event or experience.[1]
—Andreas Huyssen, *Twilight Memories*

Like the dead-seeming, cold rocks, I have memories within that came out
of the material that went to make me. Time and place have had their say.[2]
—Zora Neale Hurston, *Dust Tracks on a Road*

Rather than invent a world, I want a different means to understand this one.[3]
—Jena Osman, *The Network*

At a slavery exhibit, "And Still We Rise," at Detroit's Charles Wright Museum,
a horrific image greets the visitor. The illustrator, Isaac Cruikshank, in a replica of the eighteenth-century sketch titled *The Abolition of the Slave Trade*,
depicts a young African girl suspended upside down on a slave ship while
the captain brandishes a whip nearby. On display is a whip in a glass frame,
flanked by a narrative panel that reads: "Captain John Kimber fell afoul of the
law in 1792. He was accused of whipping an enslaved African girl to death
because she refused to dance naked on the deck of the slave ship. He was
arrested, tried, and acquitted by a jury that said the girl died of disease."[4] In
April 1792, implying the girl's alleged pregnancy and her right to protect her
modesty, abolitionist William Wilberforce delivered a speech about the episode before the House of Commons as part of an effort to end the slave trade.
Following Wilberforce's speech, Isaac Cruikshank created the illustration,
which further sensationalized the incident.

At England's Birmingham Museum, in a special temporary exhibit in 2007
that honored author and former slave Olaudah Equiano and also commemorated the two hundredth anniversary of the ending of the slave trade, a film
short also featured the Cruikshank sketch. *Dance Is Us and Dance Is Black*,
produced by British choreographer Rodrequez King-Dorset, shows an animated reenactment of the girl's beating, complete with sounds of a cracking

whip and piercing screams. The scene then switches from past to present, from animation to live performance, and the slave girl is transformed into a ballerina who is joined in partnership by a young male dancer. This film uses Cruikshank's illustration to tell a different story: the choreographer imagines that the girl is reunited with a fantasy partner—the man of her dreams—in a pas de deux that expresses neither fear nor "sadistic pain, but [only] the joy and passion of a first love."[5]

As the museum exhibits at Detroit and Birmingham demonstrate, the enslaved girl's murder, which caused a sensation in England in 1792 and inspired the famous sketch, has regained currency more than two centuries after the incident occurred. (Indeed, images of the Cruikshank sketch exist at other museum exhibitions in the United States and in the United Kingdom.) But while the Detroit exhibit replicates the incident as yet another atrocity committed upon the body of an unidentified slave, the Birmingham exhibit disrupts time and space, and imagines the girl's autonomy to command her own performance. Rather than stage the dance as a compulsory, demeaning mode of entertainment for the slave ship's captain and crew, the choreographer offers it as a communicative cultural expression through narration and performance for the modern-day spectator.

That the exhibit at Birmingham conflates aesthetic forms long established in black expressive discourse is not a novel convention. Through a creative exhibition aided by modern technology, the choreographer transforms the enslaved girl's fate from a life brutally cut short in the eighteenth century to one that freedom and progress make possible in the twenty-first century. In so doing, the exhibition does not just transform a past traumatic event from official archival records into a revisionist reproduction or reconstructed material. It also radically alters the ways in which the event is remembered, as well as the manner in which the enslaved subject is depicted. That disconnect between archiving the slave past and altering the ways in which it is remembered and/or rewritten for public consumption in the present day is the primary focus of my study.

Through historical intervention, Rodrequez King-Dorset's *Dance Is Us and Dance Is Black* counters the demeaning, brutal "dance of death" on the deck of a slave ship by staging a "dance of deliverance" for an unnamed slave girl who will forever remain unknowable. The exhibition therefore poses as both rehabilitative art for her fate and critical engagement with colossal failures in the archival record. But it also typifies limitations of a recuperative agenda that seeks to repair or otherwise restore a disembodied slave subject in futurity. Even at trial in the eighteenth century, slavery advocates characterized the young slave girl as a prostitute, while abolitionists designated her as a virginal Venus, thus projecting her as a symbol for their respective causes, rather than as an individual in her own right. Similarly utilizing the anonymous slave girl's story as a teachable model for contemporary generations fuels debate about the potential exploitation of the slave subject that might further objectify her through a neoliberal discourse, a concept that favors leftist, well-meaning remedies that could still have negative effects. Saidiya Hartman, in "Venus in Two Acts" and in *Lose Your Mother: A Journey along the Atlantic Slave Route*, deconstructs the enslaved girl's beating death, the ship captain's subsequent acquittal at trial, and the widely circulated, prurient sketch of her by Isaac Cruikshank. But she rejects the slave girl's "resurrection" through revisionist narratives that would utilize her as a teachable moment for present-day aims. Through a call-and-response figuration with Hartman in his book *In the Break: The Aesthetics of the Black Radical Tradition*, Fred Moten insists that even excoriating such practices necessarily replicates or at least revisits that exploitation. But he also recognizes the dilemma of reporting the young girl's egregious treatment and murder by an enslaver "without exacerbating the indifference to suffering that is the consequence of the benumbing spectacle."[6]

In this study of the seemingly intractable problem described above, I find a growing number of modern-day slave sites and revisionist exhibitions in the global community particularly instructive and relatable, but only when grounded in a specific, contemporary cultural and social milieu or geopolitical framework, such as community, environment, and racial ideology, contiguous with the slave past. Consequently, I am especially interested in how select modern-day slave sites and exhibitions—including the renovated slave fort, slave burial ground, reconstructed slave ship, and Bench by the Road slave memorial at Sullivan's Island—respond to the political economy of the conditions in which they are displayed. Each of the sites that I examine in this study accesses a distinct historical dimension, such as the slave's imprisonment and deportation from an African homeland, the Middle Passage journey across the Atlantic, and burial in unmarked graves. In addition, each tells a story about the slave past, relative to the lived experiences of the disproportionately diaspora slave descendants that organize and visit these sites. Though they differ from one another, all of these sites are displayed as slave memorials or monuments that function as high-profile tourist attractions, structured mostly in outdoor settings as either fixed or movable objects, as opposed to displays inside a traditional museum edifice.

I have chosen to focus on sites associated with slave trafficking in the triangular Atlantic slave trade routes where modern-day visitation—particularly by diaspora slave descendants usually guided by an oral historian—is most prevalent. Most important for the purposes of this study, I find these sites especially readable through contemporary "flash" moments: specific circumstances and/or seminal events within a geopolitical framework that binds the history of Atlantic slavery to its continued resonance or impact in the present. Hence, my critique of diverse slave sites in the past-to-present framework of this study hinges upon the need to expose their complex intersections with the instability, volatility, and unsettledness of race and slavery in modern times.

I contend that slave recovery through visual displays is not the result of an exact process yielded through meticulous research and discovery, but rather the product of instability, uncertainty, even chaos, extracted from an ultimately irretrievable past. The most pressing critical questions that I address in this study pertain to untapped iterations culled from that instability. Whether diaspora slave descendants to these commemorative slave sites around the globe are formal museumgoers, voyeuristic spectators, or active participants, they are quite often slave descendants generally seeking healing, restitution, and/or reclamation of African and African American culture as a profoundly personal experience. This shared quest motivates many of them, perhaps because of unresolved issues pertaining to slavery, including racial disparities, economic inequities, and modern-day slave trafficking. This collective or group, whom I identify as those in the diaspora who descend from enslaved Africans, gravitates toward artifacts, objects, memorials, and other reconstructed materials as part of an effort to grasp the "real" of slavery because of an inability to retrieve the lives and histories of actual slaves, who of course remain partially or completely invisible at these sites. But stymied by the "absent presence" of the enslaved subject and often in league with exhibition organizers, visitors almost instinctively enact the daunting task of resurrecting and re-embodying a fragmented slave history through performative practices that are intensely public and sometimes controversial. Consequently, out of the residues that slavery leaves behind, the audiences in search of monuments, memorials, and traveling exhibits are themselves disproportionately diaspora slave descendants who reconstruct a world that transitions to modern-day racial dilemmas.

The creators of slave sites face a difficult choice—indeed a double bind: on the one hand, to deemphasize or ignore the legacy of slavery in order to focus on the past, and on the other, to present the slave sites as "an unforgiving mirror of the present" and thereby overshadow the past.[7] But I see reflections of slavery's legacy coterminous with ongoing, present-day racial dilemmas as the most practical and revealing aspect of the modern-day slave site. Consequently, in this study I ponder how a slave site that symbolizes the past can also express itself opportunistically as that unforgiving mirror.

To clarify my objectives, I first turn to a strident formulation of a past/present praxis that favors what Walter Benjamin has called "the time of the now," or the now of recognizability, because it exposes the interconnectedness of past and present events.[8] Though grounded in the Holocaust, Benjamin's recalibrations of a past/present dialectical constellation through "flash" moments and illuminating images, rather than through a linear temporal progression, have the potential to redefine the slave past, which still infringes upon the lives of diaspora slave descendants. The famous Klee drawing of the "Angelus Novus" represents Benjamin's conception in the *Ninth Thesis on the Philosophy of History* of an elusive historical progression.[9] That angel of history symbolizes the illusion of historical progress, warning instead of catastrophic dangers lurking in the ruin heaps of the past and potentially visited on the present and future.

For Benjamin, the flash moment is not the past in a literal sense, but a memory that arises in a moment of danger, such as when conformity or past traditions are threatened by radical change. Though Benjamin does not exactly suggest that the past will reoccur as future events, he points to ruinous devastation when lessons from the past are not heeded. Here, I adapt the concept of the flash moment, well known in Holocaust studies, to the context of racial slavery because of its potential to shed light on a recidivist slave past— that is, one that repeats itself in less recognizable form. The "flash" moment (or defining moment, somewhat interchangeably, as I refashion it) is akin to what David Crouch describes as "moments of occurrence," or "things as they happen."[10] While events ebb and flow over time, through seminal events or specific circumstances, an object or exhibition that functions as a slave site can move from a state of immobility to animation. In other words, the site exists as a celebrated object merely through its display until an idea or seminal event calls attention anew to its raison d'être. At that point, the site functions not so much as a representation of its connection with the slave past as part of a process of interactions that redefine it under specific conditions in which it is displayed in the present.

I favor, as an apt example of the flash moment process, the epistemology of Jena Osman's riveting, postmodern poetic collection titled *The Network*, which threads together past and present events about race, slavery, and empire through etymology and word derivatives. The richness of this complex work is its genealogical charting of certain words in modern usage that differ sharply from their linguistic origins, and that connect thematically with what Osman identifies as networks. Derivatives for "peace," for example, include "appease," "pay," and "propaganda," while "admonish" and "monument" share origins with "money."[11] The tracing of words in current usage to origins that define them far differently prepares the reader for Osman's ultimate tour de force—the construction of a kind of maze, cycling through five networks that thematize specific events in history. Particularly relevant to my study, she connects two networks titled "Financial District" and "The Joker" with a series of historical circumstances that pertain to race and slavery. In "Financial District," for example, she chronicles Wall Street from its construction and maintenance through enslaved labor in seventeenth century New York under Dutch and, later, British occupation—followed by American Independence—to its current status as the nation's premier financial district. The remains of enslaved decedents lie buried beneath the area that includes Wall Street near the African Burial Ground National Monument, which I examine in chapter 2 in this study.

In "The Joker," Osman traces the production of sugar from enslaved labor in the Atlantic slave trade to a curious revelation about its marketing process before its arrival on the consumer's table. She writes that dark sugar, long harvested by slaves, had to be chemically altered at a refinery through an expensive process in order to produce purity through whiteness deemed highly marketable and appealing for consumers. Osman writes, "Before the dark sugar / is put on the / American table / it must go to a refinery to be whitened" (25). But the chemical whitening process that was needed to obtain purity—"above No. 16 Dutch standard color"—led to a prohibitively high tariff on imported sugar (25). Osman cites congressional hearings held in 1912 in which legislators challenged the American Sugar Refining Company's monopoly on the industry.

At those hearings, Representative Thomas Hardwick, chair of the proceedings, stated, "The contention is often made, and it is popular throughout the country among a great many people, that the Dutch standard is the real "nigger in the woodpile," as we say down South."[12] Hardwick further mused that if the white sugar were nonexistent, the consumer would be none the wiser, because the dark sugar, while less attractive and appealing, would be just as healthy and much cheaper in price. Through these congressional hearings—a "flash" moment in time—Osman reveals the circuitous route of enslaved laborers' contributions, literally and figuratively, to the financial difference of a "pure" brand of sugar that finds its way to the consumer's table. She thus aligns an originary moment in the slave past with a surprising revelation about its trajectory into the present.

A reconception of Osman's methodology for the modern-day slave site in my study discloses the unique relationship between certain interlocking events and circumstances that move the site well beyond its literal perception as an object or artifact. Like the paint factory scene in Ralph Ellison's *Invisible Man* in which optic white paint actually contains black and white traces, the premium sugar approved by the industry contained an amalgamation of dark and light ingredients. When Osman writes, "How to map a changing thing, rather than a target of frozen / particulars," I perceive that while objects and artifacts remain unchanged, transformative events that occur over time can alter the way that we interpret them (3). Put another way, Osman later makes an observation that serves as a key premise for *The Network*—and reinforces my own objectives in the process. She writes, "Rather than invent a world, I want a different means to understand this one" (38). I believe that the legacy that slavery leaves us is the way in which we view things beneath the surface, around the edges, and in the interstices.

In its saliency a defining moment or seminal event can force new scrutiny of the subject (and objects) of race and slavery. It is illuminating like a flash of light or crystalizing like an aha moment. Likened to a newsworthy item that appears without warning over an Associated Press wire, a "flash" moment can quickly change the course of events. It can make the essential difference between an awe-inspiring exhibition and the social and cultural milieu that clarifies it. The contemporary "flash" moment or seminal event raises awareness and provokes conversation about the unfinished business of slavery, such as the lack of a national dialogue on the subject, and exposes the tenets of a virulent, cyclical slavery for contemporary generations. It offers new ways to observe slavery's omnipresence in a purportedly postracial era.

Scholars of racial slavery and critical race theory disagree about whether the slave past is credibly a gloss on present-day social and political conditions for diaspora slave-descendant blacks, whether an antiquated narrative about black victimhood has run its course, or whether there is any credence at all for a shared legacy in slavery for blacks in the modern era. Orlando Patterson, for example, has long argued the importance for black Americans to shed their entrenchment in a cultural heritage. He writes, "In a world where every group still strives to be unique, to preserve its past, and to hold sacred the principle of continuity, a group which discards uniqueness and spurns tradition will by that very fact become unique in a truly revolutionary way." Charles Johnson, in "The End of the Black American Narrative," famously argued, on the cusp of Barack Obama's election as president in 2008, that a persistent pattern of victimhood had overshadowed significant progress and substantial change for black Americans. Perhaps the most controversial salvo came from Ken Warren, who argued in the book *What Was African American Literature?* that the legal ending of Jim Crow laws has upended the consistency of African American literature rooted in that context.[13] Meanwhile, in an intriguing discussion more akin to my concerns about the past/present binaries of slavery, Stephen Best finds that "a sense of racial belonging rooted in the historical dispossession of slavery" for black Americans is "unstable ground on which to base a politics."[14]

I find the turn in debate that disassociates the slave past from its continued impact in the present for slave-descendant blacks specious and premature at best. In the context of postslavery, Reconstruction policies, and Jim Crow laws, Douglas A. Blackmon, in *Slavery by Another Name: The Re-Enslavement of Blacks from the Civil War to World War II*, infers quite validly that a repetitive slavery through peonage, black codes, and other Jim Crow era practices can still account for an assortment of present-day political and socioeconomic travails for blacks. And although observers rightly point to great strides in race relations since slavery, Reconstruction, and the Jim Crow era, a backward slide that Ari Berman, in *Give Us the Ballot: The Modern Struggle for Voting Rights in America*, likens to a "third Reconstruction" enshrouds a so-called postracial climate in the Age of Obama presidency. Meanwhile, Ta-Nehisi Coates, in *We Were But Eight Years in Power: An American Tragedy*, likens President Obama's eight years in office to a "flash" moment in time during the Reconstruction era when a black congressman cited eight years as the brief time in which the Fifteenth Amendment benefited black male voters, before loopholes through peonage, black codes, and Jim Crow policies virtually nullified that amendment.

Toni Morrison, a central voice in, and contributor to, discussions about slavery's historical accountability in the present, has directly challenged some of the critical opinions expressed above. Given the unparalleled success of her Pulitzer Prize–winning novel *Beloved* (1987), Morrison's comments and observations from interviews, speeches, and writings about slavery place her at the forefront of those who validate slavery's omnipresence and vigorously champion its importance as inexhaustible subject matter. In 2006 several hundred "prominent writers, critics, and other literary sages" who answered a *New York Times Book Review* editor's request to rate contemporary fiction in America, voted *Beloved* "the single best work of American fiction published in the last 25 years."[15] Indeed, Morrison has been so forthright and effective in profoundly defending the attention currently given to slavery's continued relevance for contemporary generations, that in order to oppose her viewpoints credibly, it seems that critics must first challenge, deconstruct, or at least question her beliefs about this subject before going on to express their own ideas.

In his article "On Failing to Make the Past Present," Stephen Best discusses a shift in Morrison's views about slavery, which he channels largely through her ninth novel, *A Mercy*. Best claims that Morrison "[refuses] to make the slave past the progenitor of the existential condition of black people, or of black people alone" (473). Indeed, he makes an apt observation about a novel that maps the early, chaotic stages of colonial settlement as follows: "1682 and Virginia was still a mess" (11)! But armed with the iterations of Morrison's "latest meditation on race and slavery," he further casts doubt on "an unassailable truth that the slave past provides a ready prism for apprehending the black political present" (454). Best, in his macrocosmic approach, accounts for slavery, race, and difference as broadly conceived and disavows that a collective fate or shared personal experience exists for black or nonblack people.

But to rely upon *A Mercy* (even as Morrison's most recent publication on race and slavery) for a definitive opinion on solidarity among a black collective is highly speculative. With a fledgling nation so unsettled and unsettling before slavery was "raced" and before race was ideology, there is little wonder that Best would seek "to clear some space for a black politics not animated by a sense of collective condition or solidarity" as a benchmark of a past-to-present praxis (454). But although Morrison published *A Mercy* in 2011, the events in that novel predate those in *Beloved* by nearly two centuries, and the latter work presents an altogether different perspective on past and present connections that pertain to slavery. Would it not be just as valid, then, to read Morrison's reflections on race and slavery through the chronology of events in those novels rather than through their publication dates?

Setting aside, for the moment, the perils of touting *A Mercy*—whether in the context of a critique on a purportedly postracial society in the Age of Obama, or as a personal mouthpiece for Morrison about the slave past—it is worth noting that the author is also known for revealing comments that she has made specifically about slave memorials in a past-to-present framework. In a speech and interview published in *World Magazine* in 1989, Morrison famously expressed a desire for the construction of slave memorials—"a three-dimensional thing," as she coined it—to commemorate those captive Africans who were imported into the United States.[16] Her quest eventually led to the first Bench by the Road's placement as a slave memorial at Sullivan's Island, South Carolina, in 2008, which I discuss in this study as a slave site. At least nine out of the more than twenty additional Bench projects between 2008 and 2016 have been placed at locations that commemorate the work of abolitionists and other freedom fighters. When asked in that interview about her desire to create a commemorative slave memorial, Morrison upheld the link between the historical past and the present by commenting on its importance within her own multigenerational family. Her comments also stress the significance of past and present connections for contemporary generations, an observation that she further elaborated upon in a seminal essay titled "The Ancestor as Foundation." In the *World Magazine* interview, Morrison said that she never felt apart from or distanced from history, adding, "I can't explain to you why I think it's important but I really do."[17] And though she said that she had no particular design, individual, "or even any art form" in mind for the memorial, she said, "It can be small, some place where you can go put your feet up" (8–9).

By acknowledging the importance of a nearness to history and a "hunger for a permanent place," Morrison affirms the slave past and its present-day connections for diaspora slave descendants. Furthermore, she anticipates the Bench by the Road slave project's implementation by members of the Toni Morrison Society, a nonprofit group of scholars who study the author's canon. Later, in an essay titled "The Site of Memory," Morrison negotiated how that past can be made available as a living memory to contemporary generations that never experienced or witnessed slavery. She addressed this conundrum through "rememory," the complex evocative concept that she coined in *Beloved*, which explains the importance of knowing the slave past but without the perils of its repetitive practices. For example, she writes that one can access the imagination in order to "journey to a site to see what remains were left behind and to reconstruct the world that these remains imply."[18]

In "The Site of Memory," Morrison alludes to archival gaps, silences, and omissions in the slave past: "the absence of the interior life, the deliberate excising of it from the records that the slaves themselves told is the problem in the discourse that proceeded without us."[19] She adds that one can access the imagination to "journey to a site to see what remains were left behind and to reconstruct the world that these remains imply." But that nuanced process, which Morrison refers to as "literary archaeology," transcends the fictive realm that she intends and also enacts a "visual archaeology" of slavery for site organizers and spectators that reconstruct that past through commemorative sites. While Morrison looms large, here, through incisive theoretical commentaries and epistemologies about a past/present dialectic that governs slavery, I focus broadly on these slave sites in which fiction plays only an ancillary role. I contend that Morrison's call for—and the later installation of—a commemorative slave memorial mediates the dialectic between disparate ideas about race and slavery that she posits in *A Mercy* and *Beloved*. Since unresolved issues pertaining to the slave past remain a core concern, contemporary "flash" moments and/or seminal events, placed in conversation with modern-day slave sites, fuel a larger debate about why policies fail, why slavery lingers, why it still wounds, and how slave sites can heal.

Overview of Slave Sites

In a historical context, the slave fort as a black heritage site functions as a holding cell where slaves were imprisoned prior to their deportation from West Africa across the Atlantic through the Middle Passage in the Atlantic slave trade. But in chapter 1, "Iconic Sons of Africa 'in the Belly of the Stone Monster,'" I examine the fort as an allegorical space in which slavery's residues in the modern world distill, homogenize, and collide, especially at specific moments of racial conflict, politicization, and contestation. At the House of Slaves at Dakar, Senegal, for example, official appearances by then-sitting presidents Bill Clinton, George W. Bush, and Barack Obama, respectively (who also visited Ghana's Cape Coast Castle), opportunistically cede the international heritage site as a magnet for discussion about apologies, reparations, and responsibility for the Atlantic slave trade. But in spite of these historical events, none discussed apologies, reparations, modern-day slave trafficking, or the US role in the Atlantic slave trade.

Standing in the infamous "Door of No Return" at the fort, President Bush spoke movingly about Olaudah Equiano's captivity in Africa, but on the cusp of academic debate about his true identity as an African-born, eighteenth-century slave.[20] As another iconic, transnational "Son of Africa" in appearance at Cape Coast Castle, President Obama stood at the epicenter of discourse about belonging, dispossession, and the myth of return. His presidential visit to the House of Slaves renewed conversation about whether that fort actually functioned as an authentic slave deportation site, as told to tourists for over forty years by renowned griot-oral historian the late Joseph N'diaye. Through these "flash" moments or seminal events, the slave fort exposes deep tensions and ironic implications about slavery's long reach to its present-day consequences. I explore here the possibility that the signifiers of authenticity are symptomatic of an imperial lens in an academic or dominant culture arena, regardless of, and perhaps in tandem with, claims of archival evidence. In other words, the slave fort plays host, then, to seminal defining moments that document the struggle of marginalized groups for control of narrative, knowledge, and racial ideologies that pertain to slavery.

I am inspired by Arjun Appadurai, who theorizes "authenticity" in the context of an imperial authority, albeit mostly to determine the value of commodities and things. He writes, "There is an increasingly ironic dialogue between the need for ever-shifting criteria of authenticity in the West and the economic motives of . . . producers and dealers."[21] While the prestige of objects can be determined in this way, altering or manipulating the criteria of authenticity can also explain how groups can be marginalized through practices that exclude them from belonging and that devalue their cultural traditions.

The remains of up to ten thousand Africans whose ancestors made the passage from forts like Elmina Castle, Cape Coast Castle, and the House of Slaves may well be entombed in unmarked graves at the African Burial Ground in New York's Lower Manhattan. As I explore in chapter 2, "'Talking Bones' at the African Burial Ground in New York," seminal events in the creation of the slave site necessarily begin with the burial ground's (re)discovery during construction of the Ted Weiss Federal Office Building in 1991. But they also extend to massive demonstrations that predominantly slave-descendant groups necessarily undertook in order to ensure respect for the humanity of the burial ground decedents through the handling of remains. Indeed, the African Burial Ground National Monument at 290 Broadway that now marks the mass gravesite signals a significant shift in empowerment for diaspora slave-descendant Africans, or what Pierre Nora calls "a process of interior decolonization [that] has affected ethnic minorities, families, and groups that until now possessed reserves of memory but little or no historical capital."[22]

It is worth noting that post–civil rights era endeavors to transform the status of anonymous slave decedents at the African Burial Ground through forensic analysis, burial rites, and installation of an official monument wholly converge with activists' reassertion of a formidable self-identity (by proxy) with enslaved remains. But through its close proximity to Wall Street and Broadway—New York's premier financial and entertainment districts—the African Burial Ground National Monument also demonstrates a subsistence on, and entrenchment in, the slave past for slave decedents and their descendants. In other words, while the former participated in Wall Street's very construction and maintenance, the latter now occupy its margins.

Unlike the African Burial Ground in New York, slave burial sites at iconic presidential estates foreground the political economy of a self-identity sustained by historical memory through what I refer to as "genealogical dispossession." I submit that in spite of slave-descendants' influence on new slave memorials and special exhibitions installed at Washington's Mount Vernon, Jefferson's Monticello, and Jackson's Hermitage in recent years, a conspiratorial silencing of the "familial" slave masks their broader implications for racial ideology. Allegations through oral testimonies have long linked some slave-descendant African American families with Washington, Jefferson, and Jackson through master–slave "miscegenated" relationships (though only Jefferson's lineage has been subjected to genetic testing that validated familial slavery). The enslaved laborer at presidential estates therefore transforms from a liminal status to an emergent oneness within a patrilineal society. The slave's preeminence thus resides not only in "nation building" through brick and mortar or flora and fauna at Washington's Mount Vernon, Jefferson's Monticello, and Jackson's Hermitage but also in iconography and imaging. In chapter 3, "Founding Fathers, Chimeras, and 'American Africanisms' at Presidential Estates," I therefore subscribe to what Pierre Nora aptly refers to as "a completely new economy of the identity of the self."[23] In other words, I place the addition of modern-day slave memorials at these residences in conversation with disclosures about the familial slave and genealogical dispossession. These disclosures address consequences of a multiracial heritage for slaves and their descendants in the face of continued denial, erasure, amnesia, or willful neglect.

In chapter 4, "The Postmodern, Traveling Slave Ship Exhibitions and the 'Neo' Middle Passenger," or the only moving museum sites that I examine in this study, I explore a series of seminal moments that occur during exhibitions of the reconstructed *Zong*, the *Freedom Schooner Amistad*, and the *Henrietta Marie* slave ships. Here, I refigure the globally dispersed transnational patron—namely, diaspora slave-descendant Africans that disproportionately view these ships—as secondary witnesses, not so much to slavery itself as to present-day inequities that mirror or even mimic past forms of bondage. Those individuals and collectives whom I refer to in this chapter as "neo" Middle Passengers include a multiethnic Christian group at the *Zong* exhibit in London, an aging, slave-descendant seafarer aboard the *Freedom Schooner Amistad* at Charleston, and docents at the *Henrietta Marie* exhibition in US cities. Collectively, they reconstitute the enigmatic Atlantic Middle Passage experience through reconstructed materials and commemorative practices. But while celebrating historical progression in the demise of Atlantic slavery on their respective expeditions, these "neo Middle Passengers" also reignite debate about slave reparations, the *Zong* ship replica; continued racial discrimination in contemporary society, the *Freedom Schooner Amistad*; and even conflict in the very portrayal of the enslaved subject and Middle Passage, the *Henrietta Marie*. To tout a vanquished Atlantic slavery (a common practice at some sites) often mutes important conversations about inequities, modern-day human trafficking, and other residues of slavery that continue today.

In her 1989 article in *World Literature*, Toni Morrison lamented the lack of a fitting symbol "to summon the presences of, or recollect the absences of slaves" on the Middle Passage journey in the Atlantic Slave trade. In a direct response to the author's complaint about the lack of an appropriate slave memorial, the Toni Morrison Society installed the Bench by the Road on Sullivan's Island in 2008, the first of more than twenty proposed bench installations in the US and abroad, which I discuss in chapter 5. The Bench by the Road's ceremonial placement at Sullivan's Island as a slave memorial responds to a social and cultural milieu through its location near a dilapidated slave quarantine facility, a gentrified community, and a Gullah Geechee slave-descendant group that can no longer afford to live in the region. However, in light of a uniquely identifiable "watershed" moment—the tragic murders of nine parishioners at Charleston's Mother Emanuel Church in 2015 and subsequent removal of the Confederate flag from the state's capitol—I also reflect on the bench memorial's link to the region's centrality in slavery's legacy.

I discuss museum theory, especially as it pertains to freestanding sites as visual markers of material culture in an open-air, nontraditional museum setting, external to and apart from traditional museum structure. The slave sites that I examine in this study have significantly altered stereotypical depictions of so-called primitive societies and cultures that traditional anthropological "museums of mankind" have erstwhile shown, such as the Pitt Rivers Museum at Oxford in the United Kingdom or the Musée de l'Homme in Paris. In the design, construction, and sponsorship surrounding the seminal artifact, gone are displays (such as those still exhibited at these museums) that feature the Great Chain of Being, the missing link ideology, and the divisions of humanity. Andreas Huyssen describes the postmodern museum's shift away from "the guardian of treasures and artifacts from the past discreetly exhibited for the select group of experts and connoisseurs."[24] Site organizers and curators have replaced such antiquated, offensive displays with seminal artifacts, objects, and special exhibitions that appeal to a diverse audience that rejects collections merely as acquisitions, and favors purposeful displays that advance knowledge about slaves' cultural and economic contributions.

To date, only one freestanding museum exists that is wholly devoted to slavery, partly because of political pressures to minimize slave horrors and to emphasize racial uplift. The Whitney Plantation Museum in Wallace, Louisiana, about thirty-five miles from New Orleans, opened on December 7, 2014.[25] Focusing heavily on Louisiana, creole culture, and slavery in the southern region, the Whitney Museum was founded by John Cummings, a white trial lawyer who spent fifteen years and over $8 million of his own money to start the project. Liverpool's International Slavery Museum, the largest "gallery" in the massive Merseyside Museum complex, opened in the United Kingdom in August 2007. The Smithsonian's African American Museum of History and Culture includes an extensive slavery exhibition as a substantial part of its holdings. Therefore, in the epilogue to this study, I mark the museum's opening on the Washington Mall on September 24, 2016, as a signature defining moment.

The United Nations Educational, Scientific and Cultural Organization (UNESCO), known for designating places of cultural significance as World Heritage Sites, funds the renovation of numerous West African slave forts, including Gorée Isle's House of Slaves and Ghana's Elmina and Cape Coast Castles, as international heritage sites. The organization recognizes the slaves imprisoned there prior to their departure across the Atlantic in the Middle Passage. For slave forts, UNESCO set in motion unprecedented travels to these sites. They also shifted the meaning of the modern-day museum.

While numerous critical studies have examined neo-slave narratives, visual displays of slavery at slavery museums and black heritage sites remain under-explored. Intense interest in the increasing number of slave sites signals the need for a national dialogue on shared responsibility in healing the wounds of slavery. The modern-day slave memorial and heritage site roughly parallels the proliferation of contemporary slavery fiction at least since the publication of Toni Morrison's seminal novel *Beloved* in 1987. Contemporary slavery fiction, also known as neo-slave narratives, adopts certain conventions found in nonfiction narratives by former slaves in the antebellum period; however, modern stories about the slave past also reflect its legacy in the present day. In contrast to these narratives, slave sites consist primarily of artifacts that convey immediacy through visual and other sensory modalities that have a profound impact on the spectator.

A growing cluster of publications offers different ways to read or assess slave sites. But despite their recent proliferation, slave sites and exhibitions as freestanding practices in the context of specific contemporary circumstances have received proportionately little scholarly coverage. And no publication reads the slave site uniquely through flash moments—specific circumstances and seminal events—as I do in this study. Lisa Wool-fork, in *Embodying American Slavery in Contemporary Culture* (University of Illinois Press, 2008), constructs a bodily epistemology in order to connect present-day audiences with a slave past through speculative fiction and other "time travel" opportunities. Two works of great help to my own work focus narrowly on slave sites in Louisiana. Lynell Thomas, in *Desire and Disaster in New Orleans: Tourism, Race, and Historical Memory* (2014), challenges perspectives about slavery through still-trenchant nostalgic, Lost Cause ideologies in tourism spread throughout the South. She argues, for example, that stereotypical artifacts, such as mammy dolls and lawn jockeys, that are associated with slavery still appear in some museum gift shops. In *Creating Freedom: Material Culture and African American Identity at Oakley Plantation, Louisiana, 1840–1950* (2000), Laurie Wilkie uses oral history and archaeology from four slave-descendant Louisiana families to examine how an identity formed independent from the slave quarters contests another identity that slavery imposes upon the enslaved.

In separate studies, Kathleen Wilson and Salamishah Tillet offer parallel perspectives on the "changing same" for blacks in the era of Atlantic slavery and in the present day, respectively, that can account for current interest in slave site development and implementation. Wilson, for example, in *A New Imperial History: Culture, Identity and Modernity in Britain and the Empire, 1660–1840* (Cambridge: Cambridge UP, 2004) identifies Africans among those groups in eighteenth-century English provinces who could publicly mimic the behaviors of citizenry "in the public sphere of association," but who still found their "membership in the nation . . . tentative and unstable."[26] Tillet, in contrast, in *Sites of Slavery: Citizenship and Racial Democracy in the Post–Civil Rights Imagination* (2012), finds a "civic estrangement" for many in the modern-day African American community who have formal legal citizenship rights, but also still lack membership in its requisite signs and symbols. Civic estrangement therefore acts as a catalyst for the production of "sites of slavery," which Tillet locates through select fiction, drama, art, and heritage tourism in an intriguing study.

As overarching trope, the slave sites analyzed in this study gather the metaphorical (and biblical) "dry bones of the valley" in order to make them live again. But only by filtering the remains of slavery through the lived experiences of the museumgoer/spectator can they also discern with greater clarity the repetitive patterns that transform slavery into less recognizable forms. The most ardent legacy of the slave site is perhaps "slavery itself" or the notion that bondage from a fixed period in the distant past remains barely separable from certain residuals in ever shifting form. I offer the following as an overarching trope for my study: each chapter reorders the temporality of the history of slavery to specific conditions of that slave site's display. Most pertinently, I contend that exclusionary practices by compilers and interpreters of the historical record—an imperial lens—if you will, combined with the lack of a national dialogue on slavery and with sustained episodes of continued racial inequality, necessitates a renewed study of the urgent, cumulative effect of slavery's legacy now more than ever.

CHAPTER ONE

Iconic Sons of Africa
"in the Belly of the Stone Monster"

> Who are we looking for; who are we looking for?
> It's Equiano we're looking for.
> Has he gone to the stream? Let him come back
> Has he gone to the farm? Let him return
> It's Equiano we're looking for.
> —Kwa chant about the disappearance of an African boy, Olaudah Equiano

The slave fort, dungeon, or what playwright Mohammed ben Abdallah refers to in *The Slaves Revisited* as the "gluttonous, fat-bellied stone monster by the sea"[1] functions both as contested site and yet most frequented slave site in the global community. While the former casts the facility in the context of its public role in the slave trade, the latter privileges it as a private and public memory space for the site organizer, griot-oral historian, diaspora slave descendants and other tourists who travel to its inner sanctum. Since its renovation as a World Heritage site by UNESCO in the 1970s and '80s, the slave fort—most prominently Senegal's House of Slaves (La Maison des Esclaves) at Gorée Island and Ghana's Cape Coast and Elmina Castles—has functioned as backdrop or partial setting for numerous creative projects and events. These include Haille Gerima's film *Sankofa*, Rachid Bouchereb's film *Little Senegal*, and Mohammed ben Abdallah's play *The Slaves* (revised as *The Slaves Revisited*.)

By virtue of its very structure—windowless cells, dank dirt floors, and the narrow aperture or proverbial Door of no Return from which slaves made the Middle Passage journey—the slave fort attests to the incalculable losses that the trade created for Africans and their descendants. In other words, diaspora slave-descendants (whom I address as premier travelers to these sites) journey far into the contours of the forts and dungeons where their African ancestors languished, in order to contemplate the impact of continued discriminatory practices on their own lives. Massive increases in the number and scale of visitations to slave forts in recent years underscore their potency as geopolitical spaces that have renewed conversation about culpability for

The Elmina Castle in Ghana. Photograph by Joanne Woodard.

The "Door of No Return" at Elmina Castle. Photograph by Joanne Woodard.

Atlantic slavery and about just who bears the lion's share of responsibility for that trade. My contention is that conflicts between purveyors of a traditional archival, historical past and propagators of a symbolic memory for the present appropriately begin with slave forts in Africa and morph outwardly to slave sites elsewhere in the global community. In this capacity, they express the tenets of a virulent, cyclical slavery and offer new ways to rethink its meaning in the modern world.

It is therefore fitting that I first examine the slave fort, specifically Senegal's House of Slaves and Ghana's Cape Coast Castle—foremost among other slave sites in this study—as ground zero, or an originary source, as sanctioned by the sizable groups that journey there from far-flung regions in the international community. I then reconceptualize these slave forts from permanent structures to fluidity through select, contemporary "flash" moments and seminal events that reorder the temporality of the history of slavery to specific conditions of the sites' display. For example, when cast in the context of certain visiting heads of state, a renowned griot-oral historian, and a heritage tourism industry, the slave fort functions not merely as a historical object from the slave past but through a process of interactions that bind slavery's historical resonance to its continued impact in the modern world.

In unprecedented visits at Senegal's House of Slaves, then-sitting US presidents Bill Clinton, George Bush, and Barack Obama in 1998, 2003, and 2013, respectively, ceded the international heritage site as a magnet for discussion about apologies, reparations, and responsibility for the Atlantic slave trade, yet none of them discussed the role of the US in that trade. (The presidents had followed luminaries to the site at Gorée that include Pope John Paul II and Nelson Mandela, former South African president.) Clinton, as the first US president to make the journey, proclaimed profound regret in a well-publicized address over the horrors of the Atlantic slave trade. But reportedly fearing liability for slave reparations, he did not issue an apology for the nation's role in that trade.

Curiously, albeit with great eloquence, President Bush delivered an encomium on July 8, 2003, at Senegal's House of Slaves that evoked the iconic African British slave Olaudah Equiano, who had no known connections to that site. In an address about the evils of slavery, the president singled out Equiano for special recognition. He spoke movingly about the eighteenth-century, formerly enslaved author and freedom fighter as one who endured the cruelties of bondage but also raised his stature in society to an exalted level. Referencing Equiano's African nativity and Middle Passage journey, Bush stated, "In the year of America's founding, a man named Olaudah Equiano was taken in bondage to the New World."[2] Standing near the Door of No Return before

Gorée's House of Slaves in Senegal, the president then read words taken from Equiano's *Interesting Narrative of Olaudah Equiano, or Gustavus Vassa, the African*: "God tells us that the oppressor and the oppressed are both in His hands. And if these are not the poor, the brokenhearted, the blind, the captive, the bruised which our Savior speaks of, who are they?"[3] Ironically, when the president delivered that speech, the slave fort that he stood before was alleged to be a total fabrication, and the formerly enslaved African that he honored would soon be caught up in a colossal academic debate about his authenticity. Vincent Carretta, in *Slavery and Abolition* (1999), challenged Olaudah Equiano's veracity as an Ibo-born African kidnapped, enslaved, and taken across the Atlantic primarily based on a baptismal record and a naval muster roll that listed his birth place as South Carolina. Paul E. Lovejoy, also in *Slavery and Abolition* (2006), expressed skepticism about Carretta's claims that Equiano faked an African birth and Middle Passage journey.[4] (I shall return to this subject later in the chapter). A magnet for contentious debate, here, the slave fort prompts discussion that attests to slavery's far-reaching tentacles and its archival instability.

As America's first African American president, Barack Obama exposed a "mythology of return" and stood at the epicenter of discourse about belonging and dispossession in historic appearances at both Cape Coast Castle and the House of Slaves. In an inescapable irony during Obama's visit to the House of Slaves in 2013, for example, questions already on the domestic front about his "authenticity" as a US-born citizen also shifted to questions about the authenticity of the slave fort itself. Unlike Clinton's or Bush's, Obama's visit at the latter fort provoked media attention and renewed scholarly conversation "outright" about whether it actually functioned as an authentic slave deportation site, as told to tourists for over forty years by the renowned griot-oral historian Joseph N'diaye, who died in February 2009. Beginning with President Obama at Cape Coast Castle, Olaudah Equiano's surprising appearance in President Bush's speech at the House of Slaves, and Joseph N'diaye's unyielding defense of that fort's authenticity as a slave deportation site, I situate these iconic Sons of Africa "in the belly of the stone monster" through a constellation of "flash" moments and seminal events that evoke the instability, volatility, and the unsettledness of race and slavery in the modern world.

Obama's Mythical "Return" at Cape Coast Castle

Before traveling to Senegal in 2013, former president Obama first visited Ghana's Cape Coast Castle in July 2009. A variety of media outlets in the global community duly noted the historical circumstances surrounding then-president Obama's address before members of the Ghanaian parliament prior to traveling to Cape Coast Castle. But while Ghanaians celebrated him as a kinsman who had returned to his ancestral homeland, the president steered a strategic, diplomatic course throughout the visit, beginning with his expressed admiration for Ghanaians who had exercised "personal responsibility" for the nation's functioning democracy.

The president's visit to Cape Coast Castle and its famed Door of No Return, some seventy-five miles west of Accra, Ghana, attracted considerably more attention than his appearance before the parliament. That visit offered Ghanaians the opportunity to greet Obama as a kindred spirit, a "long-lost brother" who had returned to Africa, an observation that someone had scribbled on a placard earlier in Accra. There, an announcer had stated, "Africa meets one of its illustrious sons, Barack Obama." Ghana's then-president, the late Atta Mills, had introduced President Obama as a long-lost relative, saying: "You're welcome. You've come home."[5] But while the president's visit to the popular slave fort proved a touching moment of historic significance, as well as a striking photo op and a made-for-television opportunity, it also exposed numerous ironies in connection with the site's history as a holding cell for enslaved Africans destined for the Middle Passage in the Atlantic slave trade, as well as its more recent designation as a UNESCO funded international heritage site in 1978 and a major tourist attraction.

As I previously stated, unanswered questions about apologies, reparations, and restitution for slavery that attended former presidents Clinton's and Bush's earlier visits to the Door of No Return at the House of Slaves all but vanished from major reports or personal interviews for President Obama while at Cape Coast Castle.[6] It were as though for America's first black president, such queries no longer seemed relevant, and hence, major media markets did not engage them. Perhaps some could construe the election itself as a kind of restitution that settled the debate. The president's visit to Cape Coast Castle might even be regarded as the very fulfillment of a "return" to Africa for the diaspora slave descendant whose "symbolic reverse passage" through the Door of No Return renewed kinship and restored a lost brotherhood in a manner that neither Clinton nor Bush could claim.

On the day of the president's arrival at Cape Coast, CNN journalist Anderson Cooper spoke with an unidentified African American woman who said that a visit to that fort years earlier had prompted her to relocate permanently from the US to Ghana in order to commiserate with kindred spirits that the site attracted. In the interview with President Obama (from which subsequent excerpts here derive),[7] Cooper asked if he understood the feelings of African

American expatriates like the woman who relocated to Ghana after being deeply moved by a prior visit to Cape Coast Castle. Cooper added that for African Americans like her, the move reflected "a sense of coming home." In a carefully worded response, President Obama replied that many white Americans with whom he had spoken also found that the visit changed their lives, and that for some African Americans, visiting the slave fort in Ghana was a matter of connecting with an "unconscious part of oneself." When Cooper interjected that Africa was, after all, the birthplace of civilization, and that everyone descended from Africa, the president posed a flipside to the African American expatriate's situation. He pointed out that numerous African Americans—with whom he had spoken—had traveled to Africa only to realize that they could never live there. He added, "You are in some ways connected to this distant land; on the other hand, you're about as American as you can get." The president attributed a profound African American rootedness in the American experience to the lack of a recent immigrant experience from which to draw. "It's that unique African American culture that has existed in North America for hundreds of years, long before we actually founded the nation," he stated.[8]

In a detail that seemed both inescapable and lost in translation, President Obama's presence at Ghana's most frequented slave site gestured to a heritage tourism industry that had a few years earlier contemplated organizing a "ceremony of return" for visiting diaspora slave descendants. Known as the Joseph Project, launched by the late tourism minister Otanka Obetsebi-Lamptey, the proposed ceremony offered these slave descendants the opportunity to "enter" rather than "exit" through the Door of No Return at the slave fort. There, Ghanaians waiting on the other side would greet them as long-lost relatives or kindred spirits. Saidiya Hartman, who wrote about the Joseph Project in *Lose Your Mother: A Journey along the Atlantic Slave Route*, says that organizers clashed with a rival company that claimed credit for the idea and sued for ownership of the project. The formal, elaborate welcoming ceremony for diaspora African slave descendants as returning long-lost brothers and sisters would function symbolically as a redressive act for those whose ancestors had been enslaved and possibly imprisoned at the fort. But for some, the planned ceremony persisted as a manifestation of commercialism, capitalist excess, and profit mongering, much like selling slavery. Since returning visitors would pay a hefty sum in order to participate in the ceremony, potentially millions of dollars were at stake. However, while the Joseph Project in its planned formality did not take place, Ghanaian officials launched the "Year of Return, Ghana 2019" project that invited African American slave descendants to visit the country and jointly commemorate the four hundredth anniversary of the first Africans' servitude in Jamestown, Virginia.

Sandra Richards has identified Elmina and Cape Coast Castles, alc other slave sites as "potentially contested spaces where a variety of cal narratives and ideological agendas are enacted."[9] Debate ensues, however, about whether tourism to these slave forts promotes healing or "sells slavery" after UNESCO-funded renovations made them a central attraction, and since the advent of "for profit" return-to-Africa tourism packages.

In a sometimes awkward mix that exposed conflicting agendas, American reporter Anderson Cooper for CNN stood "at the ready" to record, for history, the thoughts and feelings of the nation's first black president on his visit to an African slave fort. As the president entered the slave dungeon at Cape Coast Castle, Cooper stood by, microphone in hand. The reporter wanted to know what the president was thinking about as he "walk[ed] around [the] castle." The president responded that his wife and mother-in-law, who had made the trip, might best answer that question. After all, they had actually descended from slaves. Cooper assured viewers that although the president lacked a slave-descendant ancestry, his West Africa visit still resonated on a personal basis. Indeed, at one point, when Obama told Cooper that he carried the blood of Africa within him, the comment drew rousing applause from bystanders, clearly a response to his birth as the son of a Kenyan-born father.

In an intriguing report two years later, however, researchers at the Ancestry.com website reported that the nation's first African American president may have directly descended from slaves after all, but through his white mother Stanley Ann Dunham's maternal ancestry, rather than his African father's lineage. According to officials at Ancestry.com, the black man in Obama's maternal genealogy is John Punch, whom many historians regard as America's first documented chattel slave. Some whites certainly descend from enslaved and/or free blacks because of the prevalence of racial passing as well as racially mixed families. Punch is believed to have fathered children with a white woman, and by law, they assumed their mother's legal status.[10] A genealogy research team at Ancestry.com asserts that John Punch's descendants acquired the name "Bunch" and split into two factions. One group, identified as mulattoes, migrated to North Carolina. The other group settled around Virginia, intermarried with whites, and altered the family's racial identification from black to white over several generations. In accordance with this evidence, the Ancestry.com research officials believe that President Obama's mother, and hence the president himself, descends from this group of white Bunch descendants.[11]

The president likely drew particular scrutiny because of the unique circumstances of his historic visit, which may explain the carefully calibrated comments that he made to Anderson Cooper during the interview at Cape

Coast Castle. In the course of the 2008 campaign, for example, some African Americans had even groused that Obama's lack of slave descent on his father's side and his being biracial somehow disqualified him from a "real" black American experience.[12] For many blacks, Obama's visit to Cape Coast Castle, and later the House of Slaves, would presumably represent a symbolic transnational return of near mythic proportions.

Cameras recorded the scene that depicted the president, First Lady Michelle Obama, daughters Sasha and Malia, and their Ghanaian hosts as they stood beneath a sign marking the Door of No Return. Addressing the scene that depicted the windowless portal, the president said to Cooper: "Obviously it's a powerful moment, not just for myself, but I think for Michelle and the girls," for whom "seeing that portal [must] send a powerful message." Mrs. Obama did not participate in the interview. The president added, "On the one hand, it's through this door that the journey of African Americans began, and Michelle and her family, like me, draw incredible inspiration and strength from that African American journey."

In a continuation of the interview, Cooper asked President Obama whether what happened at Cape Coast Castle still had resonance in America, and whether slavery should be "remembered" and discussed on a regular basis. The president responded by broadening discussion to include the universality of crimes against humanity by recalling a visit that he had made a month earlier with author and Holocaust survivor Elie Wiesel (who died in July 2016) to the concentration camp at Buchenwald. Obama compared his personal feelings at the Ghanaian slave fort with those he experienced when visiting the concentration camp with Wiesel: "You almost feel as if the walls can speak. You try to project yourself into these incredibly harrowing moments people go through," he said. He also told Cooper that the visit to Cape Coast Castle was reminiscent of the trip that he took to Buchenwald "because it reminds us of the capacity of human beings to commit great evil."[13]

Pairing the Door of No Return at Cape Coast Castle with the concentration camp at Buchenwald links slavery with the Holocaust since the issue of exploitation has plagued both sites. Yet James Young believes that the Buchenwald artists' attention, disproportionately, to commemoration resulted in a loss of identity and historical fortitude. Young writes, "Buchenwald is a place that's so self-conscious of its potential for being appropriated for political ends that it neutralizes itself—by calling attention to itself as a memory site, and not as a history site."[14] Young's comments prove prophetic especially for Gorée's House of Slaves, though its political neutrality is hardly evident, as I shall discuss shortly. There, politicization attaches itself to a griot-tour guide that actively espouses the fort to visitors as nothing short of a Gulag for slaves who awaited deportation across the ocean.

Flanked by Ghanaian officials, a guide, and a camera crew, which signaled the official nature and historical resonance of the president's visit, Obama strolled slowly through the interiors and exteriors of Cape Coast Castle. The guide emphasized the slave fort's historic value, Ghanaian officials proudly touted the return of a long-lost brotherhood, the castle stood whitewashed from its previous form, and the president of the United States steered a decidedly diplomatic course while surrounded by vestiges of the Atlantic slave trade and European colonization. The fort's whiteness shone pristinely, and waves softly fell upon rocks around the fort, which lent an impression far removed from its function as a prison for slaves destined to be forcibly removed through the Door of No Return.[15] President Obama again cited the Holocaust and said that slavery too is "one of those things that you don't forget about," and he added that slavery should be neither taught nor regarded as a situation in which "there's simply a victim and a victimizer and that's the end of the story."[16] Widening the lens of slavery's relevance by linking it to crises in Darfur and the Congo, the president concluded that slavery ultimately teaches us that the capacity for cruelty still exists, as does the capacity for discrimination against people who differ on the basis of race, religion, sexual orientation, or gender.

The vast majority of the tens of thousands of tourists that patronize the slave forts annually are "outsiders," including many African diaspora slave descendants who travel from the United States. Numerous African scholars have noted the slave forts' enormous appeal, especially among African American slave descendants in the heritage tourism industry, as compared with the all but nonexistent treatment of slavery itself in many African communities, which some largely attribute to a state of denial. With respect to Ghana, for example, Bayo Holsey best consolidates these views in her belief that slavery's omission "from public versions of coastal Ghanaian family and community histories, its troubled presentation in the country's classrooms and nationalist narratives, and its elaboration by the transnational tourism industry" remain a factor in Ghanaians' incomplete grasping of their own past.[17]

Achille Mbembe, in "African Modes of Self-Writing," famously laments the near total absence of memories of slavery from an African perspective by African intellectuals. And Ghanaian poet Kwadwo Opoku-Agyemang writes about the imbalance in slavery's representations that "hug the bare shorelines of African history" in creative writings but "are never regarded in a sustained way or mined in any serious fashion for their lessons, their truths and their metaphors."[18] Others point out slavery's absence from school curricula and a national dialogue. Or at least they explain that when referenced at all in the school curricula, discussions about slavery heavily favor the point of view that befits colonial domination. In such instances, imitative of colonial America, Martin Kilson's "reservoir theory," which asserts that Africa teemed with slaves awaiting rescue to a superior civilizing fate in the United States, prevails.[19]

However, Laura Murphy argues persuasively in *Metaphor and the Slave Trade in West African Literature* that rather than ignore slavery in their literature, many African writers represent it "differently" through metaphors that do not follow protracted neo–slave narrative form, especially as popularized in the Americas. She finds that slavery indeed remains embedded in family oral traditions in local African communities, landscapes, and stories. Murphy insists that slave remembrance in African literature and memory studies varies and does not necessarily project the slavery-to-emancipation themes that are prevalent in African American and other Western publications. And yet there is supreme irony in discussions about the absence of overt references to or discussions of slavery in African literature while an explosive "heritage tourism" industry in public culture highlights the very forts and castles where slaves were imprisoned prior to transportation across the Atlantic in the Middle Passage.

Renovated for historical preservation by UNESCO funds to restore the memory of their roles in the Atlantic slave trade, the slave forts' modernized outer coating camouflages an inner unseemliness that marks their former use. Ensconced at practically every slave fort, the proverbial Door of No Return therefore renders a metaphor: an outer shell coating that harbors an inner illusion sustained by public memory. The penetrating questions that govern this study, such as why slavery's omnipresence remains a huge problem in the global community, and why healing and closure are so difficult for many to achieve, adhere to this place. They limn the fort's dark inner sanctum and seep through the interior walls of the tiny cells inside. Those questions lurk in silent spaces where tourists gather and enact performances that bind a remembered slave past with the wounds that they bear from residues from that past.

In *Embodying American Slavery in Contemporary Culture*, Lisa Woolfork writes that slave sites like Elmina and Cape Coast Castles in Ghana "are seriously invested in the idea that the traumatic past is waiting to be reexperienced."[20] I believe that diaspora slave descendants, who make up the majority of those patrons, do not resurrect the slave past through visitation to these sites so much as they contemplate its continuing impact on their own lives in racial, economic, and social inequalities. As travelers contemplate the past that these forts conjure, the sense of displacement from an ancestral home that a "return" purportedly fulfills somehow gets muted or misconstrued as spectacle, in part, by a heritage tourism industry that capitalizes on these visits.

Many visiting diaspora slave descendants overlook the impoverished condition of local inhabitants and focus instead on the fort's connection with slavery, while those in surrounding communities, struggling to improve their own lives, ignore both the slave forts and the slave descendants that gather there. Given the explosion in heritage tourism in Africa, or what Marita Sturken refers to as "trauma tourism," slave forts may well override Paul Gilroy's slave ship as microcosmic rallying symbol for dispersed slave descendants. Buttressed by massive UNESCO-funded renovations, these sites have remained potent symbols for Atlantic slavery. As such, they require greater recognition as a beacon for a postmodern Black Atlantic reading that metaphorizes what poet Kwesi Brew calls "the betrayal and reconciliation of departure and return" by diaspora and regional Africans.[21] The forts offer a pointed, differently focused rallying symbol for Africans as well as for diaspora slave-descendant Africans in search of identity and reflection.

The unprecedented visits to the House of Slaves by three consecutive American presidents signaled an important connection with slave (re)visitation both domestically and on the world stage. President Obama's visit to Cape Coast Castle reprised the slave fort's notoriety as a point of entry, and later an exit through the Door of No Return, as well as its historical reminder of slavery's traumatic past. For the president, the visit to Cape Coast Castle in Ghana was part of a fast-growing tradition among some African American slave descendants that also travel to slave forts in search of healing, ancestral communion, or a unique travel experience. For diaspora slave descendants, Obama's visit represented a symbolic return that perhaps mirrored for them the possibility of overcoming the past. But as I have previously stated, the president's historic visit to Cape Coast also exposes a "mythology of return" that implicates those slave descendants as well as African inhabitants who project vastly different experiences and hence different relationships with that slave past.

On the grounds of Cape Coast Castle, President Obama's journey did not exactly parallel that of an unsung spiritual sojourner who, mirroring those on the renowned tour of Santiago, treks arduously to a destination in search of wholeness and rejuvenation.[22] Rather than deliver a formal address at the Door of No Return at Cape Coast Castle as he and his predecessors had done at Gorée Island in Senegal, President Obama had spoken formally before the Ghanaian parliament at Accra, Ghana's capital. In the speech, as well as in subsequent interviews, the president steered a diplomatic rhetorical course, as I have noted. Not only had he advocated that Ghanaians determine their own future through personal responsibility, but he also pledged US support for the democratic nation while he also praised Ghanaians for preserving Cape Coast as a monument to the courage of blacks and whites alike to abolish slavery and, ultimately, to win civil rights for everyone. Having elected to travel to Ghana because of its functioning democracy, the president of the United States of America and leader of the free world who just happened to be an African American was on official duty. The president, in the guise of a transnational slave figure on a mythical "return" to a Ghanaian slave fort, deflected a private moment by reflecting on a public dilemma. Simply put, he seemed unable, politically, to shed a statesman's role and connect with the site on an intimately racialist basis.

I have already noted that President Obama's visit at Gorée's House of Slaves in 2013 renewed conversation in certain media reports about the alleged fabrication of the slave fort as an outlet for slave transportation, though that has not dampened its popularity as the slave site most frequented by tourists. However, I find it particularly perplexing that "authenticity" topically seeped into conversation about a fabricated slave fort in certain media reports during the president's visit while conspiracy theorists referred to as "birthers" questioned the personal identity of America's first African American president. On the face of it, the absurdity of those claims hardly seems worth pursuing. But the controversial issue reached such proportions that the president deemed it necessary to release his birth certificate to the media. Furthermore, numerous observers believe that the birther issue gave rise to the candidacy and quite likely the presidency of Donald J. Trump in 2016. The "flash" moments that distinguished Obama's visits to Cape Coast Castle and House of Slaves may have sprouted the seeds of a radical shift by threatening past traditions through his election as America's first black president.

Joseph N'diaye and Tempests at the House of Slaves

Several years before President Obama's visit at Senegal's House of Slaves in Gorée, a dramatically different seminal event took place there when African American videographer Debra Boyd conducted a rare interview with the internationally acclaimed Senegalese griot-oral historian Joseph N'diaye. In oral presentations that he conducted at the fort from 1960 until his death in 2009, N'diaye upset the delicate balance in the president's personal, reflective style and skillful diplomacy. For nearly fifty years of service as a guide at the House of Slaves that ended with his death, ironically in the year that President Obama visited Coast Castle, N'diaye unabashedly rejected traditional, historical, archival records and espoused an oral, symbolic memory of slavery in tours that he first organized at the slave fort.

In a 1997 article titled "Debating the History of Slavery on Senegal's Gorée Island," Carolyn J. Mooney rightly assesses the debate about the House of Slaves as an intense discussion about who governs the memory about what happened at that fort, and who is officially charged with archiving that memory. She quotes an unnamed African historian who says, astutely, "There is the historical Gorée, and there is the symbolic Gorée."[23] From a historical perspective, one must necessarily account for slaves transported across the Atlantic whether they number over a hundred thousand (1 percent) or several million that poured from Ghana's multiple slave forts. From a symbolic perspective, the deplorable state of windowless dungeons and dank dirt floors at the House of Slaves is practically identical with those at Cape Coast and prove equally inhumane for those who were incarcerated regardless of the number. Mooney's comments mirror James Young's distinction between memory sites and history sites, though ironically, Young opposes the politicization of sites where Holocaust atrocities occurred. But under the powerful influence of Joseph N'diaye, and his successor as oral historian, who recognized the fort as a major site of slave transportation, the House of Slaves remains steadfastly and unabashedly a political space where the historical past and the symbolic present converge as uneasy allies.

Villagers in Ghana have often told stories about Africans who were kidnapped from communities in the interiors and taken to slave forts on the coast before being transported across the Atlantic Ocean as slaves. Some local inhabitants believed that slaves disappeared through a tunnel beneath the sea that connected Elmina and Cape Coast Castles. Others recall being admonished as children to stay away from the castle grounds lest bad spirits harm them. Laura Murphy, who heard some of these stories from docents at Ghanaian slave forts, believes that although most have no basis in fact, these stories helped Africans to process the conundrum of the disappearing slaves, often relatives and acquaintances, when no other rational explanations were given.

Similarly, the flying African motif provides a narrative for escape to freedom. Popularized in Toni Morrison's *Song of Solomon*, the slave mythically flies back to Africa, typically from a plantation in the US. The myth is based on an 1803 incident when Ibo slaves, who arrived in Savannah from Nigeria after surviving the Middle Passage, rebelled against their buyers. The buyers jumped overboard and drowned, and the slaves later fled into South Carolina swampland and committed suicide. Legend transformed the incident into a narrative that claimed the slaves rose up to the sky and flew back to Africa rather than submit to slavery.[24] I find, opportunistically, an important reckoning in stories sorted through memory scapes rather than gleaned from written archival data. Silences and omissions in certain "official" records have failed to account for the particularities of what happened to the enslaved Africans, their ancestors, and their progeny, and have therefore opened up a space for legends to take root. The highly visible slave forts and castles near the African shoreline, alternately metaphorized as monsters and fiends, womb and tomb, convey sentiment about both the disappearing enslaved relative and the returning foreign sojourner. Certain stories about the forts and castles as structural reminders of a brutal slave past refigure the archives or form alternative ones through narratives and performances in a public memory paradigm.

This debate gives way to larger questions about the failure of traditional historical archives to represent the slave past more fully and responsibly. The move toward restorative public memory practices that account for the slave fort's existence has filled the space left by gaps and silences in a destabilized archival record that devalues the slave. The unanswered questions do not so much entail whether the Portuguese, Dutch, or English built or managed the fort. Instead, those in the indigenous population simply demand to know what happened to their ancestors who disappeared from local villages during the slave trade. Those African families whose loved ones were seized and taken to those forts wistfully pondered what atrocities occurred inside the huge stone monster by the sea where people arrived and departed across the Atlantic in the Middle Passage, and never returned. Consequently, these stories have endured intense academic scrutiny, and numerous scholars have debated the authenticity of Gorée's House of Slaves as a major site of slave transportation.

Debate about the authenticity of the House of Slaves as a major site of slave transportation opens up a space for deeper probing of slave recovery's intervention, materially, at the intersection between the historical past and symbolic memory. Such sites as spawning grounds for the public (re)memory of past traumatic events is akin to Pierre Nora's conception of "lieux de mémoire," or sites of memory. Though conceding memory's vulnerability to "manipulation and appropriation," Nora points out that its rootedness in the concrete opposes history, which "binds itself strictly to temporal continuities, to progressions, to relations between things."[25] He remains skeptical of a history that lays claims to a "universal authority" by virtue of its disconnect from specific individual or group dynamics. But as material archive and premier visual marker, the House of Slaves conveys the past through an "authorized" imperial lens and a counterhistorical intervention. Furthermore, the site's permanence as an attraction for visitors unceasingly flaunts its immutability over time. Material objects, like facts or data as words on a page may be fixed apparatus, but neither can permanently anchor memory for the observer. Conditions and circumstances shift over time, and perspectives among individuals vary. But as revisionist histories, visually and visibly displayed in commemorative public spaces for tourists, slave sites like Gorée's House of Slaves under the tutelage of a charismatic oral historian like Joseph N'diaye oblige past traumatic events to conform to demands of the present, thus creating a crisis of memory for academic disciplines. It is precisely public memory's intervention in traditional, archival history that causes angst among numerous scholars.

That angst is most evident in a prolonged dispute that involved Joseph N'diaye, amid claims that Gorée's House of Slaves never functioned as a major holding cell or departure site for slaves in the Middle Passage. Until his death at the age of eighty-seven, Senegalese oral historian Joseph N'diaye greeted visitors with his own-intricate account of untold cruelties and inhumanity that he says indeed occurred at the House of Slaves at Gorée Island, Senegal. Debra S. Boyd, a professor of French at North Carolina Central University and a three-time Fulbright Scholar, refers to N'diaye as a monument that embodies the memory of the Gorée story. Boyd produced a film about N'diaye's work at Gorée, titled *Griot of Gorée: Joseph N'diaye*, which she later translated from the French to English. She also conducted a rare interview with N'diaye in the film about his work at Gorée (from which my excerpts here derive).[26] Boyd attributed Gorée's symbolic status and popularity as a slave tourist site above and beyond Elmina and Cape Coast Castles at Ghana, as well as Quidah in Benin, to Joseph N'diaye's indefatigable work and daily presence at the House of Slaves. Abdel Kader N'diaye, *enseignant* at Gorée, said that before the World Festival in 1965, tourists rarely came to Gorée, and he also credits N'diaye for the growth in Senegal's tourism industry surrounding Gorée Island and at Dakar. In the interview with Boyd, N'diaye joked, "When my African American cousins come, and they discover I'm not here, they split; they don't hang around."[27] The fort's role in the Atlantic slave trade, in tandem with the sojourner's mission, is inextricable from N'diaye's performance, because he has inured himself in the historicity of the slave past. Without his very presence and the narrative that he dispenses—or that of his successor—the site stands as a fixed symbol, an immovable object.

In many ways the *Griot of Gorée* brings together a diaspora African American slave-descendant videographer and a renowned African griot whose respective personal stories coalesce around key aspects of the Atlantic slave past. The film unabashedly and unstintingly represents the House of Slaves as a major slave transportation site. In the opening scene Boyd approaches Gorée Island on a ferry with camera crew in tow, and her words are as passionate as they are personal: "I shiver as I listen to the silent screams of my ancestors emanating from the rives of the Slave House. Gorée! A name sullied with blood and evoking a sad past."[28] She gives no indication that her ancestors came from this specific region of Africa or through the House of Slaves or whether she expresses the sentiment metaphorically. But the impression is that it does not matter, because the nonacademic rules of public memory forgive the perceived "indiscretion."

The film is part docudrama and dramatic narrative, part history and part memoir. Boyd produced the film as part of her own series, *Genius of the Sahel*, a collection of short documentary films about extraordinary African personalities that live in the Sahel. In his role as an oral historian and storyteller, N'diaye's performance at the House of Slaves benefits inquisitive seekers like Boyd. Throughout the film she threads the story of her own ancestral past into a public memory archive that she creates for all posterity. N'diaye's and Boyd's multiple stories reveal, collaboratively, what is his, what is hers, what is theirs, and what is ours.

On a day late in May 2006, N'diaye's presentation on the grounds of the House of Slaves was roughly identical to the delivery that Boyd had recorded in her film. Conducting a tour of the House of Slaves in the film before a small group of visitors, N'diaye began by referencing the Atlantic slave trade as "one of the worst genocides that humanity has ever known." He added that while the Jewish concentration camps dominated most conversation about crimes against humanity, voices remained silent about slavery. Continuing the extended comparison, N'diaye said, "Most talk about the Jewish concentration camps in the Holocaust that lasted for around twelve years, but the black slave trade lasted for 350 years. No one ever talks about slavery, but I am going to talk about it."[29]

In Boyd's film the camera pans across a ferry filled with tourists headed toward Gorée Island, and the House of Slaves comes into full view. Tourists wear cameras like necklaces, though printed notices at the fort forbid their use. Sunglasses shield their eyes against the sun's intense rays. Some are local, while others come from far away. Boyd momentarily shifts the House of Slaves away from the camera's viewfinder. Her next comment is plaintive. "How does one portray such a practice as "unjust, cruel, tyrannical, and destructive as the Negro slave trade?" she asks. As though responding to her own question, she then alters the Sankofa maxim, which says that one must necessarily return to the past in order to move forward into the future. Boyd states, "The black man must remake his past in order to make his future." To remake the past is to revise, reinvent, or rewrite it. And by thus saying so through a creative narrative, she gives herself (and perhaps N'diaye) permission to do just that. In a direct address to Gorée that stakes a claim for the film's intended role, she concludes, "Gorée, who will speak for us?"[30]

Boubacar Joseph N'diaye, *conservateur en chef* of La Maison des Esclaves à Gorée, (lead griot at Gorée's House of Slaves) was born October 15, 1922, in Rufisque, just twenty kilometers (just over twelve miles) from Gorée. Adopted by a maternal uncle at the age of six after his father's death, N'diaye grew up listening to stories about the island's history from grandparents and other family members as they gathered around a fire after dinner. Drawn to the slave past by the oral tradition, N'diaye says, "Every Goréen who respects himself is aware of everything that happened by way of oral history." He was an infantryman during World War II, and the first Senegalese to be a military parachutist that fought for France. N'diaye began studying the history of Gorée in 1958. Then, for three years while he studied, he worked as a curator at the House of Slaves for free and received only the tips that tourists would give to him. In 1962, at the request of former mayor August Ly, he started to receive pay for his work as curator. As N'diaye tells it in the film, President Leopold Sedar Senghor heard about his work. When the mayor told Senghor about N'diaye's three years as a volunteer at the site, the president demanded that the curator be put on the payroll immediately.

After touring the House of Slaves with Boyd, N'diaye sat down with her for an interview. He said that he pursued advanced studies by utilizing archives at the Institut Fondamental de l'Afrique Noire (IFAN) "that is attached to the university where I stayed for four years." President Senghor then sent N'diaye to Nantes for further study. He pointed to certificates of appreciation and recognition that he received in the US, and he held up Le Prix de la Mémoire, or Memory Prize, that he received in Paris. N'diaye also showed photographs of famous visitors, including rhythm and blues singer James Brown, actor Danny Glover, Harry Belafonte, South Africa's Nelson Mandela, Cheikh Anta Diop, Pope John Paul II, President Bill Clinton, and many others. He told Boyd how Brown "fell apart" after looking at a cell reserved in the slave dungeon for children. And he recounted how Nelson Mandela ignored protocol and entered a space below the stairs where rebellious slaves were kept: "[Mandela] stayed there for a while. When he came out, his eyes were all red." N'diaye came to Washington, DC, for the Million Man March in 1995, and he also journeyed on a pilgrimage to Fort de Joux, where Toussaint Louverture was incarcerated.

The "official" archives of slavery do not tell Joseph N'diaye's version of what happened inside Gorée's House of Slaves or at its prominent Door of No Return. They focus more straightforwardly on the Portuguese, Dutch, and French invaders that purchased Gorée from the indigenous population at

Dakar, and then in short order occupied the island. Around the mid-fifteenth century, Portuguese traders settled on Gorée. Soon the Dutch took it over and renamed it "Goede Reede," or Good Harbor. After purchasing Gorée, they built two forts in order to protect their trade in slaves. Gorée Island soon became a place in which the trade in merchandise and slaves was commonplace. The European trading companies that took over the island sealed its fate through a brisk slave trade that peaked in the eighteenth century. Disputes and power mongering among nations that vied for control of trade resulted in first the French, then the English taking turns at running the island until early in the nineteenth century, when they officially ended slavery.[31]

Like Elmina Castle and Cape Coast Castle in Ghana, Gorée Island's House of Slaves has endured claims that it housed the concubines of European slave traders, which most experts do not dispute. However, for Gorée's House of Slaves, some historians further claim that the site never functioned as a holding cell for enslaved Africans bound for the Middle Passage journey across the Atlantic. The late Philip D. Curtin, a Johns Hopkins professor emeritus and the author of more than two dozen books on the Atlantic slave trade and African history, is quoted as referring to the site as "a hoax" and a "sham" in an internet mailing list in August 1995. Evidence produced by Curtin and other highly reputable historians suggests that Gorée Island was not the primary departure point for those sold into slavery between the fifteenth and nineteenth centuries, and that slaves probably never departed through the Door of No Return at all. Curtin also says that Gorée Island was at most a minor shipping port, because of the rugged, rocky terrain that made it precarious to dock ships. He further claimed that "30,000 total exports through Gorée would be an outside estimate" and that "the 'House of Slaves' has become an emotional shrine to the slave trade, rather than a serious museum."[32]

David Eltis estimates that perhaps 120,000 slaves (fewer than 1 percent of all slaves) left through Gorée Island. Eltis, Emory University historian (via Queens University in Canada), has completed the massive *Trans-Atlantic Slave Trade Database*, which records some 12.5 million people shipped to the New World from 1514 to 1866. Slave historian M'baye Gueye at Dakar's Université Cheikh Anta Diop puts the number "in the hundreds of thousands," and he believes that Gorée serves a similar function "as a tomb for unknown soldiers." In December 1996 an article by Emmanuel de Roux appeared in *Le Monde*, a French newspaper, claiming that the House of Slaves was a myth and that it had never been a major slave port. The article quoted Abdoulaye Camara, curator of the history of the House of Slaves, who also referred to the site as "a myth," but Camara denied making the comment. Joseph N'diaye reacted angrily to the article. *Le Monde* had followed the research done by Joseph Roger de Benoist, a Senegalese scholar who argued that the site functioned only as a local port. Benoist believes that historical truth must be respected, but that Gorée must also be valued symbolically: "Slaves were traded there and were kept in the House of Slaves and homes like it," he said.[33]

After extensive debate on "the myths and realities of Gorée," scholars that attended a conference at the Institut Fondamental d'Afrique Noire at Université Cheikh Anta Diop at Dakar, Senegal, praised N'diaye for his curatorship of the House of Slaves and for his role in remembering the slave past. Most tellingly, scholars that assembled at the conference "passed a statement" or resolution affirming Gorée's past role as a slave port. Acknowledging "the limitations of statistics," the group urged that more scholarly research be conducted on that subject.[34] That research splinters into different perspectives when it comes to fingering the parties deemed most responsible for slavery. The careful, deliberate resolution reached among conference attendees spoke to the empowerment of an individual and group collective that sent firm messages about the development and implementation of slave sites as public memory spaces. The statement almost certainly guarantees the slave fort's continued appeal in the international community as a major tourist site. Most pertinently, its affirmation of the House of Slaves as a slave transportation site—whatever the numbers—also signals strong support for the work of Joseph N'diaye. Having attracted the likes of Nelson Mandela and Barack Obama among heads of state, the fort could be viewed, symbolically, as a celebratory end to Atlantic slavery and as a progressive move forward rather than a relic of slavery's tragic past. But the site remains inescapably a magnet for contentious debate about slavery's continued impact through discriminatory practices, inequities, and modern-day slave trafficking.

In a 2010 article in the *New York Times* titled "Ending the Slavery Blame-Game," Henry Louis Gates Jr. raised the specter of African kingdoms, including the Akan of the kingdom of Asante (Ghana), the Fon of Dahomey (Benin), the Mbundu of Ndongo (Angola), and the Kongo (now Congo) that participated in the slave trade with Europeans, which many Africans do not discuss. Alluding to President Obama's opportunistic role in debate about reparations, Gates noted the complexities of determining direct responsibility for slavery for enormous financial gain. But he added that the vexing issue must nevertheless be resolved "before we can arrive at a judicious (if symbolic) gesture to match such a sustained, heinous crime" as slavery.[35] In Ghana historians focus instead on reexamining trade routes in which slaves endured an arduous journey as traders brought them down to slave forts in coffles.

Through readings of the slave fort in a dichotomy of "memory site" versus "history site," to apply James Young's terms, an increasing number of Africans and other artists personify the slave fort through fictional representations as the face of the European whose incursions into the region forever changed Africa, and they assess Africa's own role in that process. For example, the authors of *Sankofa*, *The Slaves*, and *Little Senegal*, which I previously cited, feature their own fictional versions of a Joseph N'diaye at the House of Slaves, thus tackling debate about the appropriation of that role in a contemporary setting. Through works partially or exclusively set in slave forts at Gorée Island and Ghana, the fictional griots thus open a space for deeper probing about slave recovery projects' intervention in the memory/history dialectic. Meanwhile, the legacy of Joseph N'diaye—or the griot in the trenches in collaboration with the slave forts featured in the three works—makes for a riveting cross-continental analysis of conflicting perspectives on past and present, colonialism and African independence, capitalism and globalization.[36]

Maurice Halbwachs, social memory theorist and a disciple of the Durkheim school, points out essential differences between memory and history. History is generally seen as a singular and objective discipline guided by an impartial arbiter that disseminates ideas timelessly and detached from a group collective whose support collective memory requires. Specifically, Halbwachs sees history as applying a critical distance and consistency to the conveyance of past events. He argues that unlike memory, history does not change information about the past to suit the demands of the present.[37] The erroneous assumption, however, is that historians do not cater to biased factions, or to emotionalism that sometimes emits from an individual or group collective gripped by a traumatic encounter with a painful past. I earlier alluded to gaps and silences, omissions and inconsistencies in traditional historical records that foreground the very public memory practices that historians decry. To interrogate those instabilities in archival depictions of slavery that give rise to some controversial public memory practices, I return discussion to Olaudah Equiano, another iconic Son of Africa from within the belly of the stone monster.

Equiano's "Flash" Moment at Birmingham

While President Obama has been "legitimized" as an African American that may actually descend from slaves after all, the iconic slave Olaudah Equiano has been purportedly "disqualified" from a birth and captivity in Africa through certain archival records that include a baptismal document, a naval muster roll, and a slave ship database.[38] Some supremely ironic circumstances thus find America's first black president and the world's most documented African slave in the crosscurrents of tempests at the stone monster, albeit under very different circumstances. At the core of tempestuous debate, Bush's praise of Olaudah Equiano ("who never existed") at the slave fort ("that was not") shadows Barack Obama's expulsion from an "authentic" American identity. As Arjun Appadurai writes in the introduction to *The Social Life of Things: Commodities in Cultural Perspective*, "the creation of value is a politically mediated process" whether that value flows through commodities or knowledge.[39]

For Equiano, a popular Kwa chant in the epigraph to this chapter beseeches his return from captivity, which can also be read, askance, as an appeal for his return rightfully to an Ibo-African identity. These iconic Sons of Africa converse with a public memory and archival history dialectic that implicates racial slavery, as well as sites like Gorée's House of Slaves and the 2007 exhibition of Olaudah Equiano at the Birmingham Museum in the United Kingdom in an uncanny configuration. For example, Equiano's inscriptions against a racialized construct in the eighteenth century align with Joseph N'diaye's counterhistorical, interventionist public memory performance at the House of Slaves in the twenty-first century. Like the griot or oral historian at the House of Slaves, Equiano engages in a struggle between an archival, historical past and purveyors of a symbolic present that sometimes defied that past.

On September 28, 2007, the Olaudah Equiano Society, in partnership with the Birmingham Museum and Art Gallery in the United Kingdom, opened *Equiano: An Exhibition of an Extraordinary Life from Enslavement to Best-Selling Author*, which decidedly reaffirmed the author's identity as an Ibo-born Son of Africa. After years of careful planning and fund-raising efforts led by Arthur Torrington, president of the Olaudah Equiano Society, along with other members of the London-based organization in an event that honored Equiano's achievements, invitations went out for a private viewing of the "Special Exhibition" at a prelaunch late-afternoon reception at the Birmingham Museum. The event honoring Equiano marked the bicentenary of the 1807 Act of Parliament to abolish the Atlantic slave trade. Securing and affirming Olaudah Equiano in his historical place as a formerly enslaved African of Ibo extraction, the exhibition saturated the already highly charged atmosphere with the commanding message that the African-born icon had arrived and that, at long last, he had been accorded proper recognition that befitted his stature.[40]

By far the most frequently quoted and highly visible formerly enslaved African at modern-day museums and heritage sites, Olaudah Equiano has come to define, symbolically, Atlantic slavery as well as the slave recovery movement itself. Concomitantly a best-selling author, cultural exemplar, and scholarly enigma, Olaudah Equiano graces editions and monographs, and actors have performed his role in such films as *The Old African Blasphemer* (1975), *A Son of Africa* (1995), and *Amazing Grace* (2006). In its co-optation as quintessential tour guide for some heritage sites, the scripted voice of Olaudah Equiano functions both as an eyewitness to Middle Passage slave horrors and as a modern-day griot that guides museumgoers/spectators through the lingering residuals of slavery. The popular film *A Son of Africa* (1995), produced in the United Kingdom and distributed internationally for classroom and other scholarly use, chronicles Equiano's journey from enslavement to freedom and highlights his contributions to current debate about slavery.[41] With interviews by Stuart Hall and other prominent scholars, *A Son of Africa* features a dramatic, colorful reenactment of Equiano's kidnapping in Africa and depicts scenes from disputed chapters in the *Interesting Narrative* that include the horrid Middle Passage journey.

Meanwhile, at the Birmingham Museum's special exhibition of Olaudah Equiano in 2007, organizers had duly noted and listened politely to claims of Equiano's fraudulent or inauthentic self-representation as African-born slave of Ibo extraction, and they had all but ignored those claims in the exhibition proper. The impression is not that site organizers bowed to any public or political pressure to restore Equiano's credibility as a self-identified Ibo-born slave captive that purchased his freedom before becoming an antislavery activist. Rather, they gave the impression that they simply did not believe or accept circumstantial evidence that such an iconic figure only recently canonized through academic anthologies and promoted in a long-anticipated special museum exhibition had forged a fraudulent identity. That impression was made clear in the display itself, as well as at a contentious conference titled "Olaudah Equiano: Representation and Reality," which Brycchan Carey convened in March 2003 at Kingston-upon-Thames University at Surrey. There, scholars had debated claims about Equiano's identity.

I have previously alluded to a paradoxical reliance upon, and distrust of, certain traditional historical archives in some public memory practices. But to reaffirm Equiano's credentials as an iconic slave for posterity, and by default to validate his reportage of an African birth, organizers at the Birmingham Museum both trolled assiduously through archival records and relied upon the author's own account in the *Interesting Narrative* for authenticating materials and information. Paradoxically, site organizers oscillated between reliance upon certain traditional archival evidence to authenticate objects of slavery and upon "memory work" that encouraged independent assessments of reconstructed materials. For example, the Birmingham exhibition featured Equiano's excursion with Dr. Charles Irving's sea-salt expedition and displayed clothing that resembled what Equiano might have worn in Antarctica. After securing his freedom, Equiano had joined Irving's expedition to convert salt water into drinkable water. He had also ventured to the Arctic and to the Mosquito shores of South America, facts that scholars do not dispute. Generously extracting Equiano's own words from the *Interesting Narrative*, the exhibition followed Equiano's account of his boyhood, captivity, Middle Passage voyage, ultimate freedom, and antislavery activism in later years. In other words, fully amplifying the author's own version of his origins, the Birmingham Museum prominently featured Equiano himself both as premier exhibition and archival presence. Simply put, I did not detect any overt references made to Vincent Carretta's claims that "Olaudah Equiano, the African" never existed, either at the Birmingham display or in the educational materials that I examined.

While museum officials substantiated the Equiano exhibition as a historical site by accessing certain archival records, they also steeped it in the rudiments of public memory practices by shrewdly devising public relations and marketing strategies. For example, artifacts and images selected for display at the Birmingham Museum and Art Gallery seemed specially designed to link Equiano with an enriched advanced Ibo cultural heritage. Trustees of the British Museum had loaned to exhibitors a bronze male head representing Oba, leader of Benin. Numerous other artifacts also exemplified Equiano's Nigerian heritage and culture. Musical instruments, including a double clapperless bell from Nigeria called a *kuge,* a slit drum, and two beaters from West Africa dating to the early twentieth century were also on display. A thumb piano called a *sansa* and a double-ended oval drum, both from Nigeria and both dating to the late nineteenth century, were included as well. Other items on display included a pair of shackles and a widely disseminated image of slaves tightly packed on a ship, from Thomas Clarkson's 1807 book *A History of the Slave Trade.* In addition, a two-volume first-edition copy of Equiano's *Interesting Narrative,* edited by Paul Edwards, was placed on display, along with a stately, colorful uniform similar to one likely worn by Equiano as depicted in photographs from the eighteenth century.[42]

In the summer of 1790, Olaudah Equiano arrived in Birmingham to promote his autobiography and to secure support from abolitionists. Andy Green writes in "Birmingham, Equiano, and the Transatlantic Slave Trade" that Equiano found Quakers, Industrialists, and non-conformists among a growing abolitionist surge in Birmingham. After his visit, Equiano wrote a letter of thanks to *Aris's Birmingham Gazette,* in which he praised the "great marks of kindness from the under-mentioned gentlemen of this town who have subscribed to my narrative."[43] He strategically listed some sixty names of leading citizens and supporters. But not all was so egalitarian in eighteenth-century Birmingham. Shops sold slave paraphernalia such as collars, shackles, and chains, at least one of which the museum actually displayed during the special exhibition of Equiano.

Though separated by more than two centuries, the temporal space narrows among the "spectacle" of eighteenth-century readers that first peered into *Interesting Narrative* to examine Equiano for moral worth and signs of intelligence, the spectators that viewed the exhibition at Birmingham in mutual admiration of his accomplishments, and the museum's spectacular "blockbuster" visual display that solidified his legacy in the twenty-first century. Temporality governs the politics of public memory at the Equiano exhibition through its transmutability. For example, the exhibition, in concert with the two hundredth anniversary of the ending of the slave trade in 2007, had a temporary run of several months and no longer remains in the museum. The display was assembled and then disassembled, which categorized it as an "occasional" exhibition as opposed to a permanent one. Consequently, the exhibition about Equiano and slavery is no longer available to the general public.

Organizers and local community advocates set up the exhibit in order to attract visitors to view the displays, and officials made educational information about Equiano available to local schools before opening day. That way teachers could educate their students about what they would see before bringing them to the museum. Given that the exhibition would not be a permanent part of the museum's collection, officials also provided materials and information that visitors could take away from the museum experience. In addition to attracting the general public, the Equiano exhibition at Birmingham also appealed to specialized groups that hailed from local schools and communities, as well as academics from far-flung regions in the international community, to view its display.

The Equiano Society solicited letters in 2005 from academics in the global community who, in turn, requested support from the Heritage Lottery Fund and other sources in order to finance the Equiano Exhibition.[44] Site organizers had subsequently secured that support for the Equiano Project from the Heritage Lottery Fund, as well as support from the Birmingham City Council, the MLA Museums Libraries Archives Council, and the Renaissance West Midlands. The role played by corporate donors and other supporters in the perspectives that museums convey, as well as the political ramifications of special blockbuster showings, has long been a source of inquiry, especially among some in the art history community. For example, Tony Bennett, in *The Birth of the Museum: History, Theory, Politics*, remarks on the regulative and reformatory properties of public museums as state apparatuses in general, which could enter into discussion the role played by corporate donors and other supporters for such exhibitions as Equiano at Birmingham.[45] In light of the support amassed for the Equiano exhibition, Bennett's remarks might lead some observers, whether from fair-mindedness, scholarly inquiry, or cynicism to ask the following questions: Did "corporate" or other sponsors influence or pressure site organizers to tone down rhetoric critical to discussion about the slave past or to present that information to visitors inoffensively? Or conversely, did site organizers at Birmingham—reminiscent of allegations about the oral historian at the House of Slaves—present information about Equiano propagandistically or in a biased fashion? And what consideration, if any, should site organizers have given to the controversial circumstantial evidence surrounding Equiano's birthplace in assessing the author and narrative's credibility?

In addition to Bennett's concerns about the potential influence of corporate or other donors in museum displays, which skeptics might apply to projects like Equiano at Birmingham as well as to sites like Gorée's House of Slaves, Andreas Huyssen sees shifts toward spectacular showings in modern-day museums as political and potentially problematic. He writes, "Spectators in ever larger numbers seem to be looking for emphatic experiences, instant illuminations, stellar events, and blockbuster shows rather than serious and meticulous appropriation of cultural knowledge."[46] Huyssen does not single out slave sites, and his charges would not apply to the Birmingham exhibit, which most assuredly disseminated "cultural knowledge" seriously and meticulously. Nevertheless, Huyssen's observations about the need for reflection on "the politics of exhibiting and viewing" give pause when considering both the exhibition at Birmingham and the House of Slaves at Gorée as heritage sites.[47]

In the eyes of some observers, the massive tourist site at Gorée under the auspices of an oral historian's "runaway" narrative, the desire to recognize a brutal slave trade, to fulfill a cultural heritage mandate, and to expose a nation's shameful slave past may have led inadvertently (or quite purposefully) to over-zealotry. The paradox of a burdensome remembrance or what some might refer to as a crisis of memory for site organizers and spectators may blunt or disengage critical questions concerning the efficacy of public memory practices at slave sites. For others, the production at Gorée, as well as the "over the top" exhibition of Equiano at Birmingham, seems fully justifiable for those very same reasons, given the murky claims of inaccuracy against the former and the speculative, unproven claims that attend the latter. Ironically, claims of Equiano's fraudulent identity and doubts about his authorship of the narrative surfaced in 1792 in the *Star* and the *Oracle*, which charged that

Equiano had never set foot on the African continent. But neither newspaper offered evidence for its accusations nor did not dampen Equiano's success.

Some presses, amid current charges, have shown reluctance to accept monographs for publication about Equiano, though evidence is circumstantial and claims remain unproven. Some scholars have appropriated the narrative to a fictional "history of the book" motif, while others discuss the controversy surrounding the opening chapters on Africa in classrooms, and then go on to teach the narrative, proper. If Vincent Carretta is right about Olaudah Equiano's birth in South Carolina rather than Africa, then the scholarly community in its archival sleuthing with furrowed brow and poised pen has finally caught up with the iconic former slave, but he may well be ahead of that community. If the story that Equiano tells of Africa is not his own, if it indeed stems from oral tales and readings, then it is almost certainly his father's story or that of his father before him, that first-generation African from the belly of the stone monster that endured captivity, the Middle Passage, and enslavement.[48] But what if Carretta is wrong? Without certainty about the identity of Olaudah Equiano, the academic community risks a catastrophic reenactment of his "kidnapping" and "removal" from Africa through hijacking the narrative for multifarious inventive purposes. If, on the other hand, Equiano is right and the archives have failed him, then it's "déjà vu all over again."

As I previously discussed, historians have applied similar arguments to Joseph N'diaye's work at Gorée's House of Slaves by suggesting that the needs of a brisk heritage tourism industry there exceed the importance of, or the potential for, accuracy. In a move that decidedly reaffirmed N'diaye's work through a counterhistorical, interventionist narrative at Gorée Island, a new oral historian-tour guide quickly replaced him after his death in 2009 and carries forth his methodology. To a certain extent, what the slave fort and the Equiano Exhibition communicate at Senegal, Ghana, and Birmingham therefore reverberates at other sites in the global community. The griot at the House of Slaves and site organizers for Equiano at Birmingham, for example, represent a group collective empowered to transform slavery by privileging certain symbolic memory practices over archival historical records, thus (re) shaping the politics of race as ideology. Through public relations and marketing strategies, as well as perspectives formed from a remembered or reconstructed past, these site organizers and spectators refigure slavery. For the Equiano exhibition at Birmingham, what some may see as "reverse" propaganda favorable to the iconic author's version of his life story, others see as educating the public about the unrivaled, unparalleled accomplishments of a remarkable figure who succeeded against incredible odds in slavery. (I return to this discussion in chapter 2, in which a historian, in the context of the New

York African Burial Ground memorial, questions the accuracy of the vener-able, highly valued Sankofa symbol and other African traditions.)

◆ ◆ ◆

Through seminal events, such as three consecutive American presidential vis-its and the status of an iconic griot, and instability in the archives of slavery, "originary" slave forts on the African continent stream multitextured ideo-logical perspectives about slavery. For diaspora slave descendants—those that have traversed the Atlantic in a kind of reverse Middle Passage—the slave forts and castles in Senegal and Ghana also symbolize a geopolitical space in which disparate factions offer diverse perspectives on public memory, heri-tage tourism, and slavery's continued legacy. However, for the iconic Sons of Africa—Obama, N'diaye, and Equiano, ensconced "in the belly of the stone monster"—these portals remain potent symbols that make for a riveting analysis of conflicting perspectives on the slave past and the symbolic pres-ent between traditional archivists and slave-descendant scholars and activists.

I concede to the paradox of a burdensome remembrance for site organiz-ers and spectators whose exuberance may blunt or disengage critical ques-tions concerning the efficacy of public memory practices at slave sites. But the investment in the archival, "authentic" history of the slave trade obscures the ways that even debates about those investments are really about the present-day "force" of the fact of the trade, as well as its historical and material ripples across the diaspora. That said, what I also see here is slavery's legacy through the political economy of an imperial lens through which the signifiers of authenticity, belonging, and reclamation of culture authorize an interminable struggle with marginalized groups for control of narrative, knowledge, and racial ideologies that pertain to slavery.

The New York African Burial Ground Memorial at 290 Broadway.

CHAPTER TWO

"Talking Bones" at the African Burial Ground in New York

Dig my grave with a silver spade
Mark the place where I would lay.
—Blind Lemon Jefferson, "See That My Grave Is Kept Clean"

The bones will tell us what was, is, will be.
—Suzan-Lori Parks, "Possession"

Against the backdrop of seven grassy mounds that mark 424 entombed captive Africans, and against the granite monument's sun-drenched silhouette, a charismatic park ranger-turned-tour guide steeped an unforgettable performance in historical data about slavery in New York. In a provocative expression of remembrance on a September day in 2010, Douglas Massenburg laced personal style, creativity, and archival data with ample passion and animation for slave decedents (re)interred at a slave cemetery at 290 Broadway. But he is not an elaborate symbol or a fixed material object. Through performance and articulation in a "flash" moment-in-time, Massenburg transformed from tour guide into messianic sermonizer, theatrical performer, and oral historian perhaps reminiscent of Joseph N'diaye at Gorée Island's House of Slaves in Senegal. As indicated by their questions, the visitors assembled at the site, officially known as the African Burial Ground National Monument, on that September day—nearly two decades after the burial ground's discovery—knew very little about its origins, the decedents buried there, or the decade-long skirmishes that forced its production as a formal slave site. In a "flash" moment before this uninformed yet inquisitive group, Massenburg spun a narrative that reordered the temporality of the site's 400-year-old history of slavery into a twenty-minute delivery.

While a guide at the African Burial Ground National Monument from October 1, 2006, to September 7, 2014, Massenburg developed quite a following even among colleagues that promoted the tour. In the affirmation of a popular social media forum, the performance even appeared in a YouTube adaptation. Gesticulating and spreading his hands upward, Massenburg warned visitors that sites can be misleading, that what they think they see is *not* what is there. "The African Burial Ground is a cemetery; however, it does not look like a cemetery," he said. "Here, you don't see those headstones and tombstones. Instead, there are sidewalks, there are streets, there are cars, and there are tall buildings—all are on top of the cemetery."[1]

Through performance and articulation, Massenburg provided the physical embodiment that took the stead of the absented enslaved or captive African. Private pain seemed to drive the passion that his memorable public performance conveyed for the African burial ground. Massenburg's performance was perhaps the only event that most visitors witnessed at the site. In black diaspora discourse, the griot, or oral historian, is an essential figure, and orality is a foundational context to that past. In light of the anonymity and relative invisibility of the captive African decedents, in the era of instant messaging, multitasking, sound bites, and short attention spans for viewers influenced by social media, Massenburg's performance truly stands as a seminal event for the African Burial Ground Monument in modern times.

For the formerly enslaved or captive African (terms used interchangeably for the decedents), I contend that the making of a slave site appropriately begins at the place of burial. Andreas Huyssen ascribes to the museum's "fundamentally dialectical" role both as "burial chamber of the past—with all that that entails in terms of decay, erosion, forgetting—and as site of possible resurrections, however mediated and contaminated, in the eyes of the beholder."[2] Devoid of tombstones, cornices, or other markings, the African Burial Ground renders the captive African invisible, formally archived quite literally as a mapping, or what Mary Louise Pratt refers to in *Imperial Eyes: Travel Writing and Transculturation* as "scratches on the face of the country"[3] or a perceived blight upon an otherwise pristine landscape. Invisibility equates with negation and devaluation. But in an archival prefiguration and an extension of the dialectic of burial and resurrection, the death chamber can also be a site of recovery and revaluation, for even in the absent presence of decedents, the bones can aid in telling "what was, is, [and] will be."[4]

Consequently, I discuss, in this chapter, a series of "flash" moments and seminal events that culminate with the making of a slave site—officially the African Burial Ground National Monument—by a largely slave-descendant population. Their massive protests led to the forensic analysis and consecration of remains, funeral rites, and placement of an official monument for slave decedents at the site. However, I place the African Burial Ground—the most significant anthropological, scientific, and cultural find, to date, as geopolitical space—in an uneasy alliance with a traditional archival slave past. In other words, the remains or "talking bones" from the historical past, that lie beneath the ground around Wall Street and Broadway, struggle to remain a living memory for contemporary generations through veneration at the burial site.

"Occupying Wall Street": The Negros Burial Ground

In May 1991 at 290 Broadway in New York's Lower Manhattan, during preliminary construction of the Ted Weiss Federal Office Building, workers discovered remains in what was the oldest cemetery from colonial America and the largest ever found in North America that contained black African decedents. When in a news flash at a local Fox News television station, reporters first broke the story about the discovery of remains by construction workers, protests from African American communities nearby ranged from demands to halt the federal building's construction altogether and to leave remains undisturbed to pleas to excavate them for forensic analysis, preservation, and commemoration. The largely slave-descendant population in communities nearby quickly demanded a halt to further construction of the office building because of the cemetery's presence. Some protesters insisted that only the cemetery's slave descendants should decide what to do with the remains. In a televised speech in New York City, for instance, city council member Adam Clayton Powell IV echoed the sentiments of those who feared further mutilation of formerly enslaved people who were carelessly dug up and removed so that concrete would be poured for the new office building: "You do not disturb the deceased. You leave our people alone. You let them rest in peace," Powell said.[5] But ironically, by threatening to halt construction of the Ted Weiss Building if those demands were not met, he seemed to counter the clarion call to dig the bones up and to let them speak.

It so happened that colonial maps and records had long revealed the presence of the "Negros Burial Ground" in operation from around 1673 until it filled, and city officials closed it in 1793. The cemetery was set on desolate, low-lying land "approximately 1.6 miles north of the original city limits," today's Wall Street. Because the burial ground's 6.6-acre dimensions nearly match the 5-acre property that had once belonged to Sara Roloff Kierstede Van Borsum, an Indian translator for the Dutch India Company and sponsor of black baptisms, historians believe that she, along with husband Cornelius Van Borsum, approved or donated the family's land for use as a cemetery.

The site lies next to an additional area, north of the city (now Lower Manhattan), which the Dutch originally used to settle formerly enslaved free blacks as a buffer zone against the British and Native American incursions.

Originally an area that fenced in livestock, it morphed into a protective wall that Dutch governor Peter Stuyvesant ordered laborers to build in 1653. That area, rebuilt by enslaved labor after repeated disrepair, came to be known as Wall Street. Stocks and pillories stood on Wall Street, and slaves regularly received up to forty lashes there in accordance with a local law. A slave market was built at the East River pier on Wall Street in 1711. Though the slave market was later abolished, George Washington—whose inauguration took place on Wall Street—recruited slave labor to refortify the crumbling wall during the Revolutionary War. The New York Stock Exchange (now located at 68 Wall Street), which facilitated the public sale of stock, officially began in 1792.

Archaeologists disagree on the exact numbers, but estimate that the "Negros Burial Ground," coupled with a surrounding area, may contain remains from around ten thousand to as many as twenty thousand captive and freed Africans. In the seventeenth century, captive Africans, free blacks, some Native Americans, and poor whites were buried in this cemetery. (In the seventeenth and eighteenth centuries, New York City had an urban slave population second only to that of Charleston, South Carolina.) At that time, it was just a worthless low-lying landmass. But by 1991 the land's value had escalated dramatically, reflecting its proximity to premier financial and entertainment districts on Wall Street and Broadway.

Concerned citizens in African American communities near the site expressed numerous observations at town hall meetings and demonstrations about the status and treatment of remains before officials addressed questions about the proper disposal of those remains at the African Burial Ground. In a provocative comment that broached the subject of financial exploitation in 1991 in tandem with the slave burial site's (re)discovery and location, an observer made a revealing comment: "Acknowledge that the ancestors were the first and most prominent 'commodities' traded on Wall Street."[6] It is highly likely, then, that many slave decedents that lie buried beneath the area around Wall Street helped to build and maintain it, while their likely descendants, whose activism produced the monument now located at that burial site, occupy its margins.

Defacing Hallowed Ground: A Slave-Descendant Community Reacts

Because the burial ground decedents had already been ignored and disrespected as slaves, community activists regarded it as their mission to honor and protect them from defacement by halting construction of the new federal building. Their valuation of the decedents seemed compensatory as reinforcement of their own humanity against ongoing racial struggles in their lives. Through a series of confrontations, meetings, and protests, and other strategies, I document, in this section, the struggle of a marginalized people newly empowered to reverse near total anonymity for the African Burial Ground decedents who occupied "hallowed" ground. And I further identify the conditions of production for an inaugural slave site, as well as conflict among government officials, community activists, and site organizers over how best to represent the slave past in a presentist context for the decedents. From the moment the African Burial Ground's discovery was made public in 1991, much friction occurred between African American community activists and officials at the local and national levels—the General Services Administration (GSA), federal steering committee, federal government, the Department of the Interior's National Park Service, the US Army Corps of Engineers, and the Advisory Council on Historic Preservation, among them—over how to resolve differences pertaining to the overall burial ground project. Conflict centered on what to do with remains excavated at the site, how to commemorate the decedents appropriately, and how much money to spend.

Until community protests escalated—including then New York mayor David Dinkins's expressions of concern to a GSA regional administrator in September 1991, a press conference held at the burial site in October, and a predominantly African American task force formed in December of that year—congressional approval for construction of the thirty-four-story federal office building, coupled with payment for land to New York City, seemingly took precedence over some scattered bones from a forgotten era. Community activists and concerned citizens in the region criticized GSA and other government officials for neglecting to inform them about the status of remains, failing to handle the remains with care, and lacking a plan for their proper disposal. In a particularly disturbing charge, GSA officials allegedly ignored city maps that identified the African Burial Ground and continued to pour concrete over centuries old enslaved remains, according to complaints.

At a town meeting in February 1992, Dr. William Diamond, former regional administrator for the United States General Services Administration (GSA), reported the organization's decisions about disposition of the burial ground's remains, but without taking citizens' demands into account. Diamond first claimed that the cemetery was no longer thought to exist. But he also acknowledged that although the government had located a map of the Negros Burial Ground, it had not foreseen the number of skeletons found in the cemetery. Diamond later admitted that the government perhaps would have taken a different course of action had it foreseen the level of protest and community activism that took place. In interviews and at demonstrations, concerned citizens said that the GSA provided no research documents that explained to the community how the remains would be removed. And the GSA offered obscure explanations for how it would implement such plans in accordance with the National Historic Preservation Act of 1966.

A Memorandum of Agreement (MOA) between the GSA and the Advisory Council on Historic Preservation (ACHP) was signed March 15, 1989. The National Historic Preservation Act of 1966 specifies that a research and design plan for such historic sites as cemeteries is put into place. Although an MOA offered guidelines for protecting the African Burial Ground (later amended December 20, 1991), the GSA had evidently begun archaeological fieldwork, including identification and excavation of some remains before implementing those plans. After David Dinkins had accused the GSA of violating the MOA, an emergency session of the New York City subcommittee on building was held, in which experts testified to the significance of the burial site.

In town hall meetings and interviews held subsequent to the site's discovery in 1991 and even long after work had concluded, community activists and concerned citizens drew parallels between past disregard for the enslaved population and similar treatment after remains were discovered. As one observer put it, "How [the slaves] were treated when they were living was echoed in how they were treated after they died and when they were dug up."[7] For example, archaeologists were criticized for first applying the so-called coroner's method, which included use of a backhoe to dig up the remains, and later, on February 14, 1992, when construction workers damaged four to six burials at the site, which they attributed to inaccurate maps.

Town meetings and protests subsequent to the site's discovery show that social, cultural, and community activists forced the hand of government officials to validate the historically significant story of the burial ground, as well as contributions that enslaved Africans made to New York's very existence. In a civic meeting on April 23, 1992, for instance, the city council convened at Trinity Church to determine how to pay permanent tribute to the decedents. The break-through meeting at a church built by slave labor, that once barred Africans, proved highly symbolic. In 1697 persons of African descent were barred from being buried "within the bounds & Limits of the Church Yard of Trinity Church."[8] Successfully establishing the historical, cultural, and anthropological significance of the burial ground at that meeting meant that gaining approval to stop further excavation at the site would soon follow. On July 27, 1992, Gus Savage, an African American former congressman, chaired a congressional hearing in which a decision was indeed made to halt further excavation at the African Burial Ground. Two days later GSA administrator

Richard G. Austin officially terminated the excavation after some 410 remains were retrieved from the site, and another ten or eleven remains were left exposed. Savoring victory, individuals held an all-night "Remembrance Vigil" at the burial ground in August 1992, to recognize contributions that enslaved Africans made to the building of New York.

Clearly, government officials miscalculated the surrounding slave-descendant community's collective outrage, grief, and activism toward the burial site's preservation. For example, because of community activism, the GSA had to alter original plans to construct a four-story pavilion on part of the site and revise its mission as owners of the office tower to report on ways to memorialize those remains that lay underground. But for some protesters, the politically charged environment surrounding the burial ground project extended to disagreements over forensic methodology that would be used to study the remains. After hard-fought skirmishes to gain recognition for decedents, African-descendant community members in New York, supported primarily by a Congress-approved federal steering committee, took pains to ensure that skeletal remains be treated with dignity and respect.

Double Speak: What Talking Bones Can Never Tell

Paradoxically, only through forensic analysis that community activists sought for burial ground decedents—ironically used by some nineteenth-century anatomists—could modern day anthropologists acquire any direct knowledge at all about the decedents. Mindful of potential contradictions, and after considerable disagreements about how to proceed, experts took pains to apply a forensics method that would seek specific knowledge about cultural affinity, ethnicity, and condition of servitude. Forensic analysis of the burial ground remains was initially the responsibility of the Metropolitan Forensic Anthropology Team (MFAT) at Lehman College in the Bronx. The MFAT prepared an ontological analysis that emphasized a "biogenetic conception or 'race.'" The MFAT plan focused on determining decedents' racial identity in the belief that some Native Americans and poor whites also occupy the cemetery. But a Howard University research paradigm under anthropologist, Dr. Michael Blakey, opposed this method, and instead, stressed a "DNA-based genetics" that would "link individuals from the Burial Ground with specific cultural / regional origins in Africa."[9] Blakey's plan sought to determine cultural affinities in a four-part strategy that included geographical origins, physical quality of life, bicultural transformations from African to African-American identities, and possible modes of resistance. Consequently, black activists' insistence upon entrusting the forensic analysis of remains to Blakey's team at Howard University, the nation's premier historical black college or university (HBCU), prevailed as a seminal moment in the processing of the African monument decedents.

Blakey's team also hoped that their work could be tied to archaeological findings from other past African-descendant burial sites, such as the Newton Cemetery in Barbados and later discoveries at Campeche, Mexico, and St. Helena Island in southern Africa. Indeed, later analysis showed important similarities in bead assemblage and other objects, and evidence of obeah practices have made connections between the John Newton Plantation site in Barbados and the New York African Burial Ground. Excavated in the early 1970s, the Newton Cemetery remained "the earliest and largest undisturbed plantation slave cemetery yet reported in the New World," but some remains believed to be enslaved African decedents at Campeche, Mexico, may date to the 1500s.

Excavations and forensic analysis of enslaved remains, "contemporaneous with the New York Burial Ground," took place in the West Indies in the 1970s and at Campeche, Mexico, in 2006. At the John Newton Plantation cemetery in Barbados, an excavation unearthed burial #72, identified as an obeah practitioner or folk doctor "with definite in situ [in place] configuration of beads with cultural similarities to Burial #340" in New York.[10] The burial site contained 104 remains that were interred from about 1660 to 1820. In Campeche, Mexico, construction workers renovating an area around a park stumbled upon a colonial church and burial ground containing at least 180 remains of Amerindian, European, and African descent. While researchers believe ten skeletal remains to be of African ethnicity, a strontium tooth analysis of four of the ten revealed a cultural practice known as tooth filing, which (along with other evidence) enabled archaeologists to trace their origins to slavery in the 1550s near the port of Elmina, Ghana, in West Africa.[11]

At St. Helena Island, about a thousand miles off the southwest coast of Africa, archaeologists from the University of Bristol unearthed a grave site that contained more than five thousand freed, recaptured, and formerly enslaved Africans brought there by the Royal Navy between 1840 and 1872. Some three hundred bodies were first discovered at the site in 2006–2008, most of them unconfined and in shallow graves before a new road was built in order to provide access to a proposed airport project. Osteological analyses, including dental filings, beads, bracelets, and artifacts reveal ethnic identity but not specific cause of death.[12] United similarly by ethnicity, culture, and fate, whether in the Cape region of South Africa, Barbados in the West Indies, Campeche in Mexico, St. Helena Island in southwest Africa, or Lower Manhattan in the United States, the decedents symbolize the site of burial itself as literal and figurative space in which to recover, reembody, and ultimately alter the status of the historically devalued enslaved African.

At a forum held in January 1992 by GSA, Dr. Blakey submitted a report titled "Research Design for Archaeological, Historical and Bio-anthropological Investigations of the African Burial Ground," a draft design for a study of the burial ground remains. Members of the federal steering committee cited Blakey's anthropological knowledge and experience in African cultures, though at least one newspaper account hinted at reverse racism in the replacement of a white anthropologist with a black one.[13] Working first in collaboration with the John Milner Associates Archaeology firm, Blakey assumed full administration for the project after the federal steering committee's recommendations, December 22, 1992. Under a contract with the GSA in 1993, Dr. Blakey assumed leadership over the New York African Burial Ground Project at Howard University's W. Montague Anthropology Laboratory.

Once authorized to assume guardianship of the remains and to conduct forensic analyses by the fall of 1993, Blakey's archaeological team trod the divide between painting the decedents as specimens of pathology in the sterile language of autopsy reports and honoring them as meritorious captive African ancestors that deserved respect for their contributions to society. Efforts to restore honor and dignity to the decedents without further exploiting them posed huge challenges to Blakey's team as well as to activists in a slave-descendant African American community. This is especially true since some—as shown in earlier comments by Adam Clayton Powell IV—had disapproved of the excavation in the first place. The team hoped to discover as much as possible about the decedents' ethnic identity, as well as age, gender, and cause of death. But they also sought to identify social status, rank, and other personal attributes apart from condition of servitude.[14]

Forensic analyses that merely regurgitated those violations inscribed upon the enslaved body risked further robbing the decedents of dignity and humanity, which echoes a point that Saidiya Hartman makes in *Scenes of Subjection: Terror, Slavery, and Self-Making in Nineteenth-Century America* about gratuitously displaying the violated enslaved black female body, in particular. Hartman deflects this desensitizing methodology in favor of investigating what she identifies as mundane terrors such as minstrelsy and coercive acts of making merriment in the slave cabins. She contrasts such overt slave brutalities as brutal beatings, for instance, with the less discernible, but potentially more insidious, mundane violence of performativity that enforced alcohol consumption and compelled the enslaved to participate in festivities.[15]

The display of skeletal remains from the African Burial Ground seemed gratuitous and stirred sensitivities, especially given the lengthy history of exploitative treatment of the black female body. For example, large posters of the African woman known as #340, along with other skeletal remains from the African Burial Ground excavation, were tacked to a wrought iron gate behind the Ted Weiss Building for public view. Accompanied by narrative panels, the posters, which blurred the distinction between informing the public about the decedents and exploiting them, were eventually replaced with a monument designed by architect Rodney Leon, which now occupies the space. However, the posters also reinforced the fragility of the captive Africans, who, according to forensic analyses, sustained significant invasive injuries consistent with bearing heavy loads over time. And yet some injuries could also have derived from captive Africans' participation in specific acts of slave resistance.

Historical accounts, including a book in 2005 about the African Burial Ground story titled *Slavery in New York*, along with a special exhibition held at the New-York Historical Society, would report that instances of slave resistance took place far more extensively than previously known. For example, on April 6, 1712, nine whites were killed and six wounded in an insurrection organized by twenty-five to fifty enslaved blacks in New York. In April 1741 thirteen Africans convicted of conspiring to burn down New York City were burned at the stake.[16] Not surprisingly, a mixed portrait emerges for the African Burial Ground decedents, which combines raw data about physical traumas and other indignities they suffered with some creative narratives about their identities and ethnic origins.

Dr. Michael Blakey's forensic team struggled to unite clinical language about the condition of remains and cause of death with personal data about the decedents' life experiences. Though the team proved successful in a number of cases, stories and aspirations for other captive Africans remain speculative, as indicated at the outset by numerical identification tags that replaced the missing names. Other difficulties prevented "certainty" in establishing ethnic identification and cultural practices for most decedents.

Perhaps the most controversial example is Burial #101, a black male decedent for whom African cultural retentions remain speculative. Because a symbol that scholars initially identified as a Sankofa decorated the man's coffin, they determined his origins to be West African, possibly Ghana or the Ivory Coast. The symbol on the man's coffin, which "originated with the Twi-speaking people of present-day Ghana and the Ivory Coast, represents the proverb 'Se wo were fi na wo sankofa a yenkyi,' meaning 'It is not a taboo to return and fetch it when you forget.'"[17] Burial #101 stood as a rare exception, a prescient model of a slave decedent whose ethnic origins and cultural practices seemed still fathomable, and fully intact, after a centuries-old burial that provided little else to go on.

Sankofa, an Akan word, loosely means that one must return to the past in order to move forward in the future. Poet Kofi Anyidoho writes in *Fon-TomFrom* that through the Sankofa, the present and the past constantly "interface." The bird flies forward into the sky and expects great things to come in the future. But the Sankofa figure, "ubiquitous and mythological," is ever cautious, and in constantly looking back, it warns of mistakes from the past that might prove destructive for the future. Anyidoho writes, "In the Sankofa bird, Ghanaian culture has found its most complex and most recurrent expression of the nation's favourite guiding principle of development." [18] Also shown in the opening scene of Haile Gerima's film *Sankofa,* and metaphorized in numerous poems and prose by Ghanaian and other writers, the mythical bird functions as a repetitive, fundamental, and prominent symbol of the nation's formation and growth.

But in 2010 historian Erik R. Seeman published an article, "Reassessing the 'Sankofa Symbol' in New York's African Burial Ground," that questions the authenticity of the heart-shaped drawing on the coffin as a Sankofa symbol. After careful probing of extensive archival evidence, Seeman asserts that the heart-shaped design, made of fifty-one iron tacks on the man's coffin, closely resembled that which appears on numerous Anglo-American coffin lids in the eighteenth and nineteenth centuries, the approximate dating of Burial #101. He further claims that "the first evidence of the Sankofa appeared in [anthropologist] R. S. Rattray's 1927 catalog of adinkra symbols" and does not appear in historical data at all from the eighteenth and nineteenth centuries, nor in mortuary practices among the Akan people of Ghana. [19] Seeman therefore believes it is more probable that the heart-shaped symbol nailed on the coffin lid of Burial #101 emulated eighteenth- and nineteenth-century Anglo-American burial practices instead of West African ones.

Erik Seeman goes on to debunk another theory that attributes the burial position of nearly all of the decedents to a tradition embedded in African cosmology. He notes that among the decedents, "98% (367 of 375) were buried with the head facing west," and 100 percent were buried "supine" or "lying face up," which is exactly the way in which white New Yorkers were buried in the eighteenth century: "coffined (with perhaps a few exceptions for indigents), west-headed, supine, single interments." [20] Seeman's findings expose barriers that often divide traditional, evidentiary historians and memory devotees. I note in chapter 1 the iconic Sankofa's symbolic appearance and thematic role in the opening scene of Ethiopian filmmaker Haile Gerima's classic film also titled *Sankofa.* And I discuss herein controversy surrounding the authenticity of Gorée's House of Slaves as a major holding cell for slaves before the dreaded Middle Passage journey. Of course, I engage the archival history versus the living memory debate, which surfaces at other slave sites in this study, albeit under different circumstances. The former method scours archival, historical evidence for an important but exacting standard of accuracy that is not always possible to attain, while the latter method embraces a symbolic cultural collective, or a bigger picture based on a remembered or reconstructed past that may obscure the uncertainty of minute details.

Seeman goes on to point out that other decedents in the forensic study, such as burial #340, do show strong evidence of West African origins and cultural retentions. He acknowledges that African-descendant people pointedly placed artifacts in the coffin to accompany the deceased to the next world. And he links a probable "conjuring bundle" located in a burial with an African cultural practice that many scholars have associated with conjuring traditions. Taken collectively with similarities in forensic analyses of slave remains in Barbados and other diaspora-dispersion sites that I mentioned earlier in the chapter, African Burial Ground decedents affirm the existence and survival of some African funerary practices. Ultimately, Seeman assigns "hybridity" as a requisite descriptive term for the captive Africans removed from their homeland and enslaved in foreign lands. For example, he concludes that the Sankofa symbol, "with its suggestion of the unmediated transfer of African cultural forms, stands in for the more complex story of adaptation and hybridity that defines how Africans became African Americans."[21]

Should devotees maintain fidelity to the cherished Sankofa symbol, now prominently inscribed on the African Burial Ground National Monument, in light of Seeman's findings? The question of the historical past and symbolic Sankofa conjures debate about whether Gorée's House of Slaves ever functioned as an authentic deportation site for enslaved Africans, and even extends to claims about Olaudah Equiano's identity on the periphery of the 2007 exhibition at Birmingham. These treasured slavery mementos encode a message of material cultural survival, resilience against an Atlantic slave trade, and the viability of an enslaved African's identity. The House of Slaves still draws countless tourists under the tutelage of an African griot-oral historian. Olaudah Equiano remains a stalwart symbol of slave resistance and the author of a compelling personal narrative. And the Sankofa symbol still circulates wistfully in scholarship and mass culture just as it did before Seeman's data appeared in print. As I have previously observed, healthy discussion and profound debate about such controversial subjects forge a pathway through historical amnesia about and neglect of the slave past. In *Against Amnesia: Contemporary Women Writers and the Crises of Historical Memory*, Nancy J. Peterson convincingly argues that like selective remembrance, the archival exclusion or discarding of some ethnic minorities' past historical contributions to nation building, has been a deliberate undertaking.[22] However, such exclusionary practices about abhorrent conditions may well have led to the creation of a renovated House of Slaves, the iconic status of an Olaudah Equiano, or even the production of a Sankofa symbol.

In spite of Herculean efforts by the forensic team at cultural diversification among decedents, and uncertainty about the Sankofa symbol, the dominant impression given by the decedents still remains that of the crushing physical impact of enslaved labor from which one might easily discern an attendant psychological and emotional traumatic impact. Autopsies reveal extensive damage resulting from torn ligaments and muscle detachment from bone, indicative of strain from excessive work and load-bearing stress. Physical pathologies sustained by the enslaved population, such as degenerative arthritis, joint problems, and muscle strain typically derived from "axial loading" or lifting and carrying heavy loads directly on top of the head, dominate the portraits.[23] Areas of bone showed scarring and enlargement probably caused by repeated stress. A man, estimated at twenty-five years of age when he died, was identified as a member of the Fulbe ethnicity from modern-day Benin. A chemical study of his teeth, as well as the customary filing of one of them, led researchers to this conclusion. Five buttons—two decorated with anchors—were found in his coffin, prompting investigators to connect him with the British navy, though as cautioned in the GSA reports, he may have randomly selected the buttons to sew on his coat in order to provide warmth. But, overriding speculation about the man's identity, the autopsy revealed that he had suffered from arthritis and had sustained small fractures in his neck and numerous other injuries and ailments, such as anemia and rickets, commonly found among other enslaved Africans in the New York population. The autopsy team concluded that the twenty-five-year-old man's ailments and injuries—and subsequent early death—were the result of lifting heavy loads, some of which he may have carried on his head. Like most of the decedents, he was buried with his head tilted to the west, establishing a link with an African cosmology practice that Erik Seeman also disputes.[24]

Seventy-five percent of males and 65 percent of females exhibited similar pathologies. These indicators resulted from strain upon muscles and ligaments sufficient to tear bones away from their attachments. The frequency of these injuries suggests work and load-bearing stresses at the margins of human biological capacity. For example, the skeletal distribution of these wounds, which is particular muscle attachments of the arms, legs, and shoulders, points to heavy lifting. As reported by Mark E. Mack, "at least four different types of spinal fractures" have been identified among remains in the African Burial Ground.[25]

For the most part, autopsies could determine only the trauma, injury, or pathology that caused death. For example, a woman identified as burial #335, who likely died from complications of childbirth, cradled a newborn infant (burial #336) "on her flexed right arm" in a hexagonal coffin. Like many other decedents, she lay supine, with her head tilted to the west. In a particularly disturbing report, the remains of a twenty-to twenty-four-year-old woman, identified as burial #25, contained "a flattened lead musket ball" lodged in her ribs, the probable cause of death. She had also suffered "blunt force trauma to her face" and several bone fractures, "one indicating that her right arm had been twisted and pulled." New bone tracings found around those fractures indicated that she had lived for only a few days after sustaining the injuries.[26] One can also speculate about psychological damage resulting from such cruelties as constant surveillance, verbal abuse, threats of sales or the actual selling of family members that the autopsy reports neither detect nor could document definitively.

Perhaps most notable among the remains, a woman known only as #340, aged between 39.4 and 64.4 years, had originally been buried wearing a strand of simple drawn, multicolored glass beads and cowrie shells at her hips and a bracelet of beads encircling the right wrist, perhaps indicating great rank and stature, and offering keys to an African identity. When found, the deceased woman had been laid to rest with her body supine, head tilted to the west.[27] Ironically, #340, like other decedents, required a forensic analysis of her dissected parts conducted at Howard University laboratories in an effort to recognize her humanity.

After autopsies had been conducted on the remains, New York's Schomburg Center for Research in Black Culture organized an elaborate six-day "Rites of Ancestral Return" or reinterment ceremony, which proved to be a concluding seminal event to memorialize the decedents. The formality of these burial ceremonies signals more than the burial and reinterment of remains, which of course could have occurred without fanfare. These ceremonies represent the burial of an old order or political ideology—a master text that marks the historical preservation of the slave past through unidentified bodies discarded in unmarked graves and banished to remote places. Organizers at the center not only reversed a process of annihilation and disregard for the decedents when they were first buried but also favored an African cosmology-based performance tradition over traditional Western rites, which included drumbeats, ring shouts, prayers, sacred rites, and the pouring of libations. Formally referred to as "Rites of Ancestral Return," the ceremony is a strong example of a ritual and/or performance as alternative archive that acts both as an essential cultural practice and as a vehicle for processing the traumatic aftermath of slavery, or healing and emotional repair, particularly for slave-descendant African American program organizers and spectators.

The Burial Rites Ceremony began on the Howard University campus and ended in New York on October 4, 2003. Each of four caskets contained one girl, one boy, an adult woman, and an adult man who were memorialized in the reinterment ceremony. They were selected to represent the 419 enslaved and free African decedents that were inventoried (out of 424 graves excavated and identified) dating to the colonial period. In a eulogy given at Howard University's Rankin Memorial Chapel, Dean Bernard L. Richardson said that the ancestors were part of history even if not identified by name: "We give thanks for the opportunity to connect with our past and our future. Oh God, you have made these bones live again."

The four caskets, made from cedar, pine, and spruce wood, were hand carved in Ghana. Libations were poured as coffins were sprinkled with holy water and sacred oils. An African drum corps performed to mark the arrival of the coffins. Church bells rang out, the anthem "Lift Every Voice and Sing" was played, and both the Boys and Girls Choirs of Harlem performed. Such dignitaries as Charles Rangel, David Dinkins, Michael Bloomberg, David Patterson, Jesse Jackson, and Maya Angelou gave speeches. Children performed a ring shout ceremony as they formed a perimeter ring around the commemorative floor sculpture. They held signs with handwritten messages for the ancestors. Pallbearers then placed the four coffins into crypts.

Snatched from Oblivion amid Moments of Reflection

"Flash" moments and seminal events that began with the burial ground's (re)discovery and extended to massive demonstrations ensured respect for the burial ground decedents' humanity through the handling of remains. For example, after ancestral funeral rites had concluded, attention turned to selecting an artist to design a monument. The move from forensic analysis and (re) interment of burial ground remains to constructing a monument seems an inevitable resolution to repair what began as historical neglect and negation. A monument might also serve as a permanent reminder about the incident for tourists drawn to the site. Furthermore, it could safeguard the burial ground story from sinking into oblivion over time. These endeavors to transform the status of anonymous slave decedents at the African Burial Ground through forensic analysis, burial rites, and installation of an official monument wholly converge with activists' reassertion of a formidable self-identity (by proxy) with enslaved remains.

I am reminded here of African American artist Kerry James Marshall, who says that his propensity for reanimating his own African art serves to counteract its undervaluation. For the African Burial Ground, the National Park Service, in partnership with the General Services Administration, set objectives for a design that closely mirrored other "modern" monuments and memorials that honor the dead, including Mia Lin's Vietnam Memorial, the Oklahoma City Memorial, and the September 11 Memorial at the World Trade Center. Rather than merely occupy a physical space or place, these sites connect intimately with visitors. Andreas Huyssen envisions the modern museum as a "testing ground for reflections on temporality and subjectivity, identity and alterity" and adds that it can be viewed "as our own memento mori, and as such, a life-enhancing rather than mummifying institution in an age bent on the destructive denial of death."[28] These observations call attention to the unusual predicament of memorializing an estimated twenty thousand decedents, none of whom bears a single name or mark of identification, that lie in unmarked graves in one of the most highly valued tracts of land in the world.

In April 2005, after conducting a public review process, the selection team for the African Burial Ground National Monument chose a design created by architect Rodney Leon, making it the first monument in the United States to honor the contributions of people of African descent.[29] The African Burial Ground had been officially designated a New York City Historic District and a National Landmark in 1993. Considered in expert testimony to be the most important archaeological find in the United States in this century, the burial ground was proclaimed a national monument by President George W. Bush on February 27, 2006.

The African Burial Ground draws attention to multiple ironies that attend public urban space, such as its close proximity to the wealth of Wall Street and the entertainment district at Broadway, as well as to nearby impoverished communities occupied by a slave-descendant population. I ponder how individuals gripped by poverty and racial inequities in communities near the burial ground respond to a past traumatic event in the face of traumas that occur for them on a daily basis. Therefore, an African Burial Ground National Monument asks the question, Just what does commemoration (re)produce for the unknown, unidentified decedents? Does it stabilize, anchor, and clarify cultural and spiritual memory for the African descendant community, as Paul Connerton's and Patrick Hutton's ideas contend? Does it forge a community collective or reinforce cleavage amid a wealth of poverty?

Paul Connerton's observations in *How Societies Remember* vigorously renew debate about how commemorative practices serve present-day needs or rewrite the past in the context of the present. He writes, "Commemoration reproduces the past for present-day aims, by bringing the original narrative of the community into focus."[30] Commemorative practices stimulate group solidarity and aid the formation of a collective memory. Hutton also suggests, in *History as an Art of Memory*, that commemoration stabilizes collective memory, and that it supports a community's efforts to maintain solidarity in the formation of a conceptual identity. Commemoration for the burial ground's urban landscape means generating discussion about the need to keep alive cultural and spiritual memory, and to stress its importance both locally and globally. But the burial ground resists attempts to reorder the past in a seamless narrative for the present and future. As I have discussed, although an individual and group collective united to create the site, differences in how to organize protests around the discovery, how best to remember the decedents, and what to do with the remains attended the process.

A monument as a permanent fixture seemed a ready answer to questions about how the African Burial Ground might connect local communities, as well as the general public, with this important story. Furthermore, as I have noted, a monument would symbolize slave remembrance for a contemporary generation that never experienced or witnessed slavery. The presence of a monument could also address the question of temporality and fluidity in individual interpretations and perspectives that tend to shift with the winds of time. But these ideas can be misleading, because they evade questions about the geopolitical context that binds local communities, landscape, and urban space with a commemorative site such as the African Burial Ground.

Just as Dr. Michael Blakey's archaeological team confronted the challenge in a laboratory setting to raise the dead or to make the bones live again, Rodney Leon addressed the living from an artist's den by designing a monument that would accomplish exactly that mission. The African Burial Ground National Monument merges creativity with purpose by first fulfilling Leon's objectives to connect visitors intimately with the memorial proper. For example, the structure offers space for guided and self-guided tours in which visitors can express their feelings or engage in dialogue about events that the monument commemorates. Leon also steeps the design in an African cosmology tradition—including the controversial Sankofa symbol and the west–east axis that I have previously addressed—which he meticulously outlines on his website for the lay observer.

Though the monument preceded Seeman's findings, there are no plans to remove or alter the Sankofa symbol. Like the Equiano exhibition at Birmingham that I discuss in chapter 1, site organizers—disproportionately slave descendants—have ignored certain "protocols" of traditional, archival history and have opted for memory in the tradition of an oral history tradition. Through the monument's design Leon aims to satisfy individuals' desire to remember past traumatic events like slavery, but he also seeks to promote healing and to reinforce an Afrocentric cultural education for contemporary generations.

The idea that visitors must be active participants that engage intimately with the monument, structurally, is not mutually exclusive from tenets of an African cosmology tradition that foremost encourages personal reflection. I reproduce Leon's detailed descriptions in tandem with some personal observations of the site. Having visited the African Burial Ground and examined the African Burial Ground National Monument on three occasions, I have witnessed the progression from skeletal remains photographed on large posters tacked to a wrought iron gate behind the Ted Weiss Building to Leon's finished monument, complete with guided tour conducted by park rangers. A detailed narrative of Rodney Leon's memorial design can be accessed at his website through AARRIS Architects, as well as from the final report titled "Memorial" at the United States General Services Administration website.[31]

Leon identifies the monument's seven composite features—the Wall of Remembrance, the Ancestral Re-interment Grove, the Memorial Wall, the Ancestral Chamber, the Circle of the Diaspora, the Spiral Processional Ramp, and the Ancestral Libation Court, which call attention to the site as hallowed ground and encourage participation and uninhibited expressions by visitors. The twenty-four-foot Ancestral Chamber matches the depth that construction workers descended before locating the remains. In recognition of the Middle Passage, the Ancestral Chamber and its parameters resemble the hull of a slave ship, with flooring that simulates planks. Two waterfalls constructed on either side of the chamber represent the pouring of libations, and they spill into a deeper pool of water that stands for the Atlantic Ocean. The chamber opens to the sky. Coins thrown by visitors fill the pool. A cosmogram that represents the crossroads of birth, life, death, and rebirth in Congo cosmology lies at the chamber's center.

The Ancestral Chamber reflects aspects of African cosmology that touch upon cultural, spiritual, and ancestral essence, and it is oriented toward the east, permitting natural light to flow into the interior space. The chamber's interior contains an area in which individuals can choose to meditate, reflect, contemplate, and pray. The following libation text is inscribed upon a polished granite wall of remembrance: "For all those who were lost / For all those who were stolen / For all those who were left behind / For all those who were not forgotten." The remains of the 419 African decedents were reinterred among seven sarcophagi, marked by seven burial mounds along a path extending north to south from Duane Street in the Ancestral Re-interment Grove. The monument runs parallel with the direction in which the decedents are buried, along the west–east axis in the direction of the rising sun.

Rodney Leon designed his monument to connect the living world, or the public urban space that surrounds Lower Manhattan, with the spiritual or sacred space of the Libation Court and Ancestral Chamber that culminate with the burial site itself. For example, the Spiral Processional Ramp, which descends four feet below street level, is designed to bridge the gap between those two worlds. But as a heritage site, the African Burial Ground National Monument competes with the artist's creative interpretations of a material object and those perspectives that visitors and spectators may form independently. Leon's complex interpretive narrative makes key features of the monument accessible for most visitors. Consequently, the design mediates the dialectic between authorizing memory and opening up space for visitors to govern their own perspectives.

Ironically, the attack on the World Trade Center on September 11, 2001, destroyed sixteen hundred boxes of artifacts from the African Burial Ground that were stored in a room at the center's North Tower. But this example of thematic cross-fertilization, or the storage of artifacts from one tragic episode in the bowels of another location in which a tragic event also took place, is not the only symbolism that binds together seemingly disparate episodes. Both the African Burial Ground National Monument and the World Trade Center have become compelling places where remembrance of the dead is sacrosanct. Therefore, it should come as no surprise that these crimes against humanity, however different, produced similar objectives that guided artists' designs for the African Burial Ground National Monument and the World Trade Center as modern memorials. Guided by a jury's mission statement for construction of a September 11 memorial that emphasized reflection and contemplation, architect Michael Arad beat out more than five thousand competitors and produced a winning design around principles similar to those adopted by Rodney Leon for the African Burial Ground National Monument. Titled "Reflecting Absence," Arad's design features a cluster of trees surrounding two large, sunken reflecting pools that occupy the spot where the Twin Towers once stood.

Reminiscent of the modern Vietnam Memorial designed by Maya Lin, and in a move that gestures to the memorial's spinoff museum, officials at the African Burial Ground collected "nearly 8,000 personal handwritten messages from the living to the African ancestors" that were buried with the remains, according to Christopher Moore, writer for the 1994 video recording *The African Burial Ground: An American Discovery*. These notes were generic messages to anonymous ancestors that lived and died centuries before visitors appeared at the memorial site. The curatorship of the spinoff museum—truly a people's museum—was authorized solely by visitors (along with officials wise enough to save the artifacts for further display), whose unscripted mementos brought further clarity to the lives of individuals behind the hand-written messages. A special exhibit in February 2010 also unveiled handwritten notes left at the African Burial Ground by schoolchildren that expressed their feelings during a visit to the site. Yet the African Burial Ground National Monument adds unique features to the structure and format of the traditional museum.

The burial ground's complex odyssey has led to additional projects that further explain the site's origins, as well as the history of slavery in New York. These additional materials support a "living memory" of the slave past for contemporary generations. They also reinforce the idea that as "flash moments" or seminal events reoccur, they renew and revise the legacy of slavery, as well as expand the dimensions of the monument. Located in a gallery on the first floor of the Ted Weiss Federal Building, these items include maps, sample coffins, books, brochures, and other artifacts, as well as a film that historicizes the making of the Burial Ground as a heritage site. The information about the burial ground's history enlightens visitors that tour the site, but that may know very little about its origins. Therefore, the indoor exhibitions add pedagogical value to the burial ground, proper, in the hopes of leaving a lasting effect on those that leave the site.

The burial ground story reveals how official archives nullified the site's historical, cultural, and political importance, but it also documents the struggle of a marginalized people newly empowered to reverse near-total anonymity for the "talking bones" that would rearticulate a veiled history for thousands of anonymous enslaved Africans. Perhaps most poignantly, the African Burial Ground proves how integrally past traumatic events like slavery remain connected with present-day politics about race, culture, human rights, and economic stability, particularly for some in the slave-descendant community.

I return, here, to the charismatic park ranger who narrated the burial ground story on an organized tour in a gesture of remembrance for museum-goers/spectators who showed great enthusiasm for the guide's delivery. But Douglas Massenburg, a guide at the African Burial Ground National Monument since October 1, 2006, was reassigned as the lead park ranger at the General Grant National Memorial on September 7, 2014. His replacement by another park ranger-guide, who devised his own narrative about the African Burial Ground, typifies the fluidity and fleeting "flash" moments that such displays entail. Though a significant memento of a rich, complex historical past, the slave cemetery, as well as Rodney Leon's granite "slave ship" monument—like the slave forts of Ghana and Senegal—remains a mute, immobile object without an accompanying story for the casual listener to take away from the site. A static fixture cemented in time and space, the African Burial Ground National Monument is thus animated for the visitor-spectator, but only through appropriately knowledgeable site organizers and guides, governed by the constraints of time.

◆ ◆ ◆

For the African Burial Ground in New York, grassroots efforts from a slave-descendant community challenged officialdom en masse, perhaps for the first time, and altered perceptions of an enslaved people's placement in history as discounted, discarded, and devalued. Through significant protest, coupled with mobilization and intervention, community activists overrode traditional authoritative channels and rewrote the story of slavery for thousands of captive Africans. The turn from private mourning of decedents to reflection and remembrance of their legacy goes well beyond discovery, excavation, forensic analysis, and commemoration, however. Some in the region's slave-descendant community had envisioned that the burial ground site would be seen as a penetrating wedge into a historical vacuum that discounted enslaved ancestors' contributions to the nation's construction, and they called for revisionist histories to accommodate those contributions. Others refused to accept the federal office building's construction and excavation of remains and have declined to visit the site altogether. Still others saw more ambitious ramifications for the African Burial Ground that shifted public dialogue from forgotten or erased captive Africans to their movement from margin to center among the ranks of nation builders.

Civil rights activist the Reverend Herbert Daughtry said that without the bones and the enslaved labor, there would have been no United States of America and no wealth in the Western world. He expressed the notion that the ancestors' contributions benefited the nation, not just African American pride. As another observer put it, "The African Burial Ground can be a beacon, not only to tell the story of the Africans in New York City, but in Delaware, in Maryland, from Albany to Argentina—and that's primarily that they are 'colony builders.' That, to me, would be the greatest hope: that a child or adult would think of the worked slave as being synonymous with colony builder."[32]

Henceforth, community activists like Daughtry would participate in a full-fledged resurrection of the captive African in a new guise as nation builder. By recognizing and reassessing enslaved laborers' role as colony builders, observers and organizers of the African Burial Ground slave recovery would thus shift the focus from memorializing decedents predominantly as victims of horrific abuse. However, attention to the enslaved community's contributions at the local and state level would inevitably shine a spotlight on their refiguration, not only as nation builders, but also as arbiters of culture at the seats of power, including the White House, the Capitol, and even some presidential plantation sites. As I discuss in chapter 3, locating slave burial grounds and memorializing enslaved decedents, in a series of seminal events recently undertaken at presidential estates, would also further conversation about their embeddedness in the nation through patrilineal connections long silenced in official records.

CHAPTER THREE

Founding Fathers, Chimeras, and "American Africanisms" at Presidential Estates

> Nothing could be worse, for the work of mourning, than confusion or
> doubt: one has to know who is buried where—and it is necessary (to
> know—to make certain) that, in what remains of him, he remain there.
> —Jacques Derrida, *Specters of Marx* (1994)

> Thus strangely are our souls constructed, and by slight
> ligaments are we bound to prosperity and ruin.
> —Mary Shelley, *Frankenstein* (1818)

In the early nineteenth century, P. T. Barnum purchased for exhibition a gnarled, blind, partially paralyzed African American woman. She boldly claimed to be the former nurse of George Washington, which, were it true, would have made her 161 years old. Joice Heth, enslaved itinerant carnival performer that brought Barnum wealth and notoriety, said she was the first to clothe the newborn babe who would become the nation's first president. Spellbound and inordinately curious multitudes attended her performances, and she regaled them with hymns that she claimed to have sung to the young Washington. To the fascination of spectators at her performances, she would then reveal anecdotes about the president, and would emphasize her superior treatment as more befitting a servant than a slave. Heth's purported connection with Washington as wet nurse and mammy figure propelled her own fame as performer, curiously blending a patriotic fervor with naked voyeurism, race science, and a blackface minstrelsy tradition that were all in vogue in nineteenth-century America.

When she died in 1836, more than a thousand people paid fifty cents each to witness the autopsy procedure.[1] At least one newspaper chastised plans to dissect the body of the woman who had purportedly clothed the revered first president of the United States as an infant. Editors at the *New York Sun* thought that Heth should have been spared mutilation "not so much on account of her extreme old age, and the public curiosity which she had already gratified for

A reconstructed slave cabin at Mount Vernon.

Slave cemetery at Andrew Jackson's Hermitage.

the gain of others, as for the high honor with which she was endowed in being the nurse of the immortal Washington."[2] Heth's pending autopsy hovered for a brief chivalrous moment, not as personally exploitative, but as an affront to the nation and, most importantly, to the honor of a president known to be exceedingly conscious and protective of his public image. Of course, the autopsy went ahead, because, for Joice Heth, advancement for the cause of science, as well as settling the question of her age, superseded any qualms about honor. The results revealed her age to be no more than eighty years.[3]

The spectacle that Heth employed through repetitive exploitative performances renders multiple versions of a destabilized history. Heth's "grotesque" body and presumed inferior mind in the context of pseudo race science contrasted sharply with the intellect, moral rectitude, and well-proportioned physical carriage of Washington, and "created a carnivalesque juxtaposition."[4] That "collaborative performance" aggrandized Washington, who quintessentially defined the nation through iconic imaging, but it also exposed certain imperfections, including his copious reliance upon enslaved labor.

Heth's misshapen body simultaneously proved an essential component of a ghoulish command performance that both validated and demeaned her. For Heth, her performances—in spite of doubts about her authenticity—fulfilled spectators' desire for a nostalgic return to the safe bosom of a domestic slave figure and to Heth's own capitulation to a trickster's motif by accommodating those desires. If Heth could not control her enslaved status or deformed physique (she weighed only forty-six pounds), perhaps she could at least enrapture her audiences with yarns about the nation's First Founder. Heth's curious resurrection of Washington, combined with mythmaking and presidential iconography, pivots at burial sites on presidential estates where anonymous, unidentified decedents are subjected to reinvention as individuals intricately interwoven with their enslavers.

In this chapter I am interested in multiple iterations of slave recovery and commemoration for those decedents that remain buried at three high-profile presidential plantations or estates. In recent years, officials at the presidential estates of George Washington, Thomas Jefferson, and Andrew Jackson— in tandem with slave-descendant communities' active involvement—have made special efforts to locate slave burial grounds, construct memorials or monuments, and recognize enslaved laborers' contributions. Memorials and commemorative projects honoring enslaved decedents have been dedicated at Washington's Mount Vernon and Andrew Jackson's Hermitage estates. At Jefferson's Monticello, archaeologists have identified a probable slave burial ground, and memorial exhibitions have been added, including a special

Sally Hemings exhibit that opened on Saturday, June 16, 2018. While specific graves remain unmarked—with one exception at the Hermitage—archaeologists have located the approximate vicinity of slave burial sites at all three presidential estates. In reversing long-standing practice that silenced the slave's presence and contributions at presidential estates, officials reordered the temporality of the history of slavery through these newly added memorials and special exhibits.

Significant progress notwithstanding, my aim in this chapter is to canvass these sites in order to offer a renewed reading of the enslaved subject—not only as interwoven with—but also as more ensconced in the nation's very identity and iconic imaging than has often been acknowledged. I therefore place disclosures about the familial slave and genealogical dispossession or the political economy of Pierre Nora's "completely new identity of the self" in conversation with modern-day slave memorials placed at these presidential estates. The interconnectedness in private and public memory spaces between presidential enslavers and those that they enslaved extends well beyond involuntary servitude. It ranges from the exploitative performances of Joice Heth to an ambiguous paternity that crosses the threshold of the "familial slave" in plantation society at presidential estates.

Heth's story highlights the idea of an ambiguous paternity intertwined with race, slavery, nation, and iconic imaging. As such, her story embodies the concoction of an organism in Greek mythology known as the "chimera," which is at once biological mutant, genetic foundling, and philosophical illusion. This mythical organism comprises the head of a lion, the body of a goat, and the tail of a snake. Biologically, the chimera originates from two genetically distinct types of cells as a result of embryonic twins merging into a single fetus in the mother's womb. Consequently, in DNA testing, the chimera as parent would prove to be genetically unrelated to its own offspring if that offspring contained tissue from the recessive twin.

From a philosophical perspective, the chimera is defined as "a creation of the imagination; an impossible and foolish fancy."[5] Perhaps the most famous allusion to the chimera in both its biological and philosophical complexities appears in Mary Shelley's nineteenth-century novel *Frankenstein*. M. Waldman, a professor of chemistry, tells a young Victor Frankenstein that the key to understanding or unlocking the mysteries of life is sheer fancy: "The modern masters promise very little; they know that metals cannot be transmuted and that the elixir of life is a chimera."[6] Frankenstein goes on to produce a monster-offspring, but through invention rather than biological creation. Assembled from human scraps or the dismembered body parts of decedents pilfered from charnel houses, the monster-son is akin to the chimera, genetically unrelated to his inventor-father but paternally tethered to him nonetheless.

It is within this framework that Toni Morrison's "American Africanisms" intersects with the chimera as metaphor for the formerly enslaved decedent through a complex, patrilineal genetic coding that links the slave-descendant foundling with the father, but without known (or at least acknowledged) evidence of DNA tracings. Rather, like Victor Frankenstein, the enslaver subordinates, shuns, and abandons that part of himself, which he deems hideous. Chagrined, the monster says to Frankenstein, "You, my creator, detest and spurn me, thy creature, to whom thou art bound by ties only dissoluble by the annihilation of one of us."[7] Clearly, I do not regard the enslaved being as a mutated monstrosity. But the self and its recessive "other" are composite parts of the same being, not unlike the chimeric twin so hidden within that it is hardly detectable or recognizable.

The relevance of conversation about anonymous, unidentified slaves in unmarked graves at presidential estates whose occupants may very well include "slaves in the family" cannot be dismissed out of hand in the interest of full disclosure and rapidly changing circumstances in genealogical research.[8] These circumstances have seemingly come full circle in light of First Lady Michelle Obama's five-generation family odyssey from a maternal, mixed-race slavery ancestry to occupancy at the White House (I discuss former president Obama's ancestry in chapter 1.) Rachel L. Swarns explores the mixed-race slavery ancestry of Mrs. Obama in *American Tapestry: The Story of the Black, White and Multiracial Ancestors of Michelle Obama* and therefore furthers conversation about a still-sensitive subject. DNA samples suggest that Mrs. Obama's great-great-grandfather, Adolphus Shields, was the biracial son of Charles Marion Shields and Melvinia, an enslaved black woman who was Mrs. Obama's great-great-great-grandmother.

Charles Marion Shields was the third son of Melvinia's white slave master, Henry Shields. The direct descendant from Charles Shields's white family that provided the DNA requested anonymity, and "after wrestling for weeks over the matter," the family declined permission to include an ancestor's photograph in Swarns's book. The reality is that, like First Lady Michelle Obama, many slave-descendant African Americans originate from so-called miscegenated relationships—unions by force, consent, or "enforced consent"—to paraphrase John Blassingame's pronouncement in *The Slave Community: Plantation Life in the Antebellum South.*

In a haunting scene from Toni Morrison's novel *Beloved*, the formerly enslaved matriarch and community sermonizer Baby Suggs struggles to remember the scattered placement of her eight children:

Great God, she thought, where do I start? Get somebody to write old Whitlow. See who took Patty and Rosa Lee. Somebody name Dunn got Ardelia and went west, she heard. No point in trying for Tyree or John. They cut thirty years ago and, if she searched too hard and they were hiding, finding them would do them more harm than good. Nancy and Famous died in a ship off the Virginia coast before it set sail for Savannah. That much she know. The overseer at Whitlow's place brought her the news, more from a wish to have his way with her than from the kindness of his heart.[9]

As the scene realistically portrays—reminiscent of WPA interviews in the 1930s—slavery made it nearly impossible for many slave descendants to verify a requisite black genealogical history. Not coincidentally, Washington, Jefferson, and Jackson are all alleged to have fathered children by enslaved black women, which I shall discuss later in the chapter.[10] Allegations come from either oral history by certain slave-descendant African American families in the cases of Washington and Jackson, or through DNA results, for Jefferson. But verification of these claims remains untested and hence unproven for Washington and Jackson, and in spite of DNA results, Jefferson's paternity of Hemings's children is still unrecognized by some among Jefferson's white descendants and even some historians.

Silenced in certain "official" records and ambiguous in oral testimonies, the familial, genealogically dispossessed slave is mired in the nation's foundational morass. And so, in a Derridean move that insists upon the impossible task of accounting for all of the dead, I turn to where the bodies are buried at three presidential estates that exhibit significant slave presence that yearns for full accountability.

How the Slave "in Memoriam" Transforms Mount Vernon

The transformation of the slave subject into the very fabric of Americana perhaps urges a more complex reading of the master/slave relationship that bypasses the latter's indelible "otherness," faithful servitude, or contributions to nation building. The increasing addition of slave memorials and/or monuments at Washington's Mount Vernon, as well as other presidential estates, may assuage a strained relationship that some slave descendants maintain with a nation whose original sin is foregrounded in the simultaneous quest for liberty and support of slavery.

One can glean the vagaries of that complex relationship in a speech delivered by Frederick Douglass on April 14, 1876, in which he expressed ambivalence about whether blacks should celebrate the Fourth of July. In the speech, Douglass also highlighted his deep reservations about Abraham Lincoln. For millions of slaves symbolically freed in the Emancipation Proclamation—officially freed in the Thirteenth Amendment to the U.S. Constitution and accorded citizenship in the Fourteenth Amendment— Lincoln sutured a divided nation and stood emblematically as the post– Civil War patriarch of the slave "foundling." But Lincoln embodied what Douglass defined as an ambiguous paternity: "'You [white Americans] are the children of Abraham Lincoln. We [black Americans] are at best only his step-children; children by adoption, children by force of circumstances and necessity.'"[11]

In reflecting on the authenticity of paternity, Douglass seems to concede that a slave counted as three-fifths human could be perceived, metaphorically, as the unacknowledged offspring of a surrogate or "found(l)ing" father. In the 1845 *Narrative*, he quipped that "Ham's" mixed-race children were springing up throughout the South, which complicated the notion that as slaves, blacks fulfilled the biblical curse of Ham, or the so-called Hamitic hypothesis that purportedly destined them to be enslaved to their white brethren. According to historian David Blight, Douglass spent a lifetime ruminating on the identity of his father, who was rumored to be his white slave master. Douglass's discussion about genealogy across the color line places a taboo subject squarely in the public domain.

About a decade after discovery of the African Burial Ground in Lower Manhattan, two documents emerged in archives at the nation's capital that exposed the enslaved laborer's role in constructing the US Capitol building. The discovery of these documents signaled a shift in recognition and public regard for enslaved African Americans and their contributions to nation building similar to events also under way at the presidential estates of Washington, Jefferson, and Jackson. Dated 1795, these documents had evidently escaped notice or interest until, in 2001, black lawmakers insisted that they be formally displayed in the Rotunda of the National Archives Building for the duration of Black History Month. A document for receipt of payment, titled "Carpenter's Roll for the President's White House," lists five slaves: "Tom, Peter, Ben, Harry, and Daniel" (three of whom were enslaved by White House architect James Hoban). The document recorded the number of days each slave worked, and the wages paid directly to the master that signed the rolls as receipt of payment. A second document, a promissory note from the commissioners to Jasper M. Jackson, records monetary transactions for a hired slave: "'Negro Dick at the Capitol, from 1st April to 1st July 1795, 3 Months, at 5 Dollars per Month.'" A 1790s US Treasury Department note reads: "Please pay to John Hurie the balance due for the hire of Negro Emanuel for the year 1794."[12]

Identified only by their first names, enslaved laborers in the nation's capital uncover the excessive labor and rampant exploitation by enslavers that reaped financial benefits from the former's construction of the nation's premier halls of power. Hidden in plain sight, these receipts recall what Jennifer Eichstedt and Stephen Small refer to in *Representations of Slavery: Race and Ideology in Southern Plantation Museums* as "symbolic annihilation" or the "erasure of slavery," which they witnessed while touring plantation sites in the 1990s. Though Eichstedt and Small target plantation sites, parallels exist between slave labor documents and the authors' observations that by design, these sites minimize or completely erase slavery itself, as well as enslaved and legally free African Americans.[13] Outright discussion of or references to slavery and enslaved African Americans at these sites was either rare or used euphemisms such as "servitude" or "servant."

Soon after the display of the late eighteenth-century documents that exposed the enslaved laborer's role in constructing the US Capitol Building, Congress authorized a US Capitol Slave Labor Task Force to study, formally, how best to honor the slaves' work. Chaired by Representative John Lewis (D-Georgia), and cochaired by Senator Blanche Lincoln (D-Arkansas), the bipartisan, bicameral task force convened in November 2007, to explain before a commission the importance of formally recognizing the enslaved laborers. On June 16, 2010, about a decade after the documents' discovery, a bipartisan legislative group met to unveil two bronze plaques recognizing contributions that enslaved laborers made in constructing the US Capitol building. The plaques, currently on display in a room in the Capitol Visitor Center (fittingly called Emancipation Hall) contain the following inscription: "This original exterior wall was constructed between 1793 and 1800 of sandstone quarried by laborers, including enslaved African Americans who were an important part of the workforce that built the United States Capitol." At the unveiling ceremony, Senator Mitch McConnell (R-Kentucky) said, "We give them some measure of the dignity that was denied them in life."[14]

The shift in recognition and public regard for enslaved African Americans and their contributions to nation building since the new millennium proved a seminal event that clearly spoke to a more tolerant racial climate as well as the power generated by black elected officials who insisted that the documents be displayed in the first place. Nor could it escape notice that journalists recognized a spectacular human-interest story in pairing the documents with the 2008 election of the nation's first African American president. However, the occasion posed conflicting visions about racial progress. For example, slave artisans commemorated at the nation's capital bask in the aura of an African American "postracial" president that contended with questions about his identity and citizenship as I discuss in chapter 1.

The enslaved laborers at the nation's primary seat of power warrant a glance at those unidentified, unsung field workers at presidential plantation sites that remain in unmarked graves. Slave burial grounds at iconic presidential plantation sites converge with the nation's foundational moment—the signing of the Declaration of Independence—which the late Supreme Court justice Thurgood Marshall once referred to as a "flawed document" for its exclusion of slavery provisions. For years at George Washington's Mount Vernon estate, enslaved blacks—when mentioned at all—were referred to as faithful servants to the nation's first president and have only recently been recognized through memorials (1983, 2007) as contributors to the estate and nation rather than merely as servants to Washington. According to the Mount Vernon *Official Guidebook*, "ground penetrating radar indicates that as many as 75 graves may exist" on a hillside overlooking the Potomac River. The Mount Vernon enslaved laborers as field workers rarely appear in the archives, but they likely make up the majority of those that lie unidentified in unmarked graves that now bear a monument specifically designed to recognize them.[15] Though no markers indicate specific grave locations, records show that Washington's personal servant William Lee (c. 1750–1828) is buried there. Unlike with the remains found in New York, no excavation or forensic analyses have been made to determine physical condition or specific cause of death for Mount Vernon slaves. In preparing his will in July 1799, just five months before his death, Washington took a complete census of the 316 slaves at Mount Vernon (123 enslaved to him, 40 rented from a neighbor, and 143 "dower" slaves that he possessed from Martha Washington's first husband, Daniel Parke Custis), including ages and family relationships. But in spite of meticulous records pertaining to the number of slaves, their identities and specific burial locations are unknown.

In 1929 the Mount Vernon Ladies Association placed a slave memorial plaque near an area in which up to 300 slaves may be buried. The plaque contains an inscription that harks back to a different era: "In Memory of the Many Faithful Colored Servants of the Washington Family Buried at Mount Vernon from 1760 to 1860 –Their unidentified graves surround this spot." Just a few years earlier, in 1923, the United Daughters of the Confederacy lobbied Congress to approve construction of a National Mammy Monument to stand near the Lincoln Memorial in honor of loyal female domestics. Reportedly, the proposed statue, commissioned to artist George Julian Zolany, would have depicted a black maid seated while flanked by three white children assembled around her. The proposal ultimately failed. Protests from African American civil rights groups, including two thousand black women of the Phyllis [sic] Wheatley YWCA, appealed to then–vice president Calvin Coolidge to reject the measure.

The "benevolent darky" idea seems to have gained considerable momentum around this time, especially in the South. In 1926 donor Jackson Lee Bryan commissioned Baltimore sculptor Hans Schuler to construct a statue known as "Uncle Jack" at Natchitoches, Louisiana, for $4,300. Erected in 1927, the statue, which featured an aged black man tipping his hat, became a "must-see" tourist attraction that gained the notice of *National Geographic Magazine* and the *New York Times*. A plaque at the site contains the following inscription: "Erected by the city of Natchitoches in grateful recognition of the arduous and faithful service of the good darkies of Louisiana."[16] In a poem titled "The Sevignes" that addresses the statue, African American poet Ann Spencer writes, "Down in Natchitoches there is a statue in a public square / A slave replica—not of Uncle Tom, praise God / But of Uncle Remus."[17] In *Time's Unfading Garden: Ann Spencer's Life,* J. Lee Greene connects the poem with a seventeenth-century French aristocrat whose insensitivities to the lower classes, as revealed through letters, spills over into imitative behavior in the US. Shamed by the figure in the statue that bows to enslavers, but also scornful of a "polite society" complacent to his plight and that of others like him, Spencer adds, "This shameless thing set up to the intricate involvement / of human slavery / Go, see it, read it, with whatever heart you have left."[18] After weathering vandalism, highway construction, and civil rights protests of the 1960s, the statue wound up at the Louisiana State University Rural Life Museum in 1974, where it remains today.

As recently as the 1980s, a series of public relations events called attention to scant recognition of enslaved laborers at Washington's Mount Vernon estate. For example, in an article in the *Washington Post,* reporter Dorothy Gilliam noted the lack of a monument honoring the plantation's enslaved population. A local supervisor alerted a NAACP member to Gilliam's article. That member attended a meeting where the Mount Vernon Ladies Association (MVLA) had planned to request tax-exempt status for restaurants at the site. He protested the MVLA request because he believed that "it violated the spirit and letter of the county's human rights ordinance," and because the MVLA had not appropriately memorialized slaves that were buried at Mount Vernon perhaps because of the subservient tone of the 1929 slave monument. A series of meetings between the NAACP, the local black community, and the MVLA took place before reaching an agreement over a monument design. The MVLA subsequently coordinated an outreach program with the local community that includes a member of one of the oldest surviving slave-descendant families with direct ties to Mount Vernon.[19]

In 1983 architecture students at Howard University designed the Mount Vernon Slave Memorial, a granite shaft placed atop three intertwining circles. David Edge led ten students at Howard University's School of Architecture to complete the design. A tree-lined walkway contains a cut leaf column in the center, which is surrounded by the three circles symbolizing faith, hope, and love, which Edge identifies as the combined source of the slaves' strength. The monument lies in a clearing about fifty yards southwest of George and Martha Washington's tomb. The MVLA, charged with the restoration and upkeep of the plantation site, formally dedicated the monument on September 21, 1983. The winds of change over many generations have distinguished between the messages on the monuments. The following phrases were inscribed on the 1929 and 1983 monuments, respectively: "Faithful Colored Servants of the Washington Family" and "the Afro Americans Who Served As Slaves at Mount Vernon." As I have previously noted, the power of a group dynamic, notably African American slave descendants, community activists, and even university students, enacted change that revised the status that the 1929 memorial posed for Washington's deceased slaves.

Similarly, a group dynamic, consisting of some Mount Vernon slave-descendant African Americans, also participated in the dedication of yet another slave recovery project at the estate in 2007: a newly constructed slave cabin replica added as a memorial to deceased slaves. No original slave cabins have survived at Mount Vernon. However, builders patterned the reconstructed slave cabin after one that survives in a photo dated circa 1908 that, according to oral testimony, "allegedly existed at Dogue Run where the sixteen-sided barn was originally located."[20] Though an exquisite model of rusticity and sturdiness, the reconstructed cabin differs sharply in appearance from one that survives in a nineteenth-century photograph. The dilapidated cabin in that black-and-white photograph is rumored to have been located at Mount Vernon. At the ceremony in 2007, descendants of slaves that belonged to George and Martha Washington joined Dr. Thomas Battle, keynote speaker and director of the Moorland-Spingarn Research Center at Howard University, who said that the slave cabin was not just a place, but that it was also a home that "from here on . . . will be a memorial."[21] At the end of the dedication ceremony, a smaller ritual was conducted in which spectators and visitors were invited to spread soil taken from four Washington farms around the seedling plant of an apple tree near the slave cabin's entrance to symbolize the renewal of life.

The original slave cabin at Mount Vernon is believed to have housed, cumulatively, some 235 slaves who worked on one of George Washington's four outlying farms. Constructed from daubed mud and rough-hewn logs, the slave cabin replica stands sixteen feet by fourteen feet. It features a dirt floor and window areas framed by shutters against the cold; front and back entrances remain doorless. The cabin also contains a fireplace used for cooking, along with a slab bench.[22] From design to construction, the project to restore the slave cabin at Mount Vernon took a year to complete, at a cost of $100,000, donated mostly by Ann and Steven West of New Jersey. Ann West served on the Board of the Mount Vernon Ladies Association from 1989 until her retirement in 2005.

In the *Mount Vernon Gazette*, Dr. Dennis Pogue, associate director for preservation and manager of the Slave Dwelling Project, stressed the importance of the cabin to approximate the living conditions of most Mount Vernon slaves. But Pogue added that it actually took twenty years' worth of surveys to discover what people wanted to see added at Mount Vernon, which revealed slavery to be among the most-requested additions to the historic site. Nevertheless, the reconstructed slave dwelling, set near a chicken coop and tiny vegetable garden, provides a sobering contrast with Washington's white, stately mansion nearby.

The slave cabin's rough-hewn appearance, in sharp contrast with the stateliness of the mansion, is not the only visual manifestation of differences in the lives and social status of Washington and his slaves. Competing images of Mount Vernon slaves with the nation's Founder also appear in paintings by two well-known artists that date to colonial America. In a rare instance in Eastman Johnson's nineteenth-century paintings titled *The Old Mount Vernon* (1857) and *Kitchen at Mount Vernon* (1857), enslaved laborers at the estate are the focus. In the latter painting, Johnson depicts an external and internal view, respectively, of a slave cabin that dominates the painting while the president's mansion recedes. *The Old Mount Vernon* features an African American man who sits in the cabin's doorway, while *Kitchen at Mount Vernon* depicts an African American mother and children near a fireplace in a darkened, dilapidated interior. Both paintings differ significantly from Emmanuel Leutze's 1851 painting of George Washington crossing the Delaware River, which lifted a seemingly minor event in the American Revolution to seminal, even mythical, status for the president and the new nation.[23]

Long before height, weight, and thickness of hair, as opposed to the baldpate, would influence presidential elections, George Washington's image consciousness was legion, and perhaps as intertwined with his slaves as were the farm tallies recorded in his ledger. Furthermore, the antiquated "sound of body equals sound of mind" adage may well apply here, or what Charles Chesnutt references in *The Marrow of Tradition* as "noblesse oblige," a code of standards for post–Civil War southerners that elevated an individual's social status based on name, rank, wealth, and gentility. This conception of an aristocracy, sustained through at least three generations of social nobility, combine physiognomy with moral character and ethical behavior.

As for the dispossessed familial slave, some black descendants of West Ford, long speculated, though not proven, to be George Washington's biracial son by an enslaved woman named Venus, sought approval to test strands of the president's hair that still exist. But approval for such testing has not been granted. A Mount Vernon spokesperson, Denis Pogue, argues that even if performed, the test would at best implicate a Washington, but not specifically the president, as Ford's father. Linda Bryant, a West Ford family historian, has written the family's narrative in *I Cannot Tell a Lie: The True Story of George Washington's African American Descendants*. Meanwhile, in *An Imperfect God: George Washington, His Slaves, and the Creation of America*, historian Henry Wiencek set out to disprove the story once and for all. He instead found that circumstantial evidence could not entirely rule out Washington as Ford's father. West Ford is believed to be buried in an unmarked grave at Mount Vernon in an area with about fifty slaves.[24]

Ironically, forensic studies have recently been conducted on Washington's life mask (made in 1785 by a French sculptor), not to discover genetic blueprints that might link him with black descendants of West Ford, but in order to explain the Founder's strikingly different physical appearances in paintings and other illustrations. As I discuss in chapter 2, forensic analyses and scientific testing conducted on some remains at the New York African Burial Ground expose their condition of servitude, ethnic and cultural heritage, and lifestyle. Genetic historians have linked Washington's very different appearance in published images to scarring from a youthful bout with smallpox as well as lifelong dental woes that determined whether he sported a weak chin or a strong jaw line.

In a scene in Suzan-Lori Parks's award-winning *The America Play*, the African American protagonist referred to as the Lesser Known enters an American Hall of Wonders Museum, where he finds relics of history and popular culture that include George Washington's bones, wooden teeth, and a jewel box of cherry wood. Myths associated with Washington, such as the so-called wooden or ivory teeth, and his admission to chopping down a cherry tree as evidence of integrity or an inability to tell a lie, have long existed as endearing lore in popular culture. But Washington reportedly hired a surgeon to remove teeth from the mouths of his slaves, whom he paid, and to implant them into his own mouth.[25] The procedure, commonly performed among the French aristocracy, who purchased teeth from the poor, was completed by a French physician but did not meet with success.

In identifying human remains, coroners rely on the decedent's teeth through strontium analysis, because of dental durability as well as the certainty and viability that such tests provide. Perhaps the question on behalf of Washington's dentistry is whether it is more disconcerting that the surgery failed, that the transaction took place at all (that we should care), or that the image-conscious Founder bore a less-than-perfect visage or appearance, not to mention considerable discomfort. Long relegated to a historical footnote, the dental surgery demonstrates negotiations in private and public spaces between Washington and his slaves at the core of personal portraiture, imaging, and national prominence.

Beyond the physiological state, Washington's image cleaves as both the proverbial benevolent master and the punisher of those that sought liberty by attempting to escape from slavery. Washington's treatment of slaves that escaped or sought to purchase their liberty has long existed in letters, reports, and other archival records, but increased attention to slave memorials added at Mount Vernon has placed the master/slave relationship under closer scrutiny. Washington thought those slaves ungrateful for his benevolence and disloyal to an unwritten code in which he provided basic care in exchange for their labor. But the slaves' attempts to escape perhaps elevated their perception of themselves as independent beings whose interest in life, liberty, and the pursuit of happiness matched Washington's own desires. Furthermore, slaves that attempted to escape cast an unfavorable pall over a Founder that thought himself the premier architect of a principle of gratitude, which claimed that a slave treated well would neither rebel nor attempt to escape their plight. Perhaps most disturbingly for Washington, the escaped slave threatened to upset the so-called natural order that hierarchized racial, ethnic, and class boundaries. Michel-Rolph Trouillot, in his book titled *Silencing the Past: Power and the Production of History*, notes that the highly touted contented slave stood alongside a litany of laws, punishments, and measures secured to thwart any attempts to escape.[26] Against the backdrop of those laws and measures, slave recovery projects frame Mount Vernon's "slave in memoriam" as a transformative figure, revealing both the unsavory side of the nation's founding and efforts to amend that past. Consequently, those unidentified, unsung field workers that remain in unmarked graves reveal continued flux for the slave descendant and instability for the Founder's legacy as shown, not only in the 2007 reconstruction of the slave cabin at Mount Vernon, but also in the renovation of Washington's mansion in Philadelphia in the same year. While slave descendants celebrated plans to reconstruct the slave cabin at Mount Vernon, community activists fought to include a slave site at the President's House in Philadelphia, honoring nine Mount Vernon slaves that Washington transported there in the 1790s under controversial circumstances.

While excavating the president's home in Philadelphia in 2007 for a renovation project titled "The President's House: Freedom and Slavery in the Making of a New Nation," archaeologists discovered the remains of a hidden passageway evidently used by the nine Mount Vernon slaves. Between 1790 and 1800, Washington and Adams (who did not own slaves) lived at the mansion on Independence Mall, which was then the nation's capital. Local laws in Philadelphia granted freedom to slaves after they spent six months in residence. To get around that law, Washington used the hidden passageway to shuttle the nine slaves in and out of the city before the six-month period expired.

When word spread that the project to prepare "an open-air footprint of [the president's original Philadelphia house]"[27] for exhibition initially excluded plans to recognize the slave passageway, as well as slave quarters near the Liberty Pavilion, a largely African American slave-descendant community insisted that the National Park Service and city official planners commemorate the site. In the meantime, community activists organized their own ceremonies, including a funeral conducted by nine children that eulogized the slaves and cited them by their first names. Once city and National Park Service officials decided to include a slave memorial, designed by Kelly/Maiello Architects & Planners of Philadelphia at the site in Philadelphia, reactions ranged from those opposed to honoring the president at all to those that found the site's recognition too "politically correct."

The slave burial site at Mount Vernon, as well as the process from excavation and community protests to recognition and memorialization for the slaves Washington transported to the Philadelphia President's House echoes events that took place at the New York African Burial Ground some two decades earlier, though some of the president's slaves have been identified by name. Among the nine Mount Vernon slaves that were also associated with the Philadelphia house, the stories of Oney Judge, a mulatto seamstress, and Hercules, a highly skilled chef, coalesce most notably around an iconic presidency and recognition of the slave subject by a slave-descendant community. Hercules, offended that Washington might have thought him interested in escaping while in Philadelphia, later did escape from Mount Vernon after enduring a situation that he found unbearable. The highly prized cook, once given the opportunity to earn personal money by selling leftover kitchen scraps, was demoted and relegated to hard field labor. He later did escape— on Washington's sixty-fifth birthday (his final one as president)—and was never recaptured.

Oney ("Ona") Judge, an accomplished seamstress enslaved to Martha Washington, escaped from the Washingtons' Philadelphia house after discovering that after their deaths, she would not be emancipated but would be enslaved to Martha's daughter. Washington, who kept moving his slaves out of Philadelphia in order to get around a law that permitted them to claim freedom after six months' residence, wrote that Judge left "without the least provocation." Ever conscious of his image as Founder and president, he sought discreet but extraordinary measures over many years to retrieve her. When discovered in New Hampshire, Judge offered to return if her freedom were guaranteed after Martha Washington's death, but the president refused to negotiate with a slave, because he believed strongly in the contract that exchanged their labor for his care of them. Before her death some forty years after Washington's, Judge said in an interview that she never regretted her freedom, because, although impoverished, she had become literate and a Christian. She added that while enslaved to Washington, she had received no mental or moral instruction, and that the Washingtons had only played cards and consumed wine.

The renewed attention paid to the slave "in memoriam" at Mount Vernon, including monuments and the reconstructed cabin, spotlights Washington's relationship with his slaves in the private and public spaces between hearth and nation. The unsung Mount Vernon enslaved laborers that likely make up the majority of those that lie unidentified in unmarked graves now garner recognition for their contributions. However, these sites do not just pay homage to those enslaved laborers in order to reverse their historical annihilation. Rather, they make their presence known in the awkward glare of modern-day scrutiny, which demands accountability for the lingering effects of slavery.

In the year of his death, 1799, not only did Washington free his slaves in his will, but he also explicitly instructed that the children be educated and trained so that they could support themselves as free people. Washington thus did what no other Founding Father had done. He wrote, "Upon the decease of my wife, it is my Will & desire that all the Slaves which I hold in my own right, shall receive their freedom."[28] This portrait of Washington contrasts, even perhaps clashes, with his complex public policies and private practices regarding race and slavery. As I have discussed, perhaps the most compelling interest in the intimate and tenuous link between slave and Founder is not only through imaging or even nation building but also in the very real presence of the slave in Washington's own family.

In addition to West Ford's uncertain paternity, Martha's biracial half-sister, Ann Dandridge Costin (whom historians have not disputed), was born into slavery but later acquired a different, more favorable legal status than other slaves in the Washington household. Furthermore, the biracial half-brother of Martha's first husband, Daniel Parke Custis, very nearly altered the course of history when his slave owner father, John, sought to confer upon him the sole ownership of a vast estate. But under legal and family pressure, John Custis destroyed the will and prepared a final one that formally bestowed freedom, land, money, and other amenities on his biracial son, also named John. When the biracial son died unexpectedly at an early age, his half-brother, Daniel Custis, inherited the estate in its entirety, which Washington eventually acquired through his marriage to the former Martha Custis after her first husband's death.[29] The slave's elision into the families of George and Martha Washington, and the reckoning that it portended for the nation through genealogical dispossession, may well have played a role in compelling the Founder to soften his position on slavery near the end of his life, a belief that Henry Wiencek advances in *An Imperfect God*. In any case, Washington's instructions through his will to free and educate his slaves played a role in burnishing his legacy.

Where the Bodies Are Buried at Monticello

In a groundbreaking effort to observe historical accuracy, an exhibit titled *The Life of Sally Hemings* opened on Saturday, June 16, 2018, to much acclaim. Based on information provided long ago by a white grandson of Jefferson, a "14-foot, 8-inch-by-13-foot, 2-inch room" near the president's own bedroom in the home's South Wing slave quarters, that was believed to be the sleeping quarters of Sally Hemings, has been renovated. That room, built in 1809, and restructured as a bathroom in 1941, has now been restored to its original structure as Hemings's sleeping quarters. Officials at Monticello have purposely kept the exhibition room empty, except for words inscribed on the walls, taken from Madison Hemings's account about his mother's and siblings' relationship with Jefferson.

Madison's account, as well as Jefferson's grandson's claims about the room's identity, have been dismissed by some of the president's white descendants. They, along with members of the Thomas Jefferson Heritage Society, dispute that Jefferson fathered any of Hemings's children at all. While some, like white Jefferson descendant John H. Works Jr., accuse "the nonprofit organization that runs Monticello of bowing to political correctness, others like his brother, David Works, accept the Hemings' descendants as "'cousins.'"[30] Nevertheless, a majority of the Thomas Jefferson Memorial Foundation members—including a division that governs burial in the Jefferson family cemetery at

Monticello—barred Hemings-family descendants from membership in that organization. That prohibition emerges from the controversy surrounding the relationship between Jefferson and Hemings, along with DNA results confirming that Jefferson probably fathered all six of Hemings's children.

My interest goes beyond acknowledgment of the familial slave, however. I am primarily concerned with the patrilineal dilemma of acknowledging and fully integrating familial slaves in the family of presidential patriarchs. The question of where the bodies are buried at Monticello therefore merges with a broader discussion about a past–present chasm between Thomas Jefferson's acknowledged or lineal descendants and those that descend from the relationship between Jefferson and Sally Hemings. For example, I turn to the intriguing case of Harriet Hemings Jefferson, whose burial site is unknown. The only daughter of Jefferson and Hemings, and the half-sister of Martha Jefferson Randolph and Maria Jefferson Eppes, relocated from enslavement at Monticello to freedom in Washington, DC, after the president sent her there with financial support. She passed for white and lived a life shrouded in mystery. Catherine Kerrison, in *Jefferson's Daughters: Three Sisters, White and Black, in a Young America,* rightly notes that Harriet likely feared that without secrecy, she could have been returned to slavery, since her father never drew up manumission papers for her and her siblings, though he allowed them to go free unofficially.[31] As the president's black daughter, Harriet illustrates the complexities associated with the young nation's reckoning with race and slavery through backdoor channels.

And so I return discussion to the familial slave and genealogical dispossession as a lingering racial taboo. For example, the descendants of Hemings and Jefferson are forbidden from burial in the family cemetery at Monticello, where Jefferson himself, along with hundreds of lineal descendants, are buried. Moreover, the contrast between unidentified slaves' remains a few thousand feet from Jefferson's home and the stately cemetery that houses the president and acknowledged white descendants is stark.

As slave recovery projects, burial sites yield some surprising, albeit practical, findings about the lives and working conditions of enslaved laborers, even in cases where information is limited. Excavations further dispute the notion that the plantation owner always held absolute sway, and they contest strict delineations between house and field slaves on the basis of class. Instead, they reveal that slaves constructed hierarchies based on the skills borne by slave laborers.[32] A more autonomous existence for the enslaved population in preserving religious and cultural practices defines them differently than what some historians and planters have proclaimed. This idea harks to still-relevant, mid-twentieth-century debate between E. Franklin Frazier, *The Negro Family in the United States* (1939), and Melville Herskovits, *The Myth of the Negro Past* (1941), about whether slavery was so horrendous that blacks lost knowledge of cultural practices rooted in the African past.[32] As reconstructions of historical memory, however, the slave burial ground acts as a uniquely visual performance of past events that reaffirms the continuity and viability of those practices.

Still, Sally Hemings's more fully acknowledged presence in Jefferson's life and at Monticello through the exhibition in 2018 proves to be a seminal, progressive event. The Jefferson estate has made unprecedented changes in recognizing Jefferson as the father of all six of Hemings's children, initiating conversation about Hemings's presence at Monticello, and focusing on contributions by the hundreds of slaves that Jefferson held in bondage. Consequently, officials acknowledge slavery's central role in docents' guided tours.

On the day that I visited Jefferson's Monticello in August 2006, docents organized tours in three categories: the house tour, the gardens and grounds tour, and a special tour on slaves at Monticello. In this manner visitors could choose to include or to avoid discussion about Sally Hemings or slavery at Monticello. I took all three tours and observed that young African American women dressed in colonial period costumes conducted both the house tour and the slavery tour. The docent that conducted the slavery tour identified herself as a young college student under summer employment at Monticello. At the beginning of the tour, the young woman demonstrated the cramped condition of slave family quarters by asking several children to stand in an empty, rectangular space that approximated a slave quarter's dimensions. In the house tour, the docent described a dumbwaiter, one of Jefferson's premier inventions. Wine and food were sent up from the cellar to guests that never saw the slaves below who prepared the food. The dining experience for Jefferson's guests lent the impression that the elaborate meal appeared spontaneously, obscuring the role that intense slave labor played in its preparation. The docent, however, offered a different perspective; she marveled at the dumbwaiter as a practical invention and a highly efficient method for delivering food to the table. The double interpretation affixed to Jefferson's prized invention aptly characterizes his own dual, contradictory positions as both Founder and enslaver, and as father of two distinct families: one white and one black.

After the release of DNA evidence showing that Jefferson likely fathered at least one child with his slave Sally Hemings, the Thomas Jefferson Memorial Foundation president insisted that tour guides were not compelled to follow a specific script. Instead, they were permitted to form their own interpretations but had to observe historical accuracy. The tour guides shepherd some 550,000 visitors a year through the house.[33] With the addition of the Sally Hemings exhibit, however, tour guides now acknowledge Jefferson as the father of all of her children.

An excavation by archaeologists at Jefferson's estate positively identified a slave burial site as far back as 2002. The identities of slaves buried at the site of the excavation are unknown, though some relatives of Sally Hemings may be among them. The exact location of Sally Hemings's grave in Charlottesville, Virginia, is also unknown. The archaeologists discovered twenty graves in a wooded area about two thousand feet from the main house, but they dug only far enough "to identify the tops of the grave shafts," so as not to disturb the graves further. Though Jefferson never identified a burial ground for the Monticello slaves, archaeologists relied on oral tradition as well as linear depressions in rows that indicated individual burial sites, in order to make a positive identification. Further supportive evidence likens the burial site to other area slave cemeteries from around the late eighteenth and early nineteenth centuries. For example, the unmarked head and foot stones, nails contemporaneous with the period, the east–west orientation of the graves, and their relatively remote location offer further supporting data. This evidence suggests that ten graves belong to adults, while eight belong to children. Up to forty graves may exist at the site, though only twenty were identified.

Even without specific data about the total number of slave decedents buried at Monticello, excavations during the 1980s along an area known as Mulberry Row resulted in the discovery of artifacts that have proven central to understanding their lives and working conditions. Facilities for blacksmithing and carpentry, along with housing for enslaved artisans and domestics were found in the area. The current Thomas Jefferson Foundation consists of a two-hundred-acre tract, and the site marks the approximate place where a slave cabin once stood. Findings include a single small subfloor pit similar to those discovered in other archeological digs in the Chesapeake area. Slaves may have dug these small rectangular pits into the floor and used them as safe-deposit boxes. These pits were clever inventions that increased the security of food and personal belongings that the slaves acquired independent of their owners. In 1980 a divining stick was found nailed inside the wall of the Horton Grove Slave Quarters at Oxford, North Carolina's historic Stagville Plantation. The device, common to African religion, was utilized to summon protective spirits for the cabin's inhabitants. Consequently, like artifacts found at Monticello, Chesapeake, and other slave cabins, the divining stick qualifies as an aspect of cultural survival.

William Kelso, in *Archaeology at Monticello*, notes that root cellars found at Monticello's slave buildings contained tools, ceramics, buttons, and animal remains. He adds that similarities in artifacts at a number of plantation archaeological sites may indicate that slaves rebelled against the labor system through pilfering and passive resistance to conditions of labor. Since these floor pits were more likely to be present in large barracks-like dwellings than in smaller dwellings occupied by fewer people, they might also have protected slaves' privacy. Other artifacts such as African cowry shells used as currency, pierced coins, and a finger ring made of horn traceable to Jamaica believed to be a magical charm indicate cultural survival.[34]

As a material artifact in slave recovery, a simulated slave cabin constructed at Monticello seemed a natural progression to discoveries made from archaeological excavations at Mulberry Row. Indeed, in May 2015 a slave cabin replica was "formally unveiled" as over one hundred Monticello slave descendants looked on. Leslie Greene Bowman, president of the Monticello foundation, lauded the cabin as "probably the most transformational project we've mounted at Monticello in 90 years."[35]

The project was made possible when in 2013, David Rubenstein, co-CEO of the Carlyle Group private equity firm, donated $10 million—among the largest gifts to Monticello—to reconstruct a single-family slave cabin at Mulberry Row, to renovate two floors at Jefferson's home, and other projects. The project at Monticello follows the decision by officials at Mount Vernon to reconstruct a slave cabin there in 2007. Original slave cabins still survive at Jackson's Hermitage estate, but none survives at Monticello and Mount Vernon. The attention paid to slave cabins at the three presidential plantations as aspects of slave recovery revises slaves' images from invisible, dutiful servants to builders and skilled artisans that secured a measure of autonomy in their personal lives. For example, a brother of Sally Hemings lived in one of the original slave cabins at Mulberry Row, and the reconstruction project is projected to highlight his work as a joiner and cabinetmaker. In grateful acknowledgment of Rubenstein's multimillion-dollar donation, Leslie Green Bowman, head of the Thomas Jefferson Foundation, referred to the gift as "transformational" for Monticello and hinted at slavery by emphasizing the importance of knowing all facets of life at Monticello.

In *Thomas Jefferson: Negro President*, Gary Wills writes that contemporaries referred to Jefferson as the "Negro President," not because of a liberal regard for blacks, but because he owed his very presidency to the nonvoting power of enslaved blacks in the South, a product of the three-fifths compromise in which their population permitted the South to dominate Congress.[36]

But in that sense, Jefferson's position perhaps signified an uncanniness already instantiated in the founder, slave, and nation.

In January 2012 curators at the Smithsonian's National Museum of American History (NMAH) on the Washington Mall unveiled a scene chock full of symbolism and worthy of exhibition at an American Hall of Wonders, full of bewilderment and curiosity: Thomas Jefferson's mahogany desk—built by John Hemings, his slave—upon which Jefferson wrote the first draft of the Declaration of Independence. After much planning, the Thomas Jefferson Foundation joined with the Smithsonian's National Museum of African American History and Culture to sponsor an exhibition titled *Slavery at Jefferson's Monticello: Paradox of Liberty*, which ran from January 2012 through October 2012.

Because the National Museum of African American History and Culture was still under construction in 2012, the exhibition was hosted on the second floor at the NMAH. Artifacts included a bill of sale for a girl for fifty pounds, shackles, household objects, tools, other memorabilia from six enslaved families, and, of course, Jefferson's mahogany desk. A permanent counterpart to the NMAH exhibit, titled *Landscape of Slavery: Mulberry Row at Monticello*, opened at Monticello in February 2012. The exhibition at Monticello consisted of "outdoor displays mounted alongside sites of labor uncovered through archeological digs."[37]

The *Landscape of Slavery* exhibition in 2012 and David Rubenstein's donation in 2013 for future renovations at Monticello follow long-term plans to construct a slave memorial at the estate. According to the *Monticello Newsletter*, published by the Thomas Jefferson Foundation, a public call went out as far back as 2001 seeking proposals for a permanent memorial. The *Newsletter* reports that a memorial for the site will be selected from over 116 designs that were received, and that the winning designer is slated to receive a $1,000 honorarium.[38] To date, these plans have not been implemented. Jefferson freed few slaves, and although a memorial to the enslaved laborers at Monticello has been in the works, none has yet been dedicated at the site.

For the unsung slave laborer who lies in unspecified, unmarked graves at presidential estates and will never be identified, the construction of memorials or monuments, slave cabins, and other slave recovery projects may seem both reciprocal and effacing. There is one exception, however, for one slave at the Hermitage estate of President Andrew Jackson. And although archaeologists have been unsuccessful in locating the burial site for Jackson's additional slaves, officials at the Hermitage have placed a slave cemetery there from a different plantation under unusual circumstances.

Why Slave Remains Were Relocated to the Hermitage

At the Hermitage estate of President Andrew Jackson in the spring of 2009, officials dedicated a memorial near a site where the remains of sixty slaves had recently been buried. But curiously, these decedents were not directly affiliated with Jackson or his plantation. The sixty enslaved remains were disinterred from their previous burial site on the grounds of a former plantation near the Hermitage in order to clear the way for completion of a development project at the site. While these decedents were not directly affiliated with the Hermitage, they were believed to be slaves from the Ingleside and Cleveland Hall Plantations (also known as the Donelson Plantation) that were owned by Jackson's wife's nephews. An agreement between the state, the project developer, and the Hermitage led to the bodies being removed and reinterred on the grounds of the Hermitage. The burials took place after archaeologists were unable to locate, definitively, gravesites for Jackson's own slaves, in spite of years of searching, reportedly with the aid of cadaver dogs. The exact location of gravesites for Jackson's slaves remains undetermined because the cemeteries were unmarked. In light of that futility, transferring the slave remains rather than discarding them made sense, but presumably their disinterment and reinterment would also permit developers to proceed with replacing the former slave cemetery with modern real estate development without protest. But that's not exactly how things happened.

Around 2000 a private developer purchased land on a two-acre tract near the Lakewood area in northeastern Nashville in order to construct condominiums tentatively called Hermitage Springs. But the land had already been found in 1998 to be an ancient Native American burial site, which called for special handling of any excavated remains. Similar to the New York African Burial Ground, the cemetery was afforded some legal protection as hallowed ground. Specifically, "Tennessee law requires compliance" with statutes that govern "the termination of land [used] as a cemetery to legally remove and relocate any human burial [in] Tennessee, including ancient Native American graves."[39] Though a previous owner had not developed the site, the new owner began construction work that unearthed skeletal remains and burial artifacts. When the Tennessee Division of Archaeology was alerted to the situation, the state archaeologist ordered the work halted. The law required the developer to procure a chancery court order to obtain permission to remove human remains from his property. According to Pat Cummins, former president of the Alliance for Native American Indian Rights of Tennessee (the Alliance), construction work continued at the site. The Alliance consulted an attorney to intercede in stopping the work that threatened the graves. Then, in August 2000, a court order ceasing all excavations near the burial ground site was issued.

While Cummins and other Alliance members gained permission from the developer to monitor the site for theft and destruction, construction work continued to desecrate the graves and to destroy artifacts. Cummins writes that by 2004, when archaeologists became involved with the site, their unique layer-stripping techniques revealed "over 360 ancient burials dating from the early Archaic period forward to perhaps the Middle Mississippian era—a span of nearly 10,000 years of continuous use as a ceremonial burial ground."[40] Contemporaneous with the New York African Burial Ground, then, this site is among the most exclusive and rare Native American sacred sites in Tennessee and the American Southeastern region.

Two years later, in 2006, archaeologists moved to the outer boundaries of the Native American burial site and discovered rectangular forms identifiable as additional burial grounds. Since this outer region coincided with the fifteen-hundred-acre Donelson Plantation, archaeologists were certain that these additional cemeteries contained African American slave decedents. (President Jackson had close ties with the Donelson Plantation owners, who were nephews of Mrs. Rachel Jackson.) Indeed, some sixty remains and numerous artifacts were excavated and studied forensically by anthropologists at the Middle Tennessee State University. Their findings revealed pathologies similar to those of decedents at the New York African Burial Ground. As Cummins concludes, as of 2012 the multimillion-dollar investment that the developer made to the Hermitage Springs property fell through, and it remains undeveloped. In 2009 the official dedication of the reinterment ceremony, and placement of a memorial at the burial site, took place near the Donelson Plantation (which was later renamed Tulip Grove) on the grounds of the Hermitage Plantation. Jackson's wife's nephew owned a plantation house and slaves at Tulip Grove on the Hermitage grounds. Consequently, members of the African American community, the Alliance for Native American Indian Rights, the State Division of Archaeology, and management of the Hermitage itself decided that collectively "this historic setting would provide a well maintained and dignified place for the reburial of remains from the Donelson slave cemetery."[41]

Artist Lee Benson designed the memorial placed near the Hermitage burial site for the sixty slaves. Judges selected from a dozen submissions by artists after an open call went out, inviting applicants to show their qualifications. The sculpture, funded by the Cracker Barrel Foundation, is titled "Our Peace, Follow the Drinking Gourd." The memorial consists of seven oak trees that take the form of Ursa Minor, the Little Dipper constellation, which includes the symbol of Polaris, the North Star. The trees are spread across a circle of thirty boulders. The memorial is adjacent to a cemetery that contains the remains of Confederate soldiers of Tennessee. Small headstones, some bearing the birth and death dates of soldiers, dot the landscape, and a huge white memorial sculpture stands at the cemetery's fore.

Although the slave memorial's title shares the name of a slave spiritual that helped runaway slaves find and follow the North Star to freedom, Benson emphatically points out that his sculpture was neither conceived nor constructed "to make a civil, political, cultural or religious statement on slavery."[42] Rather, he says, "It is proposed as a singular declaration of our greater hopes, of a renewing of our faith in one another—a simple but eternal reminder that we are one people and one race: the human race." But the memorial's title clearly links to themes associated with spirituals, such as sublimated coded messages for escape, easing the burdens of enslavement, and embracing a power deemed superior to that of the slave master.

Benson's slave memorial, like those at Mount Vernon, shows how progression through the passage of time factors into formal acknowledgment of slaves' contributions to society and the nation at presidential sites. When I visited the Hermitage in April 2004, docents provided few details about the enslaved laborers' contributions to the mansion and plantation overall. At first glance, scant details might seem a fitting parallel to Jackson's unapologetic stance toward slavery, acknowledged by Jackson biographer Jon Meacham and others. But upon returning in August 2012 to examine the Benson slave memorial, I noticed a more pronounced effort by docents to offer frank observations about enslaved life at the Hermitage. As Brian W. Thomas writes, "The mansion was the symbolic seat of power and authority on the plantation where whites resided and the planter reigned supreme. For the overwhelmingly white audience that visits the site, this message must be a comfortable one."[43] In tours conducted for visitors, the docents' scant recognition of slaves at the Hermitage differs sharply from extensive efforts to obtain information about slaves by archaeologists whose work was fully approved, supported— and in some cases funded—by the Andrew Jackson Ladies Hermitage Association (LHA). In 1989, a hundred years after the LHA assumed the operations and upkeep of the Hermitage and the Andrew Jackson Center complex, archaeologist Larry McKee initiated a program that researched the enslaved community at the site. McKee, who spent more than a decade studying the site, wrote in a 2001 interview that no telltale scattered stones or depressions to indicate burial sites were found, in spite of a vague 1930s reference to a "grave field" on a farm map.[44] Nevertheless, he believes that hundreds may be buried there.

Thomas writes that artifacts such as beads, particularly a disproportionate number of surviving "good luck" blue beads, pendants, etc., point to community cohesion in religious and/or cultural practices preservation that were independent of the planters' control.[45] Archaeologists have been permitted for years to conduct excavations around the site in order to search for slave remains and/or memorabilia, but to no avail. Yellow tape encircled an area on the plantation's more than a thousand acres where a slave burial site was believed to be located.

I have previously noted that only one formerly enslaved laborer is buried at the Hermitage in a grave that is clearly marked, and it lies only a few feet from the graves of President Andrew and Mrs. Rachel Jackson. In relating detailed information about the lives of slaves on the plantation, docents made an exception for Alfred Jackson, aka "Uncle Alfred," Andrew Jackson's wagoner and personal servant who took care of carriages on the estate. But Alfred Jackson bears no known or claimed genetic kinship with Andrew Jackson. References to him as "Uncle Alfred" at the Hermitage estate and in publications follow a disrespectful, patronistic tradition for a slave that avoids the title "Mr." or "Mrs." before surnames. And yet "Uncle" Alfred is an ironic substitution for a (non)genetic kinship that acknowledges Jackson's benevolent regard for him as "family."

Built in the 1840s, Alfred's cabin consists of log construction and a center chimney. The President's adopted son, Andrew Jackson Jr., deeded Alfred, his wife, Gracy, and their two children to his own wife, Sarah, in order to keep them out of the hands of his creditors. After Emancipation, Alfred's family remained on the estate by choice and worked for Sarah, Andrew Jackson Jr.'s wife. In addition to farming, Alfred built up a small business conducting personal tours of the Hermitage house and grounds, telling colorful stories about the president. Ironically, Alfred probably knew more about the president and the plantation's history than anyone else in the vicinity. And while not charging fees outright, he would reportedly tip his hat at the end of each tour, humbly beseeching compensation, which he usually received. This part of Alfred's story generally concurs with that which the guides told on the day that I visited the Hermitage in April 2004. At his own request, Alfred Jackson asked to be buried near the gravesite of Andrew and Rachel Jackson. According to docents at the Hermitage, Jackson exacted a promise from the LHA that they would bury him beside the president in exchange for a mirror that he gave to them, which he had purchased in an auction from the estate of Andrew Jackson Jr. Reminiscent of the 1929 plaque at Mount Vernon, the following words are inscribed on the tombstone: "Uncle Alfred, Faithful servant of Andrew Jackson."

The original cabin occupied by Alfred's family still stands in the Hermitage backyard, though its furnishings are imitations. However, there are two compelling versions about a certain bed at the Hermitage mansion. Because of transactions pertaining to the bed, the stories' sources would almost certainly have been Alfred Jackson himself and/or members of the LHA. One story is told to tourists at the site by docents through narrative panels and an audio guide, while the other comes from a prominent member of the Hermitage slave-descendant community. According to the "official" version, in order to furnish his log cabin, Alfred purchased a bed, a water cooler, a mirror, and other items at an auction in 1867 from the estate that then belonged to Andrew Jackson Jr. The site had fallen into disrepair, and the auction was held to settle the junior Jackson's debts. The bed had come from the Jackson mansion, but because it was too large to fit into Alfred's cabin, he sawed off the legs. After his death, Alfred's heirs sold the bed to the LHA, who returned it to the mansion and restored it to its former state.

But David Steele Ewing offers a story that identifies the bed as actually belonging to President Jackson. In this version Alfred is quoted as saying that he always wanted to know what it was like to sleep on such a fancy bed. Ewing, a prominent African American attorney, claims to be a direct descendant of Andrew Jackson and an enslaved woman, based on generations of oral family history. In a conversation with this author, the ninth-generation Tennessean stated that oral family history has long identified him as Jackson's direct descendant[46] and the great-great-grandson of Prince Albert Ewing, one of the first African Americans to practice law in Tennessee, and a six-time judge. Ewing is married to Alice Randall, author of *The Wind Done Gone*, a neo–slave narrative and parody of Margaret Mitchell's *Gone with the Wind*.

Upon my visit to the Hermitage on August 9, 2012, a guide said that she was unable to confirm or deny that the bed was the same one that the president slept on. Docents point out that the bed did indeed come from the mansion and that it now resides there, but they do not say whether it was Andrew Jackson's personal bed. Another docent noted that although references to Alfred Jackson as "Uncle Alfred" may have seemed endearing in the context of slavery, the name would be offensive today. At Alfred's cabin audio explained that furniture in the cabin simulated that which Alfred had accumulated after Emancipation, but that the cabin's holdings were not indicative of its condition during slavery. A notably larger cabin nearby first belonged to President and Mrs. Jackson, before they built the Hermitage mansion. The two-level cabin was downsized considerably in order to look more presentable as one belonging to a slave. Audio at the Hermitage explained that the cabin's former state was simply too fancy for a slave to occupy. Furthermore, a narrative panel records an anecdote in which Alfred Jackson once told a visitor, "You white folks live much better than slaves." When the visitor pointed out that freedom was a heavy load to bear and that Alfred seemed to be well cared for, the wagoner asked him, "How would you like to be a slave?"

Alfred Jackson's loyalty and fondness for Andrew Jackson earned him a burial space next to the president and Mrs. Jackson as he requested. But Alfred Jackson's desire need not be perceived as cloying or fawning behavior, as it destined his burial site to be the only identifiable, fully inscribed slave's grave on the Hermitage plantation. Loyalty did not preclude Jackson from making his true feelings known—however subtly—about his own enslavement. But deed, more so than verbal expression, ensured his own survival (to a ripe old age) through business savvy, masking, and even resistance. Alfred Jackson's story is a relatively common one for enslaved blacks whose labor supported the economic wealth of slave owners as well as the nation in a colonial capitalist system. Solomon Northup, in *Twelve Years a Slave*, refers to this slave economy as "Sunday money" or "hiring out" work done on Sundays, in which slaves sometimes earned money or supplemented their foodstuffs with work completed off the plantation. Northup writes that compensation for Sunday labor generally afforded slaves a chance to earn money "sufficient to purchase a knife, a kettle, tobacco, and so forth."[47] However, Jackson illustrates that dual version of a culture and plantation economy for blacks both apart from and tethered to a local and national one after Emancipation, as it is not altogether clear that he had the opportunity to earn money independently during his enslavement.

◆ ◆ ◆

As slave recovery site at both the presidential estate and Lower Manhattan, the burial ground is an apt foundational space in which to study a chattel slave society. Decedents buried at these sites, as early representatives of the African diaspora in the Americas, cede the grave's prominence in the re-embodiment and revaluation of the historically fragmented slave. But lessons gleaned from remains and/or archaeological data far exceed teachable moments that simply reclaim the slave from obscurity. Memorials and commemorative ceremonies may quiet angst about past slave atrocities, but gratitude can be fleeting, especially when it masks slavery's continued impact through genealogical dispossession, reoccurrence through modern-day trafficking, and other means.

I next turn to the reconstructed slave ship exhibition in chapter 4, which some spectators have challenged to call greater attention to global slave trafficking, reparations for slave descendants, economic inequities, and continued racial strife. But above all, they clamor for a fitting memorial and formal recognition of unknown slaves lost in the Atlantic Ocean—arguably the world's largest graveyard. The enormity of slave burial sites pales when paired with the Atlantic as a tomb that yields incalculable losses from deaths in the Middle Passage. But captive African occupants in that death chamber are completely invisible and mostly undocumented in official records. Their existence is known through estimates and/or catastrophic incidents of slaves that were thrown or jumped overboard through defiance, resistance, and sickness. The reconstructed slave ship unites with the African Burial Ground and the presidential estate in defining a legacy for those that, displaced through geography and genealogy, speak from the grave.

First Captain William Pinkney.

The *Freedom Schooner Amistad* at Charleston.

CHAPTER FOUR

The "Neo Middle Passenger" and the Traveling Slave Ship Exhibition

> Where are your monuments, your battles, martyrs?
> Where is your tribal memory? Sirs,
> In that grey vault. The sea. The sea
> Has locked them up. The sea is History.
> —Derek Walcott, "The Sea Is History"

> A slaver is a ghost ship sailing on the edges of modern consciousness.
> —Marcus Rediker, *The Slave Ship*

On March 29, 2007, a replica of the slave ship *Zong*, site of perhaps the most horrific crime in recorded maritime history,[1] sailed across the Thames from Greenwich through Tower Bridge to dock at the Tower Pier accompanied by the Royal Navy Frigate HMS *Northumberland* in a seminal event that commemorated the two hundredth anniversary of the ending of the slave trade. On board the *Zong* replica, a group of English, African, and Afro-Caribbean members of the "Free at Last" project sang "Amazing Grace," probably the most recognizable religious hymn in modern Christendom, and the title of a 2006 film about William Wilberforce's role in the movement to end the slave trade in the British Empire. As organizers of the *Zong* exhibition, the Free at Last project members could boast of having created the historic conclusion to a traumatic chapter in the Atlantic slave trade.[2]

A year after the *Zong* replica sailed across the Thames in London, a similar ceremony took place at Cape Verde, where President Pedro Pires welcomed the *Freedom Schooner Amistad*, a reconstruction of the original slave ship *La Amistad*, as it wound its way from Praia, Cape Verde's capital, to Cidade Velha on the island of Santiago.[3] The original *Amistad* was the site of slave piracy. It traveled to the United States from Cuba in 1839, after slaves headed by Joseph Cinque took over the ship from its Portuguese captain. After a historic case that John Quincy Adams successfully argued before the US Supreme Court, the thirty-five former captives returned to Africa in 1841.

In yet another seminal event in Austin, Texas, artifacts from the slave ship *Henrietta Marie*—the first and only traveling slave ship exhibition of its kind in North America—went on display at the Bob Bullock Museum from February 11, 2006, until April 15, 2006, one of the more than twenty-five US cities that it has toured. The *Henrietta Marie*, which began its journey in London in 1699 before heading to Africa—possibly to New Calabar in modern-day Nigeria, sank off the coast of Key West, Florida, en route back to London after slaves disembarked in Jamaica. Raised by divers in 1972, the ship will eventually be housed in the Mel Fisher Maritime Museum at Key West.

In this chapter I explore a series of "flash" moments and seminal events that pertain to exhibitions of the reconstructed *Zong*, the *Freedom Schooner Amistad*, and the *Henrietta Marie* slave ships. Here, I refigure the globally dispersed transnational patron—namely, diaspora slave-descendant Africans that disproportionately view these ships. I identify these patrons as "neo Middle Passengers," or secondary witnesses—not so much to slavery itself but to present-day inequities that mirror or even mimic past forms of bondage. A multiethnic Christian group at the *Zong* exhibit in London, an aging, slave-descendant seafarer aboard the *Freedom Schooner Amistad* at Charleston, and docents at the *Henrietta Marie* exhibition in Jacksonville, Florida, and Austin, Texas, confront the ships' archival, historical slave past but also contend with its aftermath through racial discrimination, modern-day slavery, and human rights abuses relevant to their own lives and experiences.[4] The reconstructed slave ship exhibitions in this chapter thus reorder the temporality of the history of slavery through alignment with the neo Middle Passenger, or modern-day patron, in an individual and group collective. A major tenet of this study assesses the efforts of such a collective to influence site development and to read them through perspectives that often counter traditional, archival records. I have shown, for example, how a venerable tour guide at Gorée Island's House of Slaves in Senegal dispensed an oral narrative as performance about slave deportations from that site for over four decades. I described a park-ranger-turned griot's delivery of an informal, impromptu, twenty-minute oral "memory history" lesson for underinformed tourists, about the African Burial Ground decedents in New York. And I have discussed how slave-descendant community activists influenced production of memorials and other reconstructed materials for the African Burial Ground National Monument, and at presidential estates that transformed the status of anonymous slave decedents. At slave ship exhibitions—the only "slave sites" in this study that also function as "traveling museums"—the vessel itself is the reconstructed material through which an individual and group collective reimagines the impact of the dreaded, enigmatic Middle Passage experience in a presentist, global context.

The slave ship exhibitions that I examine in this chapter provide a framework through subject positions that befit their unique status as traveling sites, including representation of the enslaved, perspective of the slave-descendant spectator, and past-to-present residues of slavery. Through official appearances at stops in the US, the UK, Africa, and the Caribbean, among them, these slave ship exhibitions not only encounter diaspora slave-descendants and other spectators who offer different perspectives on the slave past but also provoke confrontations about slave residuals that differently affect these regions. For example, the *Zong* exhibition in London seemed overwrought with bombastic symbolism and emotionalism, which threatened to obscure slavery's continued presence in the form of modern-day slave trafficking and litigation for reparations, as observed by Anita Rupprecht.[5] The *Freedom Schooner Amistad*'s arrival in Cuba—the original site of its launching—ignited controversy about continued human rights abuses and racial discrimination in local communities there. And the prepackaged *Henrietta Marie* exhibition met with disapproval from some museumgoers/spectators in US cities over the "absent presence" of the slave subject and the arrangement of slave replicas in its Middle Passage display. I have noted that differences in perspectives about the value and effectiveness of slave sites can generate healthy and productive discussion. By virtue of their status as traveling exhibitions, reconstructed slave ships reinforce certain critiques about the slave past and its aftermath through modern-day trafficking, reparations, and other issues in a global context.

Slave ship replicas as both traveling exhibitions and as artifacts in existing museums reclaim the enslaved subject from biased or one-sided accounts in Atlantic slavery by slave ship authorities. Collectively, these modern-day exhibitions purport to promote education, healing, and reconciliation, but they also allow for reflection on slavery's legacy in the international community as an insatiable desire for closure that has not been fulfilled. The exhibitions therefore reveal evidence of transgenerational trauma fermented between an individual and group collective that appropriates or transforms history into a living or symbolic memory.[6]

The large audience, or disproportionately slave-descendant neo Middle Passengers at these slave ship exhibitions share a prolonged investment in a mission that focuses on a massive ancestral graveyard on the ocean floor, but they also reveal motives grounded in personal pain and/or self-interest. For example, the Free at Last Christian group on the *Zong* ship replica invoked a religious-themed message of healing and forgiveness. The slave-descendant seafarer that organized the *Freedom Schooner Amistad*'s decade-long global circulation boasted of splinters embedded in his hands, which resulted from his role as one of the ship's builders. And grief-stricken at the sight of artifacts from the *Henrietta Marie*, a founder of the National Association of Black Scuba Divers designed a memorial that he, along with other members, placed on the ocean floor to commemorate slaves transported on the ship's final journey. Their investment as patrons for these slave ship exhibitions therefore derives emphatically from circumstances in their own lives and experiences that serve as reminders of the slave past. By inserting a visual dimension and an activist component ostensibly through these individuals, contiguous with public memory practices and reconstructed materials, the slave ship exhibitions reinscribe an alternative material archive for the Middle Passage.

In the arsenal of slave recovery projects that pertain to the Middle Passage, the traveling slave ship exhibition is the "new museum," transformed from its prior assignation as structured edifice in a fixed location, typically patronized by well-heeled visitors, to a museum-in-motion filled with globally dispersed, transnational subjects, most notably diaspora African slave descendants. These neo Middle Passengers board slave ship replicas and revisit that aspect of slavery regarded as most elusive and enigmatic, or what Marcus Rediker refers to as "a violence of abstraction" obscured through ledgers, maps, and balance sheets.[7] A huge, fearsome vessel that symbolized the captive African's final exit through the Door of No Return at slave forts in Africa, the slave ship morphs into a broad canvas at modern-day slave sites. In this chapter I discuss a series of seminal events for organizers and spectators at the reconstructed *Zong* ship, the *Amistad* replica, and the *Henrietta Marie* exhibitions about the residues of slavery and instabilities in race relations in the modern era.

A Reconstructed *Zong* Slave Ship Arrives in London

In April 2007, aboard the reconstructed *Zong*, an exhibition and audio narrative depicted the horrors of slavery, including the *Zong* massacre. Officially opening the event, London mayor Ken Livingstone cut apart a huge iron chain. Brought on board in thirty-minute intervals, ticketed spectators filed past the slave ship's cargo hold, where each section contained a number to identify the simulated slaves. There was no shortage of iron on display, as thick shackles were attached to the necks of slave replicas that resembled cardboard cutouts. Heavy chains looped throughout the quarters, revealing the cramped conditions that slaves experienced. Narrative panels contained quotes—some taken from slavers' accounts—that described the stench and horrid conditions that enslaved Africans endured.

Members of the Free at Last group organized the exhibition, which they designated the Spirit of Wilberforce Project, to honor William Wilberforce and the Clapham abolitionists for their work to end the slave trade in 1807. They believed that a replica of the *Zong* slave ship would be an appropriate reminder of the cramped quarters and living conditions that slaves endured during the Middle Passage. Built in the 1940s, the *Zong* replica had served as a prop in the 2006 film *Amazing Grace*. The naval frigate HMS *Northumberland*, which accompanied the replica, displayed its own exhibition to publicize the navy's role in ending the slave trade. On their website the European, African, and Caribbean members of Free at Last posted as primary objectives for the *Zong* exhibition a desire to inform the public about historical data pertaining to the slave trade and "[to] provide [an] appropriate emotional experience." [8] The latter objective suggests that a fitting response would be a passionate and reactive one that might erupt through group organizers and museumgoers/spectators' direct engagement with the exhibition.

The Free at Last group gathered in the cargo hold, where they performed a symbolic foot-washing ceremony "to remember the horrors of the slave trade and to lament before God the involvement of our forebears." The ritual observed by numerous Christian denominations where members wash each other's feet, imitative of Christ's actions, harks back to John Newton's conversion to Christianity. The ceremony recalls his creation of the spiritual "Amazing Grace," as a redemptive act for years that he spent as a slave ship captain. The ritual also generated grousing about the knowledge that some Christian groups had invested heavily in the Atlantic slave trade. An observation made by poet Marlene Nourbese Philip, albeit in a different context, explains how the slave trade still contaminates international monetary systems through what she refers to as "speculative financing." Philip wrote that a buyer somewhere in the United Kingdom could purchase a slave in Africa, "transport him or her to the Caribbean, sell him to a plantation owner there and collect payment in England or anywhere else in Europe." [9]

For observers of the *Zong* exhibition, the teachable moment of unity and healing on board the ship's replica seemed marked as mere ceremony, at least when paired with hardcore tangible objectives, such as efforts by groups to obtain reparations from large corporations and insurance companies that made huge profits from slave trading, which lost out in litigation two years earlier. In "'A Limited Sort of Property': History, Memory and the Slave Ship *Zong*," literary and cultural studies scholar Anita Rupprecht thought the replica and the navy frigate a spectacle that presented a confusing image on the dark, turbulent waters of the Thames. She wrote, "Redolent of the current vogue for historical re-enactment, its very theatricality risked enclosing its own object, yet it was unclear precisely what that object was."[10] Rupprecht further questioned the group's appropriation of an emotional reaction to the exhibition as a primary objective. And she pondered what forms of representation might be appropriate recollections of the slave past when "these images inevitably were compromised in their inception" and have been "shaped by repression and narrative disguise, by a desire to re-erase and re-inscribe."[11]

While litigation efforts in the United Kingdom for failed reparations point to irresolution in the slave past, the *Zong* exhibition suggests that finality to the slavery question has been achieved. To shift from mourning to healing, programmatically, for past horrors of slavery is to maneuver from behind. New abuses in Atlantic slavery's historical wake, such as modern-day slave trafficking, have already taken its place. However, a desire by event organizers to bring about an emotional response, wedged into hardcore meaningful discussion about modern-day slavery and reparations, need not be adduced as theatricality. Instead, the *Zong* ship exhibition means to usher spectators into the slave ship's bowels so that they can imagine the horrors that slaves experienced in the Middle Passage. Perhaps a more effective strategy would shift the paradigmatic microcosmic slave ship that Paul Gilroy identifies as a rallying symbol for the diaspora African slave descendant in *The Black Atlantic: Modernity and Double Consciousness* to a more complex, macrocosmic fusion between the globally dispersed, transnational African slave descendant and the fetishized slave.[12]

Highly symbolic ceremonies, such as those that took place on the *Zong* and other slave ship exhibitions, reconfigure the modern-day museum through the ubiquitous symbol of a postmodern slave-ship-in-motion. The image of captive Africans packed spoon-style, traversing a shark-infested Atlantic, is therefore replaced by a neo Middle Passenger, typically a diaspora slave descendant as spectator that boards a simulated slave ship or files past its gutted remains to contemplate the horrors of slavery. Visitors to these sites, notably diaspora slave descendants, function as neo Middle Passengers or as witnesses, not so much to slavery itself as to its continuing impact on their lives. Whether through interventionist narratives, counterhistories, or performance practices, they impose an epistemological and ontological dimension onto the Middle Passage in particular and slavery in general. Consequently, these slave ship exhibitions make the slave past more coherent and accessible.

The diaspora slave descendant, prominent among those that board the slave ship replicas, is compelled (or induced by the spectacular) to enact a stigmatic paradigm, absorbing the suffering of the absented slave while the main signifier—the reconstructed, postmodern slave ship—attempts to reproduce, metonymically, what is essentially unknowable about the Middle Passage journey. As Ian Baucom writes in *Specters of the Atlantic: Finance Capital, Slavery, and the Philosophy of History*, "The spectator suffers the idea of the slave's suffering and so sentimentally secures the 'past feelings' of the slave (or, at least a representation, image or 'memory' of the past feelings of the slave) as the experience of his or her own spectral haunting by the idea of an observed moment (an 'impression') of suffering."[13] Through well-placed visual images and artifacts on board the *Zong* and other slave ship replicas, spectators can discern the suffering that the slave subject endured. They inhabit the space between a destabilized "official" historical record and a disembodied black slave subject, a sad commentary for those slaves who died, as well as for those who survived the Middle Passage.

Indeed, intense debate ensues among those who disagree about the role that prevailing discourses play in resolving deficiencies in official historical records pertaining to slavery. Gaps and silences in archival, historical data yield what Katherine McKittrick refers to as "genealogical connections between dispossession, transparent space, and black subjectivities."[14] That transparent space discounts the slave's very existence or physical presence in official records and denies their entitlement to an identity. Meanwhile, the spectator embodies the form of the elusive slave subject who transcribes and commits to public memory those *Zong* atrocities that have no visible active presence: no hands, ears, or eyes in traditional, historical archival records. Slave-descendant spectators that board the reconstructed exhibition encase themselves, figuratively speaking, in the hull of the slave ship in the guise of neo Middle Passengers on a quest to retransform the enslaved subject back into human form.

The *Freedom Schooner Amistad* Anchors in Charleston

The *Freedom Schooner Amistad*, an *Amistad* special exhibit at a Charleston museum, and a performance of the *Amistad* opera at the city's newly renovated opera house ignited a triple play of seminal events at Charleston's Spoleto Festival in 2008. But for the slave ship exhibition known as the *Freedom Schooner Amistad*, the redemptive figure and presumptive neo Middle Passenger takes the form of an aging slave-descendant seafarer rather than a poet, fiction writer, or formal academic. On May 16, 2008, a reconstruction of the original *Amistad* slave ship sailed into Charleston Harbor, South Carolina, where it remained for several weeks berthed at the Maritime Center. But perhaps the image that lent the greatest irony to the scene, however, belonged to a seventy-three-year-old self-professed former limbo dancer and aging seafarer. First Captain William "Bill" Pinkney—hands still harboring wood chips from his role in building the *Freedom Schooner Amistad* bound for those same sites where slave ships docked more than two centuries earlier—united a personal quest for freedom with an adventure of seafaring and a conviction for settling history in his mission.

In May 2008 the *Freedom Schooner Amistad* docked at the Maritime Center in Charleston. As part of the annual Spoleto Festival in Charleston, the ship appeared alongside the *Amistad* story on display at the Old Slave Mart Museum on Chalmers Street, in tandem with an opera about the slave ship *La Amistad*, which debuted at the newly restored Memminger Auditorium on May 22, 2008. Spoleto Festival organizers had coordinated the three events in order to commemorate the two hundredth anniversary of the ending of the slave trade in the US, to educate the public about the *Amistad* revolt, and to spur more interest in the already popular festival at the start of Charleston's summer tourism season. These celebratory *Amistad* events at the Spoleto Festival, along with Bill Pinkney's personal journey as a globally dispersed, transnational slave descendant, produced an expanded story about captivity, insurrection, redemption, and return.

Upon Pinkney's arrival in South Carolina on the *Freedom Schooner Amistad*, state senators Glenn McConnell and Robert Ford introduced a measure adopted by the state General Assembly to commemorate the ship "for outstanding work in educating current and future generations on the sanctity of human freedom and on the importance of continued efforts to eliminate all vestiges of the legacy of chatted slavery everywhere." The senators gave First Captain Pinkney a copy of the resolution. But a looming Civil War anniversary would produce a reenactment of the firing on Fort Sumter, which signaled the state's secession from the Union, and gentrification measures would continue to displace the slave-descendant Gullah Geechee people from communities that they had long occupied near South Carolina's coastline, as I discuss in chapter 5.

In recognition of the *Freedom Schooner Amistad*'s arrival at the Maritime Center at Charleston Harbor in May 2008, members of the Gullah Geechee nation, led by Chieftess Queen Quet, performed a libation ceremony that was reminiscent of performances by the Free at Last members at the *Zong* exhibition in London. The *Freedom Schooner Amistad* had sailed from US cities to sites along the Thames in the United Kingdom and docked at multiple locations in West Africa and the Caribbean to commemorate the two hundredth anniversary of the ending of the slave trade in Britain (1807) and the United States (1808). Traveling as well to established museums in host cities, the ship's route roughly mirrored the triangular Atlantic slave trade route. According to

Pinkney, someone rang the ship's bell fifty-three times at each stop: once for each of the *Amistad* captives.

In 1839 fifty-three Africans were kidnapped and sold into slavery in the transatlantic slave trade. Spanish captors shackled forty-nine men and four children aboard the *Tecora*, a Portuguese slave ship. They then brought the captives to Havana, Cuba, where they were fraudulently classified as native, Cuban-born slaves. Purchased illegally by Spanish planters Jose Ruiz and Pedro Montez, they were transferred to the schooner *La Amistad*. Several days into the journey, a twenty-five-year-old rice farmer, formerly named Sengbe Pieh, but called "Cinque" by his Spanish captors, led a revolt in which the Africans seized the ship, killed the captain and the cook, and ordered the planters to sail to Africa. But instead, captors took the Africans to New London Harbor in Connecticut, where the African captives were placed on trial for murder. Former president John Quincy Adams successfully argued the historic case before the United States Supreme Court on behalf of the African captives. In 1841 the thirty-five survivors were returned to Africa.[15]

In some ways, Bill Pinkney epitomizes the macrocosmic fusion of the globally dispersed, transnational African slave descendant with fetishized slave that I argue is an essential component of the modern-day slave ship exhibition. He is quite literally and figuratively fused, ontologically, to the *Freedom Schooner*'s wooden structure and frame. In a poignant interview with Bo Petersen for the Charleston, South Carolina, *Post and Courier* newspaper, Pinkney discussed his role in the construction of the Amistad replica, his philosophy of life, and musings about the ship's mission: "I was with this boat when it was logs from places like Sierra Leone, up in Washington state, Lagos. The wood that came from Surinam. The keel came from Guyana." Pinkney gave up life in the corporate world to sail in treacherous waters, and he became the first black man to sail solo around the world, he says in the interview. He also confessed, "I have splinters still in me somewhere from it." A sailor foremost, but also a speaker and storyteller, Pinkney sees himself as intricately connected with the *Amistad*: "When I'm at speaking engagements, the boat channels its stories through me. That's where I get my personal injections of what the *Amistad* means to me," he says. He also reflects on his own life story in a memoir titled *As Long as It Takes: Meeting the Challenge*. He discusses his personal connection with the *Amistad* story as a slave-descendant African American who grew up in Bronzeville, Chicago, where he says that he was "made aware" of the odds stacked against his becoming a successful adult. Pinkney poignantly observes that in the global struggle for human rights, the *Freedom Schooner Amistad* stands as "the only iconic symbol of that whole [slavery] era that can move." The observation does not suggest the ship's power as a sentimental or romanticized healing force; rather, it sees the potential for an embodied symbol to nudge conversation toward moral suasion. Pinkney concludes the interview wistfully, "There's a chill up the spine to walk down a modern pier, past the trim steel sails and lithe hulled boats, turn past the pylon and see the almost mythic features of the ship and read 'Amistad.'"[16] But as I shall discuss shortly, while Pinkney posits the ship as a force for healing and unification in intermittent travels through stops in the United States, the United Kingdom, Africa, and the Caribbean, the exhibition also encounters disparities in local economies, racial discrimination, and human rights concerns that cannot be ignored or cast aside

A short distance from the Charleston Harbor where Pinkney conducted tours on the ship, visitors could ascend the stairs to the second floor of the Old Slave Mart Museum on Chalmers Street. There, a drumbeat and a recorded message on audiotape greeted them. Narrative panels along the walls paired past historical events with present ones. The narrative first summarized the slave piracy incident on *La Amistad* in 1839. It next described the making of the *Freedom Schooner Amistad* replica between 1998 and 2000. A small model of the original *Amistad* stood on display nearby. To guide museumgoers/spectators through each section of the exhibit, curators had placed arrows on the floor, which they labeled "slavery," "revolt," "arrival," "waiting," and "return." An interactive device invited museumgoers to translate the message, "Let us all come together as one," in four languages: English, Temne, Mende, and Spanish. And in an exhibit titled "Professor Gibbes' Break Through," visitors could push a button, which prompted a recorded voice to count to ten in Mende.

On a sunny day in May 2008, Captain Pinkney greeted visitors at the Charleston Harbor, and the crew helped everyone to board the *Freedom Schooner Amistad*. Pinkney complained mildly that his duties as the ship's tour guide prevented him from attending commencement exercises in Massachusetts for a relative. The commencement had featured then–presidential candidate Barack Obama in May 2008, who had filled in for an ailing Senator Edward Kennedy. After a brief sigh for the missed opportunity, Pinkney got down to business. Speaking in a commanding voice, he summarized the *Amistad* piracy incident. He then described how workers had constructed a replica of the *Amistad* slave ship. Captain Pinkney told the assembled spectators that modern-day regulations forced changes to the replica that differentiates it from the original nineteenth-century vessel. Those regulations meant not only that modern conveniences for cooking and sanitation would separate the *Freedom Schooner* from the original *Amistad*, but that the former would also be completely unrecognizable as a slave ship to spectators and viewers.[17]

Created in 1996 as a product of a consortium between Mystic Seaport Museum, the Connecticut Afro-American Historical Society, the Amistad Committee of New Haven, and the Amistad Affiliates of New York, the non-profit AMISTAD America, Incorporated, owns and operates the 140-foot vessel. Christened by actress Ruby Dee, the vessel was launched in March 2000. Workers reconstructed the *Amistad* based on the skills and construction methods that builders employed for wooden schooners in the nineteenth century. Even some tools utilized for the project imitated those used in nineteenth-century building techniques by shipwrights, though others were electrically powered. However, it is important to point out that the *Freedom Schooner Amistad* could not function legally as a traveling slave ship museum today were it constructed exactly as it existed in the nineteenth century. Therefore, if spectators look for simulated dank holds and pungent odors that circling sharks could detect from miles away, they won't find them here. For example, modern computer technology provided the layout for the vessel, and the Tri-Coastal Marine Company designed the *Amistad* replica. The reconstructed *Freedom Schooner Amistad* has an external ballast keel made of lead, and it is powered by two Caterpillar diesel engines. Of course, nineteenth-century ship builders lacked this kind of technology. The *Freedom Schooner* is fitted with Douglas fir masts, "dark lines of iroko and angelique wood from Africa, [and] live oak from South Carolina." The *Freedom Schooner* has been named "the official sailing ship of the state of Connecticut and the U.N. 'floating ambassador' in honor of the victims of slavery."[18]

The ship appeared at the annual Spoleto Festival in Charleston, along with *The Amistad: An Opera in Two Acts*, which featured Anthony Davis, composer; Thulani Davis, librettist; and Sam Helfrich, director. Helfrich utilized the stage at the Memminger Auditorium in order to illustrate the opera's ideas about captivity, insurrection, redemption, and return. In so doing, he emphasized the contemporaneity of the *Amistad* story, reinforcing present issues about race and erasing the element of quaintness and smugness from the past. Furthermore, he pressed the case for the *Amistad* story's omnipresence: "Its reverberations are all around us today."[19] The interdisciplinary texts—the Freedom Schooner, the *Amistad Opera*, and the Amistad exhibition at the Slave Mart Museum that tell the story of the slave ship *La Amistad*—blur distinctions between past and present events much as the *Zong* exhibition does in London. In other words, they thematize the meeting of the past with the present, modernity in confrontation with history, and the implications for slavery, freedom, and democracy.

In the playbill for the *Amistad* opera, Helfrich comments on the intimacy that the stage provides as a storytelling venue because it brings a sense of immediacy to the fore. Assuming the role of project director, Helfrich pondered why the Amistad story has prevailed while other stories about horrific slavery incidents have faded from primacy in official historical records. Referencing the *Amistad*'s link with the sordid pages of our historical past, Helfrich says that the story shows that we continue to struggle with racial strife, prejudice, and violence. He adds that as "an epic work of theater: compelling, dramatic, poetic, stage worthy," opera functions as an ideal genre for this story.[20] Helfrich notes the following ironies: The *Amistad* story is about the politics of the slave trade, which had ended in the US in 1808. But none of the captives were slaves, though slavery remained legal in the US until the passing of the Thirteenth Amendment to the Constitution. While the revolt took place at sea, its dramatic events take place in the public forum of a courtroom and news accounts. The story seems quintessentially American, but it also reveals much about African culture. The trial is set in Connecticut, though the story seems driven by events largely in the American South. Finally, Helfrich adds, "With a sly nod to the Baroque, it involves the deus ex machina interventions (sometimes dubious) of two African gods and one American ex-president."[21] Helfrich's allusions to contemporary echoes underscore Charleston's thematic triple play on the slavery past. The opera's appearance in the city, alongside the *Freedom Schooner Amistad*'s display in Charleston Harbor, and the Amistad exhibition at the Old Slave Mart Museum on Chalmers Street, exemplifies this thematic unity.

In keeping with those historical references and contemporary echoes, the *Freedom Schooner* set sail to every city connected with the rebellion on the slave ship *La Amistad* as a primary goal, including the site of its origins in Cuba. So, when the ship sailed into Havana Bay on March 25, 2010, on UNESCO's third annual International Day of Remembrance for the victims of slavery, Captain Pinkney stated, "This is something I always felt was important to do for myself, for others and for my ancestors."[22] The ship's arrival near a region east of Havana where slaves once worked on sugar plantations also marked the tenth anniversary of its launching at the Mystic Seaport Museum in Mystic, Connecticut. Greg Belanger, president and CEO of Amistad America Inc., said that the visit to Cuba, where the schooner *La Amistad*'s story began, completed the organization's goals for the schooner.[23]

The *Freedom Schooner Amistad* arrived in Cuba one day after participants observed the International Day for the Elimination of Racial Discrimination, which fermented discussion about race relations and continued racial discrimination in contemporary Cuban society. Norberto Mesa, founder of the Cofradia de la Negritud (CONEG), an association of black people that seeks to bring attention to Cuba's racial problems, acknowledged increased awareness of the problem at the community level but expressed a desire to see debate about racism taken up at the national level, such as by a Cuban parliament commission, which CONEG endorses.[24] However, Miguel Barnet, president of the Cuban Writers and Artists Union, marked the ship's presence in Havana as a testament to a shared history between the American and Cuban people that "transcends" tensions between the two governments. He added that such cultural gestures could bring about goodwill between the two countries.

It would seem almost a rite of passage for the slave ship exhibitions, upon arrival to a host city, to generate discussion among event organizers and community activists about contemporary issues related to the slave past. And yet, while those discussions have taken place for the *Zong* ship replica and the *Freedom Schooner Amistad*, we see it as mostly peripheral to their primary mission to enlighten and educate the patron, and to promote healing. But for the *Henrietta Marie*, the pre-packaged form and structure of the exhibition itself compromised that singular mission for event organizers at some host cities.

The "Pre-packaged" *Henrietta Marie* "Unpacks" in US Cities

As slides show the capture, torture, and placement of slaves aboard a slave ship in the opening scene of George Wolfe's 1985 play *The Colored Museum*, a perky flight attendant prepares passengers for takeoff: "Welcome aboard *Celebrity Slaveship*, departing the Gold Coast and making short stops at Bahia, Port Au Prince, and Havana before our final destination of Savannah."[25] She adds, "Once we reach the desired altitude, the Captain will turn off the 'fasten Your Shackle' sign." The flight attendant further admonishes passengers to "refrain from call-and-response singing between cabins to avoid rebellion." On the slave ship *Celebrity*, passengers are forbidden from bringing drums aboard, though they can dance and stretch in the aisles between flashes of the "Fasten Your Shackles" sign. And for their added comfort, earplugs and magazines can be purchased for the price of a first-born male child.

Passengers on board the *Celebrity* are told that they can exchange trivial comforts, such as magazines, music, and movies, for the cost of a human being, symbolizing the glass beads and cheap trinkets that Europeans sold to Africans for slaves. While seatbelts act as restraints for the traveler's own safety and protection, shackles function as restraints against individual freedom. Middle Passage horrors masquerade as humorous trifles and take on almost souvenir proportions at slave sites and museum exhibitions. One could almost envision a pair of shackles being offered for sale as souvenirs in museum gift shops. At its most cynical, the play warns against the perils of leaving spectators at these exhibitions with the exclusive impression that the slave is either a victim, an exotic other, or a passive, acquiescent subject.

Lending his voice to a fictional work that likens a simulated airline passenger compartment to a slave ship's cargo hold, Wolfe depicts the Middle Passage experience as a routine plane ride filled with tourists headed for a destination of fun and activities. But by disarming the Middle Passage as though to make it more palatable for the slave descendant as neo Middle Passenger who travels through time and space to slave sites as a novel experience, Wolfe seems to parody just such exhibitions as the *Zong* replica, the reconstructed *Amistad*, and the *Henrietta Marie*, as well as Middle Passage displays in established museums. Specifically, the play equates spectators and visitors with voyeurs queuing for a glimpse at slave replicas placed in assorted positions in makeshift ships. Harboring an underbelly of black comedy and tragedy beneath local-color humor, Wolfe's panorama of theatricality borders on the absurd and threatens to compromise the grave lessons that traveling slave ship exhibitions display.

After a "flash" moment that reckoned with images from the slave ship *Henrietta Marie* in 1993, retired New York State Health Administrator Oswald Sykes permanently changed his life. First, he grew angry after seeing shackles from the ship's wreckage at a 1991 Black Scuba Divers convention in Fort Lauderdale, Florida. Later, however, he channeled that anger into designing the 2,700-pound concrete memorial to honor forgotten slaves of the Atlantic slave trade. The memorial plaque, which faces east to Africa, has the following inscription: "Speak her name and gently touch the souls of our ancestors." In a seminal ceremonial event, Sykes, along with president and National Association of Black Scuba Divers founder Albert Jose Jones and other members, placed the monument on the ocean floor at the site of the *Henrietta Marie* shipwreck. Jones is an environmental science professor at the University of the District of Columbia and a marine biologist. On December 16, 2001, Sykes organized a slide show to accompany the ship's exhibition in the New York State Museum in Albany, New York. The exhibit ends with a huge photo of Sykes and members of the NABSD at the underwater site of the wreckage. Periodically, he returns to the site in order to clear the barnacles that have accumulated on the memorial with sharp-edged dental instruments.[26] A seafarer in the form of a master scuba diver—and for the sake of argument, a neo Middle Passenger—Sykes has almost singlehandedly become the vessel's most ardent messenger.

Unlike the *Zong* and *Freedom Schooner Amistad*, the *Henrietta Marie* is neither a replica nor a reconstructed slave ship. Rather, original artifacts shorn of incrustation and supplemented by a few reproductions make up the traveling exhibition that has toured more than twenty-five US cities. These include Detroit, Michigan; Los Angeles, California; Charlotte, North Carolina; Little Rock, Arkansas; Long Island, New York; Jacksonville, Florida; and Austin, Texas. Located and recovered in 1972, some thirty-five miles off the coast of Key West, Florida, by divers, the *Henrietta Marie* is the only slave ship in North America (out of five known slave ship wrecks) to be so fully researched, documented, and exhibited as a traveling slavery museum in select US cities. Officials at the Mel Fisher Maritime Museum plan to house the exhibit there permanently.

As the *Henrietta Marie* exhibition cycles through host cities in the US, a collective made up of site organizers, curators, docents, and spectators engages in a political struggle, like Oswald Sykes, to reclaim a heritage that they believe to be erroneously represented in the exhibition. Seeking moral reckoning from an under-represented Middle Passage history, slave-descendant groups, in particular, have requested the *Henrietta Marie* exhibition for museums in their cities for several decades. This primarily slave-descendant coalition also seeks to formulate an individual and collective cultural connection through identification with slave subjects that the exhibition depicts. Consequently, museum officials and docents at some host cities have restructured certain parts of the *Henrietta Marie* exhibit deemed historically inaccurate and inauthentic. Dissatisfied with some aspects of the *Henrietta Marie* exhibit, hosts in Charlotte, Jacksonville, Los Angeles, and Chicago supplemented it by adding their own exhibitions about African and/or African American history and culture.

Ordinarily, a museum at a select host city must request the *Henrietta Marie* exhibition, so it travels to sites by invitation and sponsorship. However, in some cases the exhibition went in search of a host city to display its contents. Ship officials recommend that the host museum allow for a three-thousand-square-foot space, though the exhibit can fit in less than two thousand square feet. The host city must pay a $40,000 exhibition fee, which may inhibit the ship's appearance in some impoverished predominantly African American locations where that exhibition could prove beneficial. Museums in host cities can decide whether or not to charge an admission fee. But the *Henrietta Marie* exhibition is not always shown in an enclosed edifice defined as a museum. Some of the sites are "centers," so long as they can bear the cost of the exhibit.

Mel Fisher museum officials typically dispatch a docent armed with a written guide, titled *A Slave Ship Speaks: The Wreck of the Henrietta Marie, A Docent Guide*, to educate curators in host cities on ways to set up the exhibit as a self-guiding tour for museumgoers. But dispensing written guidelines for setting up self-guided tours seems contradictory, since prearranged instructions, prepared by *Henrietta Marie* officials, guide the museumgoer through the exhibit's contents. The docent's published guide features a script that some local curators in host cities found objectionable for those very reasons. These curators have charged that instructions prepared by *Henrietta Marie* exhibition officials tend to offer a distorted, propagandistic, and Eurocentric perspective on slavery. For example, site organizers, docents, and spectators at some host cities criticized the Mel Fisher staff for including information about the illnesses, deaths, and other conditions of the slave ship's crew. Narrative panels pay inordinate attention to specific illnesses, death rate, and overall conditions of the ship's captain and crew. Museumgoers/spectators in some host cities have complained about the content of these panels. They suggest, by comparison, that no one would pay attention to the plight of the SS guard that tortured and murdered Jews. At a *Henrietta Marie* exhibit in Tallahassee, Florida, for example, a student at Florida A&M is quoted as saying, "If you're going to have something on the Jewish Holocaust, you're not going to show what the German soldiers went through. You'd show what the Jews went through."[27]

Other complaints centered on the exhibition of slaves in the ship's cargo hold. Museumgoers/spectators complained most frequently about the deplorable arrangement of life-sized slave replicas in the slave cargo hold below deck, which some host-city curators found disproportionate to its importance. For example, some slave replicas were placed in an upright sitting position, while others lay in spaces that were much roomier than those claimed in historical records. At an exhibit of the *Henrietta Marie* in Los Angeles, for instance, curator Cecil Fergerson commented that slave figures in the simulated ship's hold "look like they are on a cruise to the Caribbean in jockey shorts."[28] Consequently, museum officials and docents at some host cities have restructured certain parts of the *Henrietta Marie* exhibit deemed historically inaccurate and inauthentic.

Ironically, the most prominent aspect of the *Henrietta Marie* exhibition is the "absent presence" of enslaved Africans that were sold in the Caribbean prior to the sinking of the ship off the coast of Florida. The title of the exhibition, "A Slave Ship Speaks: The Wreck of the *Henrietta Marie*," defies accuracy and thus forces the question, Can a slave ship speak? Or rather, who speaks for the slave ship, which is another way of asking, Who can speak for the absented slave that can never be fully recovered? This idea invokes Gayatri Spivak's oft-cited rhetorical query for the subaltern as representational or represented subject that others must produce in a confluence of alternate subjectivities. Such a reading suggests that the captive African can be spoken for or represented only by others, whether European or African, slave master or slave descendant.

The work undertaken by the Mel Fisher exhibition organizers to represent the ship's anonymous, enslaved survivors is a discursive one controlled through exclusionary practices in narration, editing, and other strategies. As Pierre Bourdieu writes in *The Field of Cultural Production*, "one has to be blind not to see that discourse about a work is not a mere accompaniment, intended to assist its perception and appreciation, but a stage in the production of the work, of its meaning and value."[29] The self-guided tour arranged by officials at the Mel Fisher Maritime Museum, the home site for the *Henrietta Marie* at Key West, is a misnomer, since instructions beckon museumgoers/spectators to pull up the brass-plated flaps placed beneath each artifact, and to read the message inside. These messages do not merely inform or educate the museumgoer/spectator about the ship's final voyage, however. They also function as an interpretive discourse for a body of work. Exhibition artifacts come pre-packaged, and organizers arrange companion narrative panels that they have already constructed, along with a display of the ship's slave quarters below deck.

The journey that began in London in 1699—only the second for the *Henrietta Marie*—took the ship to West Africa, possibly New Calabar in modern-day Nigeria, which was the second leg in the triangular slave trade route. The ship next journeyed across the Atlantic Ocean, then traveled to Jamaica, where the crew unloaded slaves before heading back to England to begin the journey anew. But while en route to London, the *Henrietta Marie* sank off the coast of Key West, Florida, during a violent storm. Its wreckage lay underwater for over two centuries before being recovered by members of a diving team for Mel Fisher, an entrepreneur of similar enterprises. The shipwreck's remains included nearly eighty sets of Bilboes, or iron shackles, which indicates that at least 150 enslaved African men out of approximately three hundred captives endured the Middle Passage journey. As an established, organized, and well-funded exhibition, the *Henrietta Marie* is unique, and its contents consist of substantial artifacts from the wrecked slave vessel.

Museumgoers/spectators that view the exhibition are both "self-selecting" and "sought out" by invitation in a coordinated public relations effort by museum officials at the exhibition sites. The docent's guide for the *Henrietta Marie* carries a seal from General Motors, its corporate national tour sponsor, along with the Mel Fisher Maritime Heritage Society at Key West. But the traveling museum's reliance upon corporate sponsorship may have encouraged researchers to lower the volume on controversial discussions about the exhibition at local sites, although curators and docents at host cities may choose on their own to avoid potentially offending museumgoers/spectators. At the *Henrietta Marie*'s exhibition at the Bob Bullock Museum in Austin, Texas, a museum official said that before the exhibition arrived, curators were prompted to avoid presenting the exhibition in a manner that might offend local visitors because of the area's conservative environment.

A few years before the *Henrietta Marie* arrived at Austin, its artifacts went on display in Jacksonville, Florida, where curator Lydia Stewart and other officials at the La Villa Museum hosted the *Henrietta Marie* exhibition. During the ship's exhibition in these and other US cities, newspaper accounts and personal interviews recorded moderate to significant disagreement among some docents and museumgoers/spectators over the exhibit's structure, format, and presentation. At the same time, according to docents at La Villa Museum at Jacksonville and the Bob Bullock Museum at Austin, the largely African American slave-descendant group that patronized the exhibit generally approved it and acknowledged its importance. But the group also tended to respond with anger, frustration, and grief over the slaves' plight.

When suffering by a commonly identifiable group is based on a singular unifying event like slavery, the result is akin to what Vamik Volkan refers to as a chosen trauma that "fittingly reflects a large group unconsciously defining its identity by the transgenerational transmission of injured selves infused with the memory of the ancestors' trauma."[30] Slavery functions as that event that unifies the group because its effects linger. Docents cannot easily communicate trauma relying only on displays of restraining devices. They must measure the desire to know against the unbearable pain of knowing.

It seems inevitable that tensions would develop between Mel Fisher museum officials and curators, as well as visitors in host cities. Officials emphasize the tragedy of slavery in a context in which many, if not all, hands were dirtied. In other cities where the exhibit has traveled, forced confrontation with the past has created reactions ranging from formal detachment to discomfort, grief, anger, and hostility. For example, journalist Mike Toner writes that "the artifacts from this ship make some people cry, they make some people angry, but they cannot fail to move anyone who sees them."[31]

When the exhibit arrived in Los Angeles, local curators insisted on organizing a guided rather than self-guided tour and created an independent narrative that offered a more Afrocentric perspective to the exhibit. For example, a curator in Los Angeles objected to the guide's depiction of slavery as a cooperative venture between equal partners in Europe and Africa. But when Teryl Watkins, president of the Watts Labor Community Action Committee, read the docent guide, she expressed disappointment that the traveling exhibition suppressed atrocities of the slave trade while focusing interpretations favorably on Europe and Europeans. When she passed on her concerns to Cecil Fergerson, a former county museum curator, he agreed that the exhibit was worth mounting but needed some script changes. The Mel Fisher Maritime Heritage Society, which owns the artifacts and the exhibit, did not foresee what Fergerson had in mind, since the society preferred that a self-guided tour be conducted. But Fergerson's volunteer docents addressed issues by distributing pamphlets and brochures that challenged the exhibit's text, citing the exploitation of African people by Europeans. Rather than refer to the slavery era as Europe's "age of exploration," local curators substituted the phrase with Europe's "age of exploitation."[32]

At the Du Sable Museum of African-American History in Chicago, Illinois, curator Ramon Price supplemented the *Henrietta Marie* exhibit with additional artifacts that were deemed "inappropriate elements" by a *Henrietta Marie* representative.[33] Like curators in other host cities, Price believed that the slave hold section of the exhibit did not depict reality. Consequently, when the exhibit arrived in Chicago, he added more figures to simulate the cramped nature of slave quarters "and hid them behind a thick screen so the original figures, which he described as barely resembling humans, were less visible." Price also removed a scene in the exhibit that he believed to be an inaccurate, "misleading and amateurish" representation of an African village.

Dissatisfied with the exhibit, officials at La Villa Museum in Jacksonville, Florida, assembled their own narrative panels, which supplemented the *Henrietta Marie* exhibition. Museum administrator and curator Lydia Stewart said that the newly added panels included Africa before slavery, a description of West African civilization, and a description of the Middle Passage that contradicted the *Henrietta Marie*'s display. She says that museum officials augmented both script and artifacts primarily to defuse the image of blacks solely as slavery victims and to debunk the notion that Europeans brought civilization to Africa.

In a defense of the *Henrietta Marie*'s format, structure, and design, a sign on a wall during the planning stages of the exhibit read, "IT'S THE SHIP, STUPID." Madeline Burnside, former executive director of the Mel Fisher Maritime Heritage Society, said the exhibit's slave hold matches that of the *Henrietta Marie* specifically and is not meant to portray the spoon-style packing of slave bodies depicted in other accounts. Inetta Bell, a docent at the North Carolina Spirit Square Center for Arts and Education said, "Conditions on slave ships were much tighter than what the reproduction shows."[34] Mel Fisher Museum officials argue that they mean to show the cabin size of the *Henrietta Marie*, formerly a warship that was smaller than most slave ships.

Consequently, it transported fewer slaves, which permitted them more room to move around.

In the *Henrietta Marie* exhibition, the slave cargo hold measures thirty-six spaces, though in reality, it measured only eighteen spaces. The cargo hold in the exhibition therefore strengthens curators' arguments that the *Henrietta Marie* exhibition model misleads spectators into believing that slaves had far more room to maneuver in the real ship's cargo hold. Stewart, for instance, said that the exhibition displays replicas of slaves sitting and lying in positions inaccurate to scale, which is misleading, and she points out that the Middle Passage section is most traumatic for many people. In the cargo hold exhibit, words taken from the *Interesting Narrative of Olaudah Equiano, or Gustavus Vassa, the African*, and from the ship's surgeon are audiotaped to accompany the simulated slave hold section. Ironically, the Middle Passage that Equiano describes closely resembles the tight-packing method that some curators in host cities affirm rather than the loose-packing strategy shown in the *Henrietta Marie* exhibit. To the astute observer, the taped passage from Equiano's text simply does not match the casual display of slave replicas spread out in the cargo hold. Finding that spectators completely ignored the taped messages, La Villa Museum officials added a written panel that described the Middle Passage journey in minute detail.

Stewart said that site organizers at La Villa museum augmented both script and artifacts primarily to defuse the image of blacks solely as slave victims and to debunk the notion that Europeans brought civilization to Africa. "We can't just walk people through and say thanks for coming," Stewart said. "We wanted to educate students on the importance of Africa before the slave trade as a thriving place."[35] Stewart added that museum officials included excerpts from the film, *Lest We Forget*, a description of the Middle Passage designed to correct misconceptions in the exhibit that the *Henrietta Marie* officials arranged. Consequently, in an anteroom at the entrance, before entering the main exhibition room, museumgoers/spectators would see Benin bronzes, sculptors, and other artifacts from the La Villa's own collection. The curators added these artifacts in order to illustrate those large African kingdoms (such as Mali, Ghana, and Songhay) that thrived before sub-Saharan and transatlantic slave trading took place.

Stewart recalled that one school group arrived only to cancel its tour in order to better prepare students for what they would see. The school group returned to the museum to see the exhibit after teachers had first educated students about slavery. Some might excoriate Stewart for posing an idyllic or mythical Africa prior to the onset of slave-trading industries. But through the La Villa's exhibit-within-the-exhibition set up by *Henrietta Marie* officials,

Stewart presented a comprehensive perspective of Africa prior to the sub-Saharan and transatlantic slave trades and through the Middle Passage in order to educate patrons.

Middle-school-age children were the most vocal and volatile, sometimes accusatory, forming divisions by race and putting white classmates on the defensive, Stewart said in an interview with this author. She added that docents developed ways of talking about the exhibit, including holding question-and-answer sessions, to help meet the challenge of not being accusatory to whites. Stewart notes that the *Henrietta* produced the largest crowd ever to attend an exhibit at La Villa. (Tallies excluding weekend numbers produced 740 people; total estimates exceed a thousand people.) La Villa Museum, whose budget comes from the city of Jacksonville, charged $6 for adults, $3 for children, students, and senior citizens, and offered special group rates. The museum, which budgeted for the *Henrietta Marie* exhibit two years ahead of its arrival, is aiming for nonprofit status.

In an article titled "Shedding Light on a Grim Era in History" for the *Austin American Statesman* newspaper, Fred McGhee described his feelings after viewing the exhibit at the town's Bob Bullock Museum: "It was an emotional experience. How could this commerce become the backbone of the British empire?"[36] He added that the artifacts, especially shackles small enough to fit a child's wrist, "speak louder than words." McGhee, a visiting scholar at the University of Houston's Department of African American Studies and a maritime archaeologist, worked as a consultant to the *Henrietta Marie* exhibition in Austin, Texas. Visible in the foreground, a length of chain is connected to a double shackle. In a larger photo that dominates the page, a casually dressed Fred McGhee leans against the makeshift cargo hold that contains life-sized replicas of two slaves, one lying in a semifetal position, the other sitting, head bowed. In the same article, Ricardo Gandara also focuses on artifacts that tell the story of the slaves' suffering on the *Henrietta Marie*, compensating for the absence of detailed knowledge about them or their own perspectives. The article appeared in coordination with the exhibition at the Bob Bullock Museum. Color photographs of the ship's bell bearing the name *Henrietta Marie* permitted accurate identification by divers were included with the article, along with the images of three rusty shackles retrieved from the wreckage.

The *Zong* and the *Henrietta Marie* exhibitions have circulated in the UK and the US, respectively, while only the *Freedom Schooner Amistad* has traveled internationally. Like the traveling *Zong* and *Freedom Schooner Amistad* exhibitions, the *Henrietta Marie* occupies the metaphorical space of ship-in-motion and tests Paul Gilroy's hypothesis of a chronotype that would move beyond the strictures of the modern nation and would connect more broadly with dispersed, diaspora slave descendants. Gilroy envisioned the slave ship's ability to connect—through movement—disparate cultures and places for dispersed descendants of enslaved Africans: "The image of the ship—a living, micro-cultural, micro-political system in motion—is especially important for historical and theoretical reasons."[37] Among Gilroy's critics, Paul Zeleza sees tunnel vision in *The Black Atlantic* for its portrayal of the African American diaspora as a cultural creation. The inference, here, is that focusing on the Middle Passage erases all tracings of an African past memory vis-à-vis slave trafficking in the interiors before the Atlantic crossing. On the other hand, Houston Baker criticizes Gilroy's lack of focus on particularities in the diaspora slave-descendant mesh, such as the absence of an explanation for a route that extends from enslavement to imprisonment in an industrial prison complex, especially for African American males. In this context, Gilroy's paradigm would yoke African American, Brazilian, and Cuban diaspora slave descendants into uniform positions that would minimize the different histories that created their social conditions.[38]

The traveling slave ship exhibitions in this chapter usher in a twenty-first-century museum in which hybridity, even irreconcilability, is the new normal for the cultures of this world. Slave ship replicas depend on perpetual movement, wandering to distant shores, encountering new conditions born of old ones—and forming new alliances with diaspora slave descendants in the global community—from the remains of original slave ships. As spokespersons for the traveling slave ship exhibitions, corporate and other sponsors, event organizers, curators in host cities, and spectators all vie for control of the narratives about the slave past and ultimately the depiction of the enslaved subject. When tensions arise among them for control over the exhibit's accompanying narrative, the method by which the very history of slavery itself will be offered for public consumption is at stake. Rather than a redemptive or homogenized image, then, what threatens to erupt in this combative zone is a postmodern slave ship, the permanence of an ancient museum specimen marked by fluidity and instability. The guide or docent, arguably the single most strategic liaison between exhibition and spectator, connects most intimately and can answer impromptu questions without immediate consultation, thereby introducing the greatest potential for resisting the prepared script.[39]

The question posed by social critics like George Fredrickson, in his essay "The Skeleton in the Closet," is whether African Americans should suppress slavery "as unpleasant and dispiriting" or whether they should remember it "in the ways that Jews remember the Holocaust."[40] Fredrickson's question, placed in the context of slave ship exhibitions—or slave sites that can move—asks how they might prove beneficial as aspects of commemorative, public memory practices on an ongoing basis. Ceremonies and rituals that attend these exhibits are reminders that maintaining the memory of a foundational ancestral slave presence is vital to retaining a valid self-identity. As the manager of the Shrine of the Black Madonna Bookstore in Atlanta, Georgia, says, "Every group of people is allowed to remember the past and pay homage to those who have come before them. Why shouldn't we? It's that whole ritual of memory and honor. That's part of being human."[41] But a traumatic reckoning with the slave past, or what Orlando Patterson regards in *Rituals of Blood* as a perennial, slavery-induced trauma for slave descendants need not be tantamount to paralysis or stasis rather than progressing forward.

◆ ◆ ◆

There is much to laud as well as to give pause about "flash" moments and seminal events at traveling slave ship exhibitions as a collective. Can the traumatic slave past, or more specifically the Middle Passage, be made coherent through visual displays, a discursive lens, and personal and public reflections that traveling slave ship exhibitions provide? The *Zong* ship replica focuses heavily on healing and reconciliation as ceremony, but artifacts and images below deck remind spectators of past brutalities in the trade. One might expect the *Amistad* replica as traveling exhibition to offer the best possibility for critique of diaspora slave-descendant spectators traumatized and adrift in lands that lack equal opportunities for them. But the *Freedom Schooner* strikes a pose almost too pristine, perhaps compromised by its very proximity to, but not exact likeness of, a slave ship.

Traveling to sites connected with the triangular trade and the original *Amistad*'s journey as a kind of goodwill ambassador, the *Freedom Schooner Amistad* regards slavery in a global context, and it boasts a seasoned seafarer in Captain William Pinkney, whose personal life story lends embellishment to the journey. But that goodwill risks discouraging discussions about continued racial strife so as not to offend certain officials at host cities. In chapter 5, I examine how the Bench by the Road slave memorial at Sullivan's Island near Charleston rearticulates the discourse of slavery in connective stories that the slave and the diaspora slave descendant share through recurrent forms of bondage and oppression. That engagement with contemporaneity or present issues about race diminishes the element of remoteness and quaintness in the past.

The Toni Morrison Society Bench by the Road at Sullivan's Island near Charleston.

CHAPTER FIVE

The Bench by the Road
Slave Memorial at Sullivan's Island

There is no place you or I can go, to think about or not think about, to summon
the presences of, or recollect the absences of slaves; nothing that reminds us
of the ones who made the journey and of those who did not make it. There is
no suitable memorial or plaque or wreath or wall or park or skyscraper lobby.
There's no 300-foot tower. There's no small bench by the road.
—Toni Morrison, *World Magazine*, 1989

On October 12, 1988, Toni Morrison accepted the Frederic G. Melcher Book
Award for the publication of *Beloved*. During the acceptance speech, Morrison said that *Beloved* had to be written because "no small bench by the road"
or other "suitable memorial" existed to honor those that had been enslaved
and transported to the United States.[1] In a seminal ceremonial event that fulfilled Morrison's quest in *World Magazine* for commemoration of the enslaved,
members of the Toni Morrison Society (TMS) participated in the placement
of the Maafa Bench by the Road slave memorial on July 26, 2008, as an official
slave site at Sullivan's Island near Charleston. The memorial bench illustrates
the role that tangible markers increasingly play to increase the presence of
slave heritage sites, to alter or redefine the museum proper from formal, indoor
structure, and to renegotiate the meaning of slavery in the modern era.

I begin in this chapter by discussing how the Bench by the Road slave
memorial at Sullivan's Island responds to the political economy of the landscape, the environment, and the community in which it is displayed. Like site
organizers at the slave forts, burial grounds, and reconstructed slave ships in
this study, those who installed the Bench by the Road Slave Memorial reorder
the temporality of the history of slavery through specific conditions of its
display through a cultural milieu, geopolitical framework, and racial ideology. The bench memorial therefore forms a thematic cluster in solidarity with
those slave sites in a past-to-present dialectic. Specifically, the ceremonial
placement of the bench memorial responds to a social and cultural milieu
through its location near a dilapidated slave quarantine facility, a gentrified

community, and a Gullah Geechee slave-descendant group that can no longer afford to live in the region. While the slave past documents African Americans' dislocation from their communities during the Civil War, the present chronicles their pending displacement because of gentrification in the community that surrounds the location of the bench memorial.

This chapter exposes the Bench by the Road slave memorial, allegorically, in a geopolitical space in which slavery's residues in the modern world collide at seminal moments of contestation. But in light of a uniquely identifiable "watershed" moment—the tragic murders of nine parishioners at Charleston's Mother Emanuel Church in 2015 and subsequent removal of the Confederate flag from the state's capitol grounds—I reflect on the bench memorial in concert with the region's centrality in slavery's legacy. As a slave memorial in a region rife with contradictions over the appropriate designation and display of monuments and memorials, the Bench by the Road represents a capacity for belonging and healing, alongside one that exposes local inhabitants' disruption and alienation from community.

The Bench Memorial: Commemoration, Culture, and Commodity

On Sullivan's Island near Charleston, in South Carolina, overlooking the calm, peaceful waters of the Atlantic Ocean, sit the remains of several pest houses built in 1707. Newly transported enslaved Africans were taken there, where they were quarantined and examined for disease before being released for sale. Sullivan's Island is believed to be where some 40 percent of all enslaved Africans brought to British North America were transported.[2] The United States Census reports that as of 2010, Sullivan's Island is home to about two thousand people, the majority of whom are white. It includes valuable waterfront property, a vital part of the local economy for real estate moguls and wealthy homeowners who can afford it. Those properties that date back several generations may well have reaped the benefits of slave labor over time. Coveted areas along the state's coastlines have rapidly succumbed to the development of resorts, golf courses, and other amenities.

Prominent among those that have been displaced from long-standing homes around sea-island communities like Sullivan's Island, members of the slave-descendant Gullah Geechee population occupy a cultural space between the defunct pest houses, as symbolic relics of the slave past, and a gentrified community that gestures to the present. The Gullah Geechee people, slave descendants of eighteenth- and nineteenth-century Angola, Ashanti, Fante, Mandingo, Yoruba, and other West African ethnicities, retain one of the nation's most unique cultures, distinguished by religion, language, food, crafts, and folklore. Because of the isolation of the sea islands from the mainland—ideal for the captive Africans' rice growing skills—the Gullah Geechee community has survived mostly intact for more than three hundred years, though certain aspects of their unique culture have dimmed in recent years.

Today, a defunct pest house, which sits as a stark, unintended memento of the area's former use, must compete with a new emblem, one that reverses the muted histories of slavery and remedies the failure to memorialize those Middle Passage slaves that Morrison alluded to in her 1989 article. In other words, while the pest house harks back to a dark chapter in the area's history, the steel bench counters that oppressive image with one that marks the landscape with the enslaved's indomitable spirit. Furthermore, the bench reinforces the empowerment of the Toni Morrison Society as a group collective.

In 2000 Gullah Geechees gathered at Fort Moultrie on Sullivan's Island to form a nation, headed by Marquetta L. Goodwine (aka Queen Quet), a Gullah chieftess, historian, and founder of the Gullah Geechee Sea Island Coalition. And in 2004 Congressman James E. Clyburn (D-South Carolina) introduced the Gullah Geechee Cultural Heritage Act (H.R. 4683) to preserve the dwindling Geechee heritage culture along a coastal swath in the Carolinas, Georgia, and Florida. Therefore, it is no small irony—but with great fanfare—that a group of Gullah descendant Adande drummers, reminders of those priced out as residents to the area because they can no longer afford the high property taxes, gathered near a cove at Sullivan's Island on a steamy Saturday afternoon on July 26, 2008, along with Nobel Laureate and Pulitzer Prize–winning author Toni Morrison to participate in the installation of a slave memorial in the form of a steel bench. The Toni Morrison Society, a nonprofit organization made up of scholars devoted to studying Morrison's canon, chose Sullivan's Island as the first placement site in the Bench by the Road project.

Slavery museums and black heritage sites cohere around artifacts, objects, and other aspects of a material culture, like the Bench by the Road, that symbolically occupy the space of the absented slave, and that give coherence to the sites that house them. Specifically, this chapter focuses on a seminal artifact as a permanent exhibition in an outdoor setting that accesses a key historical function in the slave past. Here, I am especially interested in the Bench by the Road that, unlike slave forts, burial grounds, and slave ship exhibitions examined in this study, primarily exists as a singular artifact, a kind of museum unto itself. Visual markers of material culture are subject to historical reconfiguration, often fraught with tension over conflicting views offered by artists, designers, curators, and sponsors. The visual dimension of memory joins with an artifact's spatial environment, which can alter perspectives pertaining to the surrounding landscape, local economy, and racial politics.

Stephen Greenblatt, in "Resonance and Wonder," explains two different models for organizing exhibits and museum displays that clarify this interpretative process: one that evokes wonder by highlighting artifacts or objects that elicit "an exalted attention," and one that evokes resonance, which "pulls viewers away from the celebration of isolated objects and towards a series of implied, only half-visible relationships and questions."[3] Greenblatt's explanation bodes well for artifacts critiqued as abstract ideas, but I also find it especially pertinent for the unique relationship between certain seminal objects of slavery, such as the Maafa bench memorial, and its relationship with the community, local economy, and racial politics that surround it. I employ a variation of Greenblatt's idea for the bench memorial as a heritage site, which reinforces its capacity to transmit those inferred, partially discernible relationships well beyond their exaltation as wondrous objects. Often a singular artifact or object like the Toni Morrison Society Bench by the Road, rather than lengthy narrative panels or "official" written archival records, projects a most compelling visual and tactile dimension that connects intimately with visitors or spectators. I think of artifacts as artificially made objects of historical interest and significance, "object[s] produced or shaped by human workmanship; especially a simple tool, weapon, or ornament of archaeological or historical interest."[4] An artifact from the slave past can evoke the humanity of the slave or diaspora slave descendant, or it can dehumanize the slave or diaspora black, depending on context. Artifacts can help to illustrate willed forgetfulness or self-protective nostalgia, and they can provide culturally mediated information that can unblock a spectator's confusion about what is read as opposed to what is seen. An artifact or object has the potential to recall a past event or incident immediately through a mnemonic association with that event.

I categorize the bench memorial at Sullivan's Island as an artifact that originally existed as a simple, steel park bench and was later transformed by a commemorative ceremony that honored Middle Passage slaves. An object that serves one purpose can be made over or transformed into an artifact that specifically recalls or represents the slave past, such as the steel benches that the Toni Morrison Society placed in a variety of locations as memorials. Formalized with a small plaque engraved on its backside, the bench memorial therefore illustrates the transformation of a singular artifact as a slave site that stands apart from a formal museum edifice while still serving as a stalwart player in a historical legacy.

I have argued that, through a past-to-present praxis, the Bench by the Road slave memorial as a premier artifact offers new ways to rethink the meaning of slavery and to observe its omnipresence in a purportedly postracial era. I have also discussed the nuances in an interpretative process that navigates through emanations, inferences, and associations between artifacts and related events. And I have noted how Greenblatt's theory of resonance, through emanations, can prompt individuals to associate museum artifacts and objects with specific events and circumstances that they may infer. But I am also aware of contested memory when these connections may not be readily evident to the spectator without intervention from site organizers or docents.

In *The Diasporan Self: Unbreaking the Circle in Western Black Novels*, J. Lee Greene explains how racial memory can be activated for the slave-descendant spectator (whom he calls the diaspora subject) whose soul "as primordial memory" is initially inactive or dormant upon contact with an artifact. Greene writes, "A subject who comes in contact with an inanimate object (such as an artifact) that houses memory has his or her own memory reactivated."[6] Through an intriguing process that Lisa Woolfork refers to as "bodily epistemology," the spectator figuratively puts on the skin of the slave's body double or likeness when the image triggers reminders of the anonymous, enslaved African. In this way, the spectator approximates the presence of the enslaved subject when cast in a "subcutaneous transmission of the past to the present."[7] This idea is particularly effective for what I regard as the virtual slave or replica of a slave figure when positioned as a diorama in a museum setting. At best, visual displays of slavery blur distinctions between past and present, with the added benefit that the spectator concretizes the abstractness of the slave's experience. In addition, the spectator's engagement with present-day issues about race and slavery diminishes the element of remoteness and quaintness in the past.

Nearly two decades after lamenting the absence of a memorial for enslaved Africans who died and for those who survived the Middle Passage, author Toni Morrison led several hundred members of the Toni Morrison Society in a "Maafa Bench by the Road Ceremony" at Sullivan's Island. Society members moved in a procession down the pier, dressed in white and hoisting yellow umbrellas high against the stifling heat and humidity, swaying to the drumbeats of Gullah Adande performers. Morrison tossed a daisy wreath over the bridge into the Atlantic Ocean in memory of the millions of enslaved Africans who perished during the Middle Passage and those who arrived on Sullivan's Island, now the home to Fort Moultrie.

Toni Morrison Society organizers carefully orchestrated the ceremony, which was attended by reporters and spectators that were alerted in advance to the occasion. Just as organizers had done at reinterment services for the African Burial Ground in New York, and sponsors of the *Zong, Amistad,* and *Henrietta Marie* slave ship exhibitions had done, organizers of the Bench by the Road memorial performed solemn ceremonies that included drumbeats, sermons, the pouring of libations, and other rituals. In so doing they shifted slave remembrance from logs, ledgers, maps, and even historical databases to a performative archival blend. A society member and African American professor at Coppin State University in Baltimore, Kokahvah Zauditu-Selassie, alluded to the shift by calling the event a reclamation of African American literature, dance, and connection with nature. Another member read a portion of Morrison's 1989 interview in the *World Magazine* in which she lamented the absence of a slave memorial.

Another member, Judylyn Ryan, recited "The Sermon in the Clearing," a passage taken from Morrison's *Beloved* in which the character Baby Suggs implores formerly enslaved followers to love their hands, because others, whom she implies as enslavers, do not do love them. And Zauditu-Selassie recited a sermon and explained the meaning of the Maafaa, a Kiswahili word that refers to the Middle Passage as a black holocaust. Society member Don Denard poured libations as he invoked the names of such deceased African Americans as Harriet Tubman and others. The ceremony culminated with the unveiling of a six-foot, twenty-six-inch-deep black steel bench, emblazoned with a small bronze plaque mounted on its back, that was set in a place overlooking a cove and facing the waterway.

The ceremony transformed an otherwise simple steel bench overlooking a cove into a concrete historic marker, which triggered a variety of responses to its new identity as a memorial and slave heritage site. For Morrison, whose words had brought the project to fruition, visitors could "summon the presences [and] recollect the absences" of millions of enslaved Africans that perished in the Middle Passage.[8] Morrison's original edict set the tone for observers to regard the bench as designated for contemplation in silent observance, and to pay homage, long overdue, to the captive Africans. A nonprofit scholarly organization, the society selected this location as the first of at least twenty sites to answer the call that Morrison made after winning the Nobel Prize for literature in 1989.

The installation ceremony first held at Sullivan's Island sent a message that the Bench by the Road was as much about present-day interests and objectives as about honoring the estimated "60 million and more" captive Africans transported in the Middle Passage that Morrison references in the epigraph to *Beloved.* For example, the eighth bench installation also took place in South Carolina at the Mitchelville Freedom Park on Hilton Head Island. While mayor pro tem Bill Harkins reflected on the bench as an inspirational site, Preservation Project chair Randy Dolyniuk thought "to imagine the lives of Mitchelville's first residents as they experienced freedom," and project spokesperson Joyce Wright added, "It could also be simply 'a place you can sit and reflect.'"[9] The Toni Morrison Society, in concert with the Mitchelville Preservation Project, installed the bench as a tribute to a historic black settlement on the island. During the Civil War, Union troops under General Ormsby Mitchel—the settlement's namesake—drove off Confederates in 1861, then set aside land to settle marooned slaves displaced from the island. Census records in 2010 report that over five thousand Gullah Geechee slave descendants resided in Mitchelville. The community formed the Mitchelville Preservation Project to retain their culture because of encroachment by upscale buyers in search of summer homes and resorts.

The bench placement at both Sullivan's Island and Mitchelville clearly intends to preserve African American culture and identity for communities first isolated in the slave past, and under threat of displacement yet again as a result of gentrification in the modern era. African American artist Juan Logan, who exhibited a sculpture titled *Foundation, 2004,* at Charleston's Gibbes Museum during the summer that the bench memorial was placed at Sullivan's Island, referred to gentrified communities as plantation sites. Logan's *Foundation, 2004* sculpture expands from one cast ductile iron block to forty-two blocks, each one placed atop the other. The structure symbolizes the exploitation of slave labor. But it also metaphorizes an extension of that exploitation through gated communities, golf courses, resorts, and the like. These gentrified communities especially attract whites who, nostalgic for the old plantation, seek security that the new plantation offers, according to Logan.[10] In this regard, the Bench by the Road Slave Memorials at both Sullivan's Island and Mitchelville remind visitors that enslaved black laborers buttressed a plantation economy.

Out of the more than twenty Bench by the Road placement sites, ten commemorate the slave past on behalf of those abolitionists who helped slaves to escape from slavery through the Underground Railroad. In addition to Sullivan's Island and Mitchelville, a bench memorial was placed at Oberlin, Ohio, which functioned as a major, historic stop on the Underground Railroad. In Concord, Massachusetts, the fifth bench memorial resides at the reconstructed home of Caesar Robbings, a black abolitionist and landowner who held antislavery meetings there. At Walden Woods, in Lincoln, Massachusetts, the ninth bench memorial honors the memory of Brister Freeman, who gained freedom from slavery upon fighting in the American Revolutionary War. A successful landowner, he helped other African Americans to survive.[11]

The thirteenth and fourteenth bench memorials were both placed in Middletown, Delaware, to honor Samuel D. Burris, an African American Underground Railroad conductor and abolitionist who helped countless individuals and families to escape from slavery as they traveled through Delaware. The fifteenth bench memorial honors Cynthia Hesdra, a former slave who eventually became a conductor on the Underground Railroad. She also became a successful entrepreneur, landowner, and businesswoman in New York. The sixteenth bench, at Lincoln University, Pennsylvania, commemorates the Hosanna AUMP Church, an active stop on the Underground Railroad and an important site for abolitionist meetings. In addition, bench memorials were placed in Jackson, Mississippi, on April 10, 2015, and in Cleveland, Ohio. The latter memorial commemorates Cleveland's African American and white abolitionist communities.[12]

In addition to the bench memorial placement sites in the US, the Toni Morrison Society sought to extend the memory of slavery to a global community. Consequently, the first international bench memorial installation took place in Paris, France, in November 2010, and was dedicated to the memory of Martinican Louis Delgres. A man of color (*homme de couleur*) and an antislavery revolutionary, Delgres fought against Napoleon and the French reoccupation and reinstitution of slavery at Guadeloupe. Trapped in battle on the Matouba volcano, Delgres and hundreds of followers chose to commit suicide by detonating their own gunpowder supplies rather than surrender to French authority.

At the ceremony in Paris, which took place on a street named in Delgres's honor, before an international press corps and a throng of cameras and crew, Morrison praised his resistance and bravery: "I have always thought of my own work as a kind of rewriting the history of African Americans and Americans in general, and so this particular place where this bench sits is the beginning of reconfiguring and rewriting the rest of the world with certain sites."[13] She added that the reinscription ceremony for Delgres in Paris signaled that more such dedications at other international locations would be desirable and should take place.

In its transformation from park bench to a historic marker in local, national, and international settings, the Bench by the Road memorial symbolizes an enslaved people's passage across the Atlantic and stands as a permanent memento long after commemorative ceremonies have ended. Of course, the memorial also serves as a site of contemplation and reflection for visitors. Tacitly acknowledging an inability to represent the slave's authentic voice, the bench therefore functions as a "memory space" that endeavors to recover an elusive subject. Tourists and spectators might otherwise see it simply as a resting place, and responses may well range from indifference to stoicism and trauma.

Diaspora slave descendants might descend on the scene as visitors to an authentic black heritage site that deifies or enshrines the enslaved subject by proxy. Slave descendants, in particular, may gravitate toward the visual marker in the stead of the enslaved subject with whom they seek to commune, but they may also seek spiritual healing for unresolved issues in their own lives. And yet, in a geopolitical, spatial context, the bench memorial also marks its territory in an arena rife with ironies that pertain to the landscape and local economy.

In Charleston's *Post and Courier* newspaper, on the occasion of the installation ceremony at Sullivan's Island for the first bench memorial placement, the caption for a feature story stated, "'Bench by the Road' Tribute to Slaves." But the front-page story for the same newspaper attracted a different headline: "Selling Slavery: Area Business People Finding Money in Long-Shrouded History." The feature story, written by Dottie Ashley, focused primarily on the Bench by the Road ceremony itself as a tribute to slaves. But in the cover story for the *Post and Courier*, Kyle Stock raised the specter of "reverse" exploitation by suggesting that local slave sites were more about generating revenue for tourism than educating the public. Stock's story, which rankled some members of the Toni Morrison Society, charged that tourism to slave sites had taken the place of slavery as a profit-driven, thriving industry that buttressed Charleston's local economy: "Charleston has long made its fortune by bringing people here. Centuries ago, it was slaves. Today, it's tourists," Stock wrote. And he added that Charleston's business community had discovered that "the examination and discussion of [slavery] can be lucrative once again."[14]

To support his point, Stock cited Alphonso Brown, a Gullah tour guide, who operates a two-hour tour of slave history in downtown Charleston, South Carolina. Stock also noted that slave cabins at Charleston's Magnolia Plantation were in the process of being restored to their original state. "Suffering sells," he wrote, and struck a comparison between slave tourism and "carefully preserved concentration camps" in Germany.[15] "Revisiting the darkest chapters of human history is not only a cathartic exercise but a lucrative one," Stock continued.

Perhaps the greatest irony, however, that escaped notice in the local newspaper accounts, calls attention to the relationship between the natural environment and the built object. While "cultural" capital accrues to the exhibit, it is offset by "commodity" capital that prevails through trends in some modern-day realtors' market. As mentioned earlier, Sullivan's Island, like so many gentrified communities, is now the site of waterfront properties belonging to some of the area's wealthiest citizens. It seems bizarre, and it misses the mark to identify heritage tourism and slave cabin restorations as "selling slavery," while overlooking the long-term, potentially damaging impact of "selling out" a community through gentrification. Enslaved labor at least two centuries ago aided the profit margins that are still sustained today.

The reporter for the *Post and Courier* might have mentioned that prior to the restoration of Charleston's Magnolia Plantation, Johnnie Leach, a South Carolina resident, had raised thirteen children and sent three of them to college while living in "Slave Cabin C" from 1946 until 1969. Leach descends from skilled black gardeners that date to the Depression era, though the home that he occupied was built in the 1850s, then later inhabited by free blacks. Other black families lived in slave dwellings at Magnolia well into the 1980s, making their own renovations over time. Old newspapers line the walls of one cabin as insulation against cold winters.

In an article for the *Grio News* titled "South Carolina Slave Cabins Housed Family through '60s," Associated Press reporter Bruce Smith writes that the Leach family drew water from a pump, cooked on a woodstove, and used an outhouse as a toilet. They were the last to live in a slave cabin without indoor plumbing and with minimal lighting from an electric line and a few lightbulbs, though later families living in the quarters added toilets. These modern conveniences were removed when the Magnolia Cabin Project began restoring five historic structures to their 1850 status as part of a $500,000 restoration project. But Leach (a combat engineer in World War II) favors the cabins unchanged, "so some of the young ones can see what they didn't see," he said. Speaking in the lilt of a Gullah descendant, he added, "To me, it don't have the old looks."[16] But the question as to whether certain aspects of similar sites commercialize or sell slavery for monetary gains by promoting tourism has also divided some in the academic community.

The *Post and Courier* reporter who quipped that slavery sells might also have noted the struggle that some owners of slavery museums and black heritage sites experience simply to survive. In Walterboro, South Carolina, for example, Danny Drain, owner and curator of the Slave Relic Museum, which contains over two thousand artifacts—mostly of slavery—has closed his establishment. Yet the museum's small but unique collections brought it to the attention of the Smithsonian Museum and Henry Louis Gates Jr., who filmed the site for a PBS program on slavery. Drain, a slave descendant who owns most of the collection, lives upstairs in a huge house. He also recreated a slave quarters from one room and had plans to build slave cabins in the property's backyard.

The articles in the *Post and Courier* reopened a prolonged conversation broached at a conference that took place at the College of Charleston in the spring of 2000, titled "Plantations of the Mind: Marketing Myths and Memories in the Heritage Tourism Industry," which examined slave commemoration as public history. Participants, mostly from the academic community, hailed from the United Kingdom, the US, and Africa. According to organizer John Beech, after the conference ended, the group toured seven area sites, each offering a different perspective on slavery in relation to the local environment and material culture. But Beech added that the tour, which included plantation mansions, rice paddies built by slaves, and slave cabins "all sent a single message loud and clear—slavery took place here!"[17]

Some social theorists question whether heritage sites such as these engage in hyperbole, spectacle, or oversaturation of marketing practices that obscure the message that slavery should remain central to public discourse as a horrific, unforgettable crime against humanity. Andreas Huyssen finds it ironic that the nontraditional museum would capitulate to a "capitalist culture of spectacle" even as it "wrest[s] tradition away from conformity."[18] Among those that reference commodification and recovery, albeit in the context of the Holocaust, James Young suggests that an aspect of American culture that permeates artistic disciplines indeed finds death and terror commodious. Young also believes that "entertainment value, even perversely" cannot be divorced from, and ultimately gets entangled with "historical narrative."[19] But like other groups that organize commemorative projects for the enslaved, the Toni Morrison Society commemorates enslaved laborers' contributions to nation building, promotes universal healing, and reclaims a literary and cultural heritage.

In a humorous moment after the formal ceremony ended, when asked by a reporter how she felt sitting on the newly installed memorial bench, Morrison first quipped that she couldn't see the waterway because the throng of reporters had blocked her view. But she later responded to a question posed by a *New York Times* reporter: "It's never too late to honor the dead. It's never too late to applaud the living who do them honor. This [ceremony] is extremely moving to me."[20] Invoking the issue of race, along with then-senator Barack Obama's candidacy for the presidency (which she had endorsed in a letter that made headlines), Morrison suggested that whites converse among themselves about slavery's legacy, because African Americans are not owners of that institution. She also added that antislavery activists that included nonblacks sacrificed their lives to procure justice.[21]

Morrison's iterations reveal how an academic group remembers the slave past through public memory practices. The Toni Morrison Society is made up almost exclusively of university professors that give presentations at meetings held biennially, and that publish scholarly articles and monographs on

Morrison's literary canon. While committees within the organization make decisions about what constitutes a bench placement site, they enlist a variety of participants from local communities at each site to coordinate programming, performances, and public relations. Consequently, the Bench by the Road as slave recovery project mediates the dialectic—the heretofore uneasy alliance—between traditional methods of archiving historical records versus public memory practices, which results in an archival reconfiguration of information pertaining to slavery omitted from those records.

By placing the bench at the point of entry for millions of slaves, the Toni Morrison Society, the Adande Gullah Geechee drummers, and community organizers functioned as a collective group and moved to reclaim their literature, culture, and traditions, which also meant reclaiming an identity. Transformed from artifact to slave memorial by the society, the bench thus represents something far more valuable than land or waterfront property; it reprises those abstract and concrete mechanisms such as human dignity, pride, and possessions that were confiscated through historical theft. The Bench by the Road ultimately symbolizes ownership of self, as well as ownership of one's own stories.

Much debate centers on differences between objects and texts, or differences in narrative representations of "things" versus a kind of objects for objects' sake versus the site as process "through exercises of power and ideology." Individual and collective memory inures us to the study of objects, because they seer indelibly into our consciousness in ways that chronology or factual data do not. Implicit in much scholarly research is the notion that "artifacts are passive reflections of the culture that created and used them, or they are active instruments in the creation and perpetuation of culture."[22] Like the Gullah Geechee on the threshold of land loss, the concept of ownership critically becomes a matter of family and cultural preservation. But as I have previously stated, the bench memorial as a novel artifact responds, simultaneously, to the political economy of landscape, environment, and community and racial ideology.

The Bench Memorial: The Paradox of Symbolic Memory

When Toni Morrison expressed a desire for a slave memorial in *World Magazine* that later evolved as the Bench by the Road project, she thought that it would be refreshing if there were monuments about black people that could be exhibited to the public. But she added that blacks and whites alike would benefit from these monuments. "It could suggest the moral clarity among white people when they were at their best, when they risked something, when they didn't have to risk and could have chosen to be silent; there's no monument for that either," Morrison said.[23] In this section, I place the Bench by the Road slave memorial in conversation with South Carolina's centrality in slavery's legacy through its Civil War monuments and Morrison's observations. I submit that like other slave sites in this study, the bench memorial can best be read through "flash" moments and seminal events, such as its ceremonial installation and performances by a Gullah Geechee ethnicity, because these events expose the conditions of its display through culture, landscape, and community. But I also contend that seminal events that occur long after the site's installation may reassess it as a mechanism for processing ever-shifting racial ideologies that reflect the changing times.

In South Carolina's history of race relations, Confederate monuments echo the paradox of symbolic memory in a dichotomous duet with the Bench by the Road slave memorial near Charleston and at Mitchelville, along with other slave sites in the state. Competing identities born of slavery and Lost Cause ideology have long defined the formation and recognition of Confederate Civil War memorials and monuments in South Carolina and other southern states. For example, the Confederate flag has long been a controversial symbol of racism to many slave-descendant blacks. On the other hand, the bench memorial marks the archival, historical slave past as a living memory of the present for contemporary generations, although the instability and volatility of race relations in the state still endure.

On June 27, 2015, Bree Newsome, a thirty-year-old black civil rights activist, climbed over a fence, then shinnied up a thirty-foot flagpole in front of the statehouse in Columbia, South Carolina, and removed the Confederate flag. Trained to scale a pole by a New York activist, using lampposts, basketball hoops, and even a flagpole, Newsome believed that an African American female would serve as a symbolic presence because of her under-representation in the civil rights struggle overall. Newsome, along with a companion-accomplice, James Ian Tyson, was immediately arrested and jailed for "defacing monuments on state Capitol grounds."[24]

The pair faced fines of up to $5,000 and jail for up to three years, but several organizations quickly raised nearly $100,000 to pay their legal fees. Newsome was released later that night, and authorities hoisted the flag back up less than an hour later. Following her release, Newsome said in a statement to the media, "We removed the flag today because we can't wait any longer," and added, "It's time for a new chapter where we are sincere about dismantling White supremacy and building toward true racial justice and equality."[25]

The gut-wrenching, seminal moment that led to Bree Newsome's act of civil disobedience occurred when on June 17, 2015, nine black church parishioners were murdered by Dylann Roof, a nineteen-year-old white supremacist, at the venerable Mother Emanuel African Methodist Episcopal (AME) Church.[26] The deceased members included church senior pastor and South Carolina state senator the Reverend Clementa Pinckney. They also included the Reverend Sharonda Coleman-Singleton, who was a pastor at Mother Emanuel, along with the Reverend Daniel Simmons, a ministerial staff member. Cousins Ethel Lance and Susie Jackson had long attended Mother Emanuel, and Depayne Middleton Doctor was a singer in the church choir. Myra Thompson was the wife of the vicar of Holy Trinity Reformed Episcopal Church in Charleston. Cynthia Hurd, well known in her community, managed two libraries in the Charleston County Public Library system. Tywanza Sander, the youngest victim at the age of twenty-six, was a graduate in business administration from Allen University in Columbia, South Carolina.[27]

The Mother Emanuel Church, built in 1891 and the oldest AME church in the South, had a lengthy, activist history of slave resistance, opposition to Jim Crow and segregation, and support of voter registration for African Americans. The AME church replaced an earlier 1872 church that was damaged by an earthquake in 1886. Under the leadership of Morris Brown, congregants formed the Emanuel AME Church in Charleston after suffering discrimination at a segregated church and after a dispute over a burial ground. The Emanuel Church burned to the ground after authorities discovered that its founder, Denmark Vesey, had planned to organize a slave revolt. He was executed, and over three hundred alleged participants were arrested. Services at Mother Emanuel and other black churches were outlawed, and congregants had to worship in secret until 1865, when the church was reorganized.[28]

After extensive debate in the weeks after the murders of nine worshippers took place, a watershed moment in the history of race relations occurred in South Carolina at the state's capitol in Columbia. Led by Nikki Haley, South Carolina's first Indian-American governor, an overwhelming majority of members of the state's General Assembly voted to remove the Confederate flag "monument" from statehouse grounds. Representative and attorney Jenny Horne, a descendant of Jefferson Davis, gave a moving speech credited with influencing the vote on the flag's removal, and state senator Paul Thurmond, son of former Dixiecrat and segregationist Strom Thurmond, also supported its removal. A few weeks after Bree Newsome's act of civil disobedience led to her arrest, it took "one minute and 55 seconds [for] a S.C. Highway Patrol Honor Guard to slide the flag from the top of the pole, fold it twice, roll it into a thin baton and wrap it in ribbon," according to a reporter for the *Post and*

Courier.[29] Yet the flag's removal in July 2015 took place more than fifty years after officials first raised it at the site in 1962 as protest against integration. And it occurred more than 150 years after South Carolina seceded from the Union, and after the firing on Fort Sumter signaled the start of the Civil War.

Governor Nikki Haley signed into law the bill authorizing the flag's removal, using nine pens, one for a family member of each of the nine parishioners killed at the Mother Emanuel AME Church. Sustained applause erupted from a multiracial group of an estimated eight thousand to ten thousand persons gathered at the site when the flag was removed. As *the Washington Post* recorded, "Just before the ceremony, a few gray-haired white men at the front of the crowd waved Confederate flags. But many more, both black and white, waved the United States flag."[30] The Confederate flag was placed in storage at the Confederate Relic Room and Military Museum about a mile away.

Although the Confederate flag was first raised at the statehouse in 1962 to protest integration, it is not the same flag that represented the Confederacy in the Civil War, nor is it one of three flags that the Confederacy would eventually adopt. "The 'Stars and Bars' flag, currently the subject of controversy, was actually the battle flag of General Robert E. Lee's Army of Northern Virginia."[31] Many whites, especially those who descend from Civil War Confederate soldiers, identify the flag as a symbol of patriotism and southern pride. Meanwhile, the bench memorial represents the slave past, but it also responds to the shifting winds of economic and political change for a racially diverse academic group and a slave-descendant community empowered to install it. Like Dylann Roof, who murdered the Charleston "Mother Emanuel Nine," and who brandished the Confederate flag in a photograph on a social media site, some whites still see the flag as a symbol of white supremacy.

At the site where the flag flew before its removal, a Confederate soldier monument remains, alongside an African American monument. But rather than a symbol of diversity, the African American monument was added at the statehouse in Columbia, South Carolina, as a compromise to assuage blacks' opposition to the Confederate flag's original presence there, and because the NAACP boycotted tourism in the state. In its placement next to the statehouse, authorities legally sanctioned the flag as a monument and sacred symbol representing South Carolina. But the state's significant black population argued that the flag never belonged at the statehouse, because all tax-paying citizens owned that building.

Upon signing into law the bill that authorized the flag's removal, and in interviews with reporters, including an appearance on NBC's *Today* show, Governor Haley addressed the complexities and contradictions that the flag represented as symbolic memory. "In South Carolina, we honor tradition, we honor history, we honor heritage, but . . . that flag needs to be in a museum, where we will continue to make sure people will honor it appropriately," she said.[32] Governor Haley declared that the statehouse belonged to all South Carolinians. "No one should drive by the statehouse and feel pain" or "feel like they don't belong," she added. The governor's comments also acknowledged the volatility of race and slavery in the state's historical past. By connecting the flag's existence to heritage, history, and tradition while simultaneously linking its removal to the importance of healing and forgiveness in a Bible Belt arena, she offered something for all South Carolinians, which helped to ensure the success of her mission.

◆ ◆ ◆

At a bond hearing in June 2015, several relatives of the nine parishioners who were killed at Mother Emanuel Church had reinforced healing by speaking words of forgiveness to the accused murderer. "We have no room for hating, so we have to forgive," said the sister of the deceased DePayne Middleton Doctor.[33] The daughter of deceased victim Ethel Lance chose to forgive the killer for religious purposes. When addressing the removal of the Confederate flag from the statehouse, Governor Haley said, "This is a story about the history of South Carolina and how the action of nine individuals laid out this long chain of events that forever showed the state of South Carolina what love and forgiveness looks like."[34]

Through a series of "flash" moments and seminal events that culminated with the removal of the Confederate flag from the South Carolina statehouse, the governor, bipartisan lawmakers, African American activists, deceased parishioners, and their families shifted the meaning of at least one "monument" that had secured the state's legacy of plantation slavery. Rather than represent the historical chronology of the state in the context of regional pride and Civil War memories, such symbols could perhaps convey the negative impact that they have had on race relations for some two centuries. The flag's removal thus demonstrates that monuments are susceptible to shifts in perception that occur with the winds of social and political change. That past-to-present geopolitical framework exposes the unsettledness of race and slavery in modern times, but on this occasion, the outcome seemed to favor a measure of healing and recovery. To reiterate the premise of my study, I ponder the extent to which the slave sites in this study that have proliferated in the global community in recent years portend significant progress and substantial change for blacks or whether slave sites that symbolize the past can also express themselves opportunistically as unforgiving mirrors of the present.

CODA

On November 8, 2016, Donald J. Trump was elected forty-fifth president of the United States of America and assumed a radical right-wing political course. On June 19, 2018, in a building constructed by slave labor, members of the Charleston, South Carolina, City Council voted 7 to 5 to apologize, formally, for its participation in the slave trade.[35] As an indelible structure of memory in this climate, the Bench by the Road Memorial, like other slave sites in this study, shares in the labor of the historical past but marks the fluidity of slavery's legacy in the present.

EPILOGUE

Opening the Smithsonian National Museum of African American History and Culture

For all of its complex planning and implementation—even allowing for its deflection from initially establishing a planned "slavery only" museum—the Smithsonian's National Museum of African American History and Culture's (NMAAHC) celebratory opening as a quintessential part of the legacy of slavery reflects a "watershed" moment. The NMAAHC, under the curatorship of Lonnie G. Bunch III, opened to a rousing reception and dedication ceremony on September 24, 2016, in the nation's capital. At the ceremony, then-president Barack Obama (who had spoken at Ghana's Cape Coast Castle and Senegal's House of Slaves) hinted at the relationship between the historical past and the present-day unsettledness of race and perhaps slavery, observations that have guided this study through select "flash" moments and seminal events at slave forts, slave burials at the African Burial Ground Monument and presidential estates, reconstructed slave ships, and the Bench by the Road Memorial. At the NMAAHC ceremony Obama said, "This museum provides context for the debates of our times, it illuminates them, and gives us some sense of how they evolved, and perhaps keeps them in proportion."[1]

Fittingly, in appearances at slave sites that bookend this study, the president spoke words, prophetically, that reorder the temporality of the history of slavery and that seem to defy the NMAAHC's gradational display. The site moves from slavery's basement-level exhibition to Reconstruction, Jim Crow, civil rights, and the election of President Obama. But does the museum therefore account for Benjamin's angel of despair through the cyclical pattern of a third Reconstruction at its uppermost level? The president's remarks somewhat contradict certain critical assessments, such as comments published in the *New Yorker* magazine that attribute the museum's reduction of history "to a scattering of bright but unconstellated stars."[2] But Vinson Cunningham, in "Making a Home for Black History," asserts that slavery might have been better served had it been presented "without the escape hatch of freer air above."[3] Roughly 50 percent of the five-story museum, which contains some forty thousand objects and artifacts, is subterranean, including the "Slavery and

Freedom" exhibition as part of a history gallery that occupies the museum's lower levels. The "Segregation Era" and "1968 to Today" occupy the museum's uppermost levels. Noting the irony of locating both President Obama's election and the rise of the Black Lives Matter movement in the concluding exhibitions, Cunningham finds that the museum lacks an explanation for what sustains racial progress and offers no strategy by which to enlarge upon it.

The museum's outer brownish-black coloring deliberately counters the white marble tones of other museums that surround it on the coveted Washington Mall. "I wanted a darker building," Bunch explained.[4] "What I wanted to say was, there's always been a dark presence in America that people undervalue, neglect, overlook," he added, and echoed Toni Morrison's observations in *Playing in the Dark: Whiteness and the Literary Imagination*. After winning the competition in 2009, Tanzanian-born, British-Ghanaian architect David Adjaye designed the museum's glass-cubed building. Its exterior corona consists of 3,600 painted, cast-aluminum panels.

Well before the museum was built, Civil War historian Eric Foner pointed out that the nation's capital had no such edifice devoted to American slavery. "We have a museum of the Holocaust in Washington, which is a great museum, but you know, what would we think if the Germans built a big museum of slavery in Berlin and had nothing about the Holocaust?'" he asked.[5]

It took one hundred years for an African American museum dedicated to emancipated people to become a reality. That journey began in 1915 when Black Union Army veterans formed a committee to build the museum. A commission to plan it began in 1929 under President Herbert Hoover but eventually dissolved under Franklin D. Roosevelt. In 2005 the NMAAHC was placed under the direction of Dr. Lonnie G. Bunch III and broadened its focus from a proposed all-slavery museum to one that included slavery, history, and culture.

Plans to develop a second museum were also announced. The United States National Slavery Museum, under the direction of former Virginia governor Douglas Wilder, would be placed about thirty miles away in Fredericksburg, Virginia. But plans to build a slavery museum at Fredericksburg ceased after financial and other complications led organizer Doug Wilder to file in September 2011 for bankruptcy. The difficulty of maintaining two costly, high-profile African American museums located just thirty miles apart, as well as opposition from some in the Fredericksburg community to having a museum about slavery in their backyard, may well have proven insurmountable for its survival. I do not propose to write here an exposé of numerous complications that led to failure of the museum at Fredericksburg, as the case remains unresolved.[6] I do contend, however, that the progression of one museum to a spectacular, blockbuster opening and the halting of the other under still ambiguous circumstances form a cautionary tale in clues articulated in this study.

In the late 1980s, shortly after arriving to Washington, Democratic congressman and civil rights activist John Lewis of Georgia lobbied for an African American museum to be built. The late North Carolina senator Jesse Helms famously rejected the idea on the Senate floor in 1994 on the grounds that a "Yes" to African Americans would force Congress to contend with other ethnic groups seeking similar recognition. Not until 2003 did Congress authorize the creation of the Smithsonian's National Museum of African American History and Culture, which would be funded 50 percent federal support and 50 percent private donations. The museum cost totals $540 million, with private donations accounting for $270 million. It was to occupy a place on the Washington Mall between the Washington Monument and the National Museum of American History in the nation's capital.

For more than a decade, dates for the completion and opening of both the Smithsonian NMAAHC and the National Slavery Museum changed repeatedly as funds dissipated, support waxed and waned, and opinions fluctuated wildly about the efficacy of such a museum. For example, nearly half of blacks polled in a Smithsonian survey of five thousand Americans in the 1990s opposed the museum's development of a slavery exhibit, partly because of embarrassment and a lack of interest. Over 80 percent of whites in the survey believed slavery to be important to blacks but not to whites.[7] In spite of the Smithsonian's survey in the 1990s, phenomenal interest in slave remembrance through contemporary fiction, slave sites, art, and other forms of cultural expression has not abated as the nation continues to struggle with race and slavery in its multifarious contexts.

As shown by the community involvement that helped to establish Liverpool's International Slavery Museum in the United Kingdom and the New York African Burial Ground in Lower Manhattan, the clarion call to remember the slave past must be met by individuals and groups motivated and empowered to effect change through site construction. Organizers must be prepared to enter delicate negotiations likely with local, federal government, and/or corporate sponsors; secure donations from public and private sources; and prepare a clear plan of action. Suffice it to say that while the planning, development, and implementation of the museum comprise an empowered group, its identity is governed by temporality, spatiality, and ideology.

The Washington Mall as site of the National Museum of African American History and Culture reinforces its status in the ideology of race and slavery. For example, the museum occupies a site where slavery pens once stood, and it shares space near a Capitol Building built by slave labor and a commemorative MLK statue that binds it with both a shameful past and a hopeful future. But the NMAAHC's proximity to the United States Memorial Holocaust Museum near the Mall and the National Museum of the American Indian (NMAI) "within 'the monumental core' of the nation" connects it thematically with "crimes against humanity" that expose multiple forms of US involvement and/or responsibility. These competitive yet complementary placements on the Mall not only represent the weight of those crimes but also form a hierarchical construct for those that jockey for position as the group deemed most victimized. Broader, related questions pertain to the selection criteria that get these museums—or any museum—past naysayers and censors and into that desirable space.

Since the early 1900s the Washington Mall has evolved as a quintessential monumental, even sacred, space and now stands as "a repository of national identity."[8] During the planning phase of the Holocaust museum, criticism ranged from skepticism about placing it in a country where the Holocaust did not take place, as I have discussed, to balking at placing it at the presidential seat of power, when the US government failed to rescue Holocaust victims. Others insisted that African Americans and Native Americans have primacy in placing a museum on the mall because of slavery and Native American genocide. A regard for the museums at the site as expressions of democratic principles, national belonging, and cultural enrichment has prevailed.

Some of the barriers that Lonnie Bunch and officials at the NMAAHC faced also confronted organizers of the Smithsonian National Museum of the American Indian upon its creation in 1989. In addition to debate with Congress, the NMAI contended with the Smithsonian's Office of the Secretary and its National Museum of Natural History, as well as the Museum of the American Indian in New York City over different visions for the NMAI's development, structure, and implementation. For example, each offered different perspectives about the museum's narrative content. As Patricia Pierce Erikson writes, "At stake were whether or not univocal subjectivity and the Western metanarrative (encompassing and authoritatively explaining otherness while simultaneously maintaining a rational distance from it) would guide the NMAI."[9] The multiple critiques that now guide the NMAI derive from the diverse tribal groups that collect and display artifacts and dispense narratives about Native American life, history, and culture. Therefore, Native Americans themselves employ agency and take the lead in educating the museumgoer/spectator about language, literature, art, anthropology, and heritage.

For the National Museum of African American History and Culture, especially its slave recovery displays, success means managing the risks of encapsulating all the pain and trauma of "monumentality" in its making. I have discussed in this study how some public memory practices at slave sites mitigate the trauma associated with remembrance by privileging a remembered past but may encounter discrepancies through countering certain traditional historical archival records. Exuberance caught up in the fervor of an Atlantic slavery's demise occasionally mutes conversations about continued discriminatory practices stemming from that very past. Sites that reinscribe slavery through visual displays both opportunistically and obliquely expose the sheer weight of interlocking forces and events that drive a disturbing, repetitive form of slavery. Ultimately, through reconstructed materials and visual displays, slave sites—even when calibrated through a risk-benefit assessment—offer new ways to rethink slavery's legacy in a purportedly "postslavery" era.

Though the National Museum of African American History and Culture emphasizes slavery, history, and culture broadly speaking, Lonnie Bunch typically centers discussion almost exclusively on the slave past when addressing the museum. In lectures that he delivered at Austin's Bob Bullock Museum and later at Yale University, Bunch addressed the mission as well as challenges for the proposed National Museum of African American History and Culture through strategies that I find contemporaneous with many existing slave sites that take into account ideology as well as other factors like economics and location. Specifically, Bunch resuscitated the community activism and work associated with establishing the African Burial Ground by citing the centrality of New York City as under-recognized for slavery, which has been obfuscated by an overly narrow focus on antebellum slavery in the South. He applauded the New-York Historical Society and the African Burial Ground for centering slavery as a national institution, and for according agency to the enslaved subject. He also acknowledged consulting closely with organizers and officials at Liverpool's International Slavery Museum, the site most structurally and thematically comparable with the NMAAHC.

To understand slavery, one must begin with the enslaved, Bunch said, and cited the Somerset Plantation in North Carolina as another example. He stressed the particular importance of accessibility in accordance with spectators' demands that also meet with scholarly specifications: "The public needs to find heroes in unambiguous stories [and] resilience against no end in sight," he added. When Bunch lamented the insularity or dearth of coverage in the typical American museum, he called to mind global connections between reconstructed slave ship exhibitions and the diaspora transnational slave descendant. "Slavery allows America to break down its parochialism, [and] this 'inward looking' prevents us from looking globally at slavery," he stated. And when Bunch said that "to talk about slavery yesterday is to talk about today, and to talk about the past is to talk about the present," he affirms the ability of objects and artifacts to bespeak a slave corporeality in the twenty-first century. In a comment that looks askance at modern-day slave trafficking and the industrial prison complex, or that cautions against the propensity to transform slavery into less recognizable forms, he concludes, "Find ways to use slavery as an unforgiving mirror of today."[10] In other words, the perverse (and pervasive) manner in which slavery has formed and continues to shape and inform all aspects of American life urges that we remember that slave past but that we also remain vigilant about its continuing impact, resurrection in new forms, and relevance to the lives of museumgoers/spectators.

As a fitting explanation for those in the diaspora slave-descendant community who obsessively seek to recover information about the slavery past, Pierre Nora, in "Between Memory and History: *Les Lieux de Mémoire*," offers the following observation: "The defense by certain minorities of a privileged memory that has retreated to jealously protected enclaves ... intensely illuminates the truth of lieux de memoire—that without commemorative vigilance, history would soon sweep them away."[11] But this observation does not adequately explain either the protected enclaves or the vigilance within African American communities in particular, because history has already rampantly disregarded the slave's humanity. Some other explanation, deeply seared into the consciousness of diaspora slave-descendant-spectators, must account for the woundedness that slavery still imposes.

Through slave recovery practices—whether gleaned from the African Burial Ground story in New York, reconstructed slave ship exhibitions, seminal artifacts, or slave forts in West African nations—diaspora African slave-descendants have inherited a flawed historical record along with the attendant burden and the responsibility to search out and restore slavery's missing pieces. But as I have demonstrated in this study, slave sites are not formed monolithically, or implemented homogeneously with the same objectives and strategies that govern all locations for all times. These exhibitions form the building blocks of slavery, diachronically, through a patchwork metaphor, a stitching together of something fragmented or torn, painstakingly item by item and artifact by artifact. Lonnie Bunch has searched out and received a large number of artifacts from private donors and individuals' personal collections to exhibit those missing pieces of slavery in ways that history has not accounted for. Nat Turner's blood-splotched Bible, displayed with a machete—both carried in the insurrection in which he killed white men, women, and children—tells a different story than the conflicted Styron account of an enslaved black man obsessed with his white mistress. An 1876 hymnal sung by Harriet Tubman, though unable to read or write, while she conducted the Underground Railroad rounds out the image of a pistol-toting Tubman who exclaims to her passengers, "Be free or die here," at Detroit's Charles Wright exhibit.

In the development and construction of the NMAAHC significantly around artifacts of slavery, but that more broadly "embodies the story of black life in America," Lonnie Bunch exemplifies the type of leadership that can engineer such a massive and ambitious project.[12] The National Museum of African American History and Culture (NMAAHC) is poised to rival Liverpool's International Slavery Museum as the next gargantuan facility of its kind. In what hopefully symbolizes a forward trend, the Whitney Plantation Museum in Louisiana is the only major museum edifice domestic or abroad, to date, that is devoted exclusively or wholly to the institution of slavery. In the US that restraint on the NMAAHC likely eased bipartisan support from conservatives Rick Santorum (R-Pennsylvania), Sam Brownback (R-Kansas), and others, and enabled then-president George W. Bush to describe the multifaceted museum as a place of healing that would promote racial harmony. Sites that depict the traumatic slave past (or purportedly exploit or sell suffering) are tempered by triumphs shown in education, sports, the arts, and civil rights. A popular culture division includes music, visual arts, and sports, and an additional segment thematizes community.

Bunch's objectives for the NMAAHC, spoken several years before its advent, are at once deceptively simplistic and expressly nuanced in disclosing the fundamentals that would make for an appealing museum of this magnitude. For example, collaboration, which he stresses, does not allude to requisite camaraderie among principal site organizers. But the museum itself is a place that shows healing and reconciliation as the end results of a collaborative process. In a revealing comment that proves the importance of avoiding certain pitfalls of a project about an especially sensitive subject, Bunch says succinctly, "Do not underestimate the power of inspiration." In other words, he avers that the NMAAHC generates positive feelings, and it unites all facets of the nation through common ground.[13] Bunch might have added: Do not underestimate the rewards of an activist group, bipartisan congressional support, and the tenacity of a consummate, seasoned director/curator.

The literary patrons in the eighteenth and nineteenth centuries that boldly examined the stories, writings, and visages of formerly enslaved Africans for personhood, moral worth, and/or intelligence has been replaced in the twenty-first century by a likely diaspora slave descendant that journeys to black heritage sites in search of those souls lost in the wreckage of history. I have discussed in this study how slave recovery practices at select museums and black heritage sites resurrect and reembody the historically fragmented slave history in revisionist reproductions, reclamation of culture that commemorates those slaves lost, and stories that rewrite the captive African's status as nation builder and active participant rather than as passive victim in liberationist practices. Site organizers have largely purged the romanticism, nostalgia, and Lost Cause ideology that defined a shameful historical past exhibited at Old South plantations. But in peering at the slave subject's composite image at the modern-day slave site, the museumgoer/spectator receives, in return, a gaze that is both alluring and disconcerting. The place of honor that the exhibition bestows upon the slave for perseverance, endurance, and laborious contributions to nation frustrates and confuses, because it eerily reflects the unfinished business of slavery, shown through shifting laws, policies, and practices that still resonate for many in the global community. Consequently, the slavery museum and black heritage site must continually amend the paradox of slavery's continued legacy through strategies that (re) appropriate the traumatic slave past to accommodate its transformations in the present day.

NOTES

Introduction

1. Andreas Huyssen, "Introduction," *Twilight Memories: Marking Time in a Culture of Amnesia* (New York: Routledge, 1995), 3.

2. Zora Neale Hurston, *Dust Tracks on a Road* (New York: Harper Collins, 1991), 1, originally published J. B. Lippincott (1942). See also Toni Morrison, "The Site of Memory," in *Out There: Marginalization and Contemporary Cultures*, ed. Russell Ferguson et al. (New York: New Museum of Contemporary Art, 1990), 302.

3. Jena Osman, *The Network* (Albany: Fence Books, 2011), 38.

4. "A New Life in a New World?" "The Abolition of the Slave Trade," Library of Long Print and Photographs, division of the British Cartoon Collection.

5. Rodrequez King-Dorset, *Dance Is Us, and Dance Is Black*, Birmingham Museum, UK. In the context of slavery, dance proves commensurate with what Paul Gilroy and others have identified as alternative responses to prohibitions against literacy for enslaved blacks. King-Dorset's video is inspired by Isaac Cruikshank's sketch "Girl Flogged to Death" (1796). See also Captain John Stedman, *A History of Surinam* (1796). See Celeste-Marie Bernier and Judie Newman, "Public Art, Artefacts and Atlantic Slavery: Introduction," *Slavery and Abolition* 29.2 (June 2008): 146.

6. For a poignant discussion about the potential exploitation of the young girl even as a teachable moment for posterity, see Saidiya Hartman, *Lose Your Mother: A Journey along the Atlantic Slave Route*. See also Saidiya Hartman, "Venus in Two Acts," *Small Axe* 12.2 (June 2008): 1–14. (King-Dorset's Birmingham Museum exhibition postdates Hartman's writings about the enslaved girl's beating death.) See Fred Moten, *In the Break: The Aesthetics of the Black Radical Tradition* (Minneapolis: U of Minnesota P, 2003), 3.

7. I owe the concept of slavery's "unforgiving mirror" to Dr. Lonnie Bunch, director of the Smithsonian National Museum of African American History and Culture (NMAAHC). I see slavery's resurgence through alternative forms as an unpardonable reflection of the present because it suggests that contemporary generations have not heeded lessons from the slave past. In a lecture, "Race, Memory, and the Museum," at the Bob Bullock Museum in Austin, Texas (22 February 2006), Bunch said the following: "African American history and culture is a wonderful but unforgiving mirror," and he added that we should "find ways to use slavery as an unforgiving mirror of today."

8. Walter Benjamin, "Theses on the Philosophy of History," in *Illuminations*, ed. Hannah Arendt, trans. Harry Zohn (New York; SchockenBooks, 1968): 253–65.

9. I reappropriate the famous Klee drawing of the "Angelus Novus" in Walter Benjamin's *Ninth Thesis on the Philosophy of History* from its connection with the Holocaust to its relevance for slavery.

10. David Crouch, "Landscape Performance, and Performativity," in *The Routledge Companion to Landscape Studies*, ed. Peter Howard, Ian Thompson, and Emma Waterton (London: Routledge, 2013), 121. In this theoretical approach, Crouch deemphasizes affect and the power of representations and instead focuses on "moments of occurrence" in order to understand how things accrue value.

11. Osman, *Network*, 5, 63.

12. Jena Osman writes, "The 1912 Congressional hearings held to investigate the monopoly powers of the American Sugar Refining Company questioned the legislative joker that—in the name of 'purity'—caused imported sugars white in color (above No. 16 Dutch standard color) to pay a prohibitively high tariff" (*Network*, 25). See also the *Journal of Social History* (US Congress, 1911–1912).

13. See Orlando Patterson, "Toward a Future That Has No Past: Reflections on the Fate of Blacks in the Americas," *Public Interest* 27 (1972): 60–61. See also Charles Johnson's controversial comment in "The End of the Black American Narrative." Johnson writes that "the black American narrative of victimhood" has become "ahistorical" and no longer fits the reality of progress. See Salamishah Tillet's discussion of Johnson's remarks, as well as Ken Warren's comments, in *Sites of Slavery: Citizenship and Racial Democracy in the Post–Civil Rights Imagination* (Durham: Duke UP, 2012), 1–18. Ken Warren further complicates this debate in his book *What Was African American Literature?* (Cambridge: Harvard UP, 2011).

14. See Stephen Best, "On Failing to Make the Past Present," in *Modern Language Quarterly* 73.3 (September 2012): 454–74.

15. Sam Tanenhaus, Book Review editor for the *New York Times*, sent out a letter in 2006 that requested this information. See Book Review, *New York Times* 21 May 2006, print ed., Web, 5 September 2016. Not coincidentally, the production of slave sites and exhibitions closely parallel the proliferation of contemporary fiction about the slave past after the publication of Toni Morrison's *Beloved* in 1987. Bernard Bell, in *The Afro-American Novel and Its Tradition*, coined the term "neo–slave narratives" for novels in this category.

16. Toni Morrison, in *World: Journal of the Unitarian Universalists Association* 3.1 (January/February 1989): 4–5, 37–41. See also *World Magazine*, 1989, reprint.

17. Morrison, interview, *World Magazine*, 8–9.

18. Toni Morrison, "The Site of Memory," in *Out There: Marginalization and Contemporary Cultures*, ed. Russell Ferguson et al. (New York: New Museum of Contemporary Art, 1990), 302.

19. Morrison, "Site of Memory," 302.

20. See Vincent Carretta, "Olaudah Equiano or Gustavus Vassa? New Light on an Eighteenth-Century Question of Identity," *Slavery and Abolition* 20.3 (1999): 96–105. See also the "Preface" and "Equiano's Africa," in Carretta, *Equiano, the African: Biography of a Self-Made Man* (Athens: U of Georgia P, 2005). I discuss this debate further in chapter 1.

21. See Arjun Appadurai, ed., "Introduction: Commodities and the Politics of Value," *The Social Life of Things: Commodities in Cultural Perspective* (Cambridge: Cambridge UP, 1986), 44.

22. Pierre Nora, "Between Memory and History: Les Lieux de Mémoire," trans. Mark Poudebus, *Representations* 26 (Spring 1989): 15.

23. Nora, "Between Memory and History." Nora writes, "The total psychologization of contemporary memory entails a completely new economy of the identity of the self, the mechanics of memory, and the relevance of the past" (15).

24. Andreas Huyssen, "Escape from Amnesia," *Twilight Memories: Marking Time in a Culture of Amnesia* (New York: Routledge, 1995).

25. See David Amsden, "Building the First Slavery Museum in America," *New York Times Magazine*, February 2015, *New York Times*, Web, 6 July 2018.

26. See Kathleen Wilson, "Citizenship, Empire, and Modernity in the English Provinces, c. 1720–1790," *Eighteenth-Century Studies* 29.1 (1995): 69–96. See also Kathleen Wilson, *The Island Race: Englishness, Empire, and Gender in the Eighteenth Century* (London: Routledge, 2003), and *A New Imperial History: Culture, Identity and Modernity in Britain and the Empire, 1660–1840* (Cambridge: Cambridge UP, 2004).

Chapter 1. Iconic Sons of Africa "in the Belly of the Stone Monster"

1. Mohammed ben Abdallah, *The Slaves Revisited*, 2005, np. The first non-American play to win the National Association for Speech and Dramatic Arts' Randolph Edmunds Award in 1972, the date of the earlier version of the play, titled *The Slaves*, is set at Elmina Castle in Ghana. No specific slave fort is identified for Abdallah's 2005 revision of the play. See Mohammed ben Abdallah, *The Slaves* [electronic resource] (Alexandria: Alexander Street Press, 2001). See also Mohammed ben Abdallah, *The Slaves*, in *The Fall of Kumbi and Other Plays* (Accra: Woeli, 1989.)

2. See the press release "President Bush Speaks at Gorée Island in Senegal," US Department of State, released by the White House Office of the Press Secretary (8 July 2003).

3. "President Bush Speaks at Gorée Island in Senegal."

4. See Vincent Carretta, "Olaudah Equiano or Gustavus Vassa? New Light on an Eighteenth-Century Question of Identity," *Slavery and Abolition* 20.3 (1999): 96–105. See also "Preface" and "Equiano's Africa," in Vincent Carretta, *Equiano, the African: Biography of a Self-Made Man* (Athens: U of Georgia P, 2005).

After meticulous research, Carretta identifies "the Ogden as the most probable vessel bearing Equiano from the Bight of Biafra to Barbados"—if Equiano indeed came from Africa, which Carretta suggests is not the case. Carretta edited the ninth and final edition of the narrative that was approved and published by Equiano in his lifetime. See Vincent Carretta, *Olaudah Equiano: The Interesting Narrative and Other Writings* (New York: Penguin 1985). I contend that the two-volume first edition of Equiano's narrative, edited by Paul Edwards, remains the correct, official edition.

5. Peter Baker, "Obama Delivers Call for Change to a Rapt Africa," *New York Times Online* 11 July 2009, New York ed.: A1.

6. Various individuals and groups have engaged discussion, debate, and even some perfunctory legal action, intermittently, for slavery reparations in the US and Britain since around the 1980s. Ta-Nehisi Coates discusses continued activity in the reparations

movement. He reports that for twenty-five years Congressman John Conyers Jr. (D–Mich.) has introduced Bill HR 40, known as "the Commission to Study Reparation Proposals for African Americans Act." The proposed bill, which would study "slavery and its lingering effects as well as recommendations for 'appropriate remedies,'" has died each year without ever reaching the House floor. See Ta-Nehisi Coates, "The Case for Reparations," in *Atlantic*, June 2014, 62.

7. Hans Nichols and Roger Runningen, "Obama Visits West African Slave Fort, Says Is 'Source of Hope,'" *Bloomberg L.P.* 11 July 2009. See also Anderson Cooper, "Interview," *AC360*, CNN (first) broadcast 13 July 2009; "President Obama's African Journey," *Anderson Cooper 360* (aired 18 July 2009), *CNN Transcripts*: 1–19, Web, 30 August 2009.

8. Cooper, "Interview."

9. Sandra Richards, "Notes from the Road: Cultural Tourism to Slave Sites," *BTNews* 9.2&3 (Winter/Spring 1999).

10. While James Horton and other historians identify Punch, along with the first twenty Africans to arrive in Jamestown, Virginia, in 1619, as indentured servants, Linda Heywood, John Thornton, and others dispute Punch's and other blacks' identification as indentured servants in colonial America. The film *Africans in America* also depicts African Angolan Anthony "Antonio" Johnson as an indentured servant who eventually obtained freedom and acquired substantial land before purchasing black and white servants of his own.

Interestingly, top-rated geneticists hired by aides to the Obama campaign in 2008 were unable to trace Mrs. Obama's paternal ancestry beyond her great-great-grandfather, Jim Robinson. Nor was Swarns's team later able to trace Mrs. Obama's maternal ancestry beyond her great-great-great-grandmother Melvinia, which I examine in chapter 3 on the subject of slavery, miscegenation, and American presidency.

11. Sheryl Gay Stolberg, "Obama Has Ties to Slavery Not by His Father but His Mother, Research Suggests," *New York Times* 30 July 2012, A9, Web, 30 July 2012. (See also *Ancestry. com* press releases, July 2012.) Through Y-DNA tests, the research team found sub-Saharan African traits, likely from around Cameroon. Independent researcher Elizabeth Shown Mills, an expert in southern research and past president of the Board for Certification of Genealogists, reviewed the findings of Ancestry.com as a third party and concluded the following: "A careful consideration of the evidence convinces me that the Y-DNA evidence of African origin is indisputable, and the surviving paper trail points solely to John Punch as the logical candidate." She adds that though one man's fatherhood of another cannot be proven with certainty, the research conducted at Ancestry.com "meets the highest standards and can be offered with confidence."

12. See Gary Younge, "Is Obama Black Enough?" *Guardian*, US ed., 1 May 2007, *Guardian News and Media Limited*, Web, 1 July 2018. See also David A. Graham, "A Short History of Whether Obama Is Black Enough, Featuring Rupert Murdoch," *Atlantic Monthly*, October 8, 2015, Web, 1 July 2018.

13. Cooper, "Interview"; Cooper, "President Obama's African Journey."

14. Adi Gordon and Amos Goldberg, "An Interview with Professor James E. Young," English and Judaic Studies at the University of Massachusetts at Amherst, Yad Vashem, Jerusalem (24 May 1998), Shoah Resource Center, International School for Holocaust Studies.

www.yadvashem.org. Young states that the Disappearing Monument "reflects this essential ambivalence toward the memory of your own crimes" (13).

15. A. W. Lawrence, *Trade Castles and Forts of West Africa* (Stanford: Stanford UP, 1964), 29.

16. Cooper, "Interview."

17. Bayo Holsey, *Routes of Remembrance: Refashioning the Slave Trade in Ghana* (Chicago: U of Chicago P, 2008). See also Achille Mbembe, "African Modes of Self-Writing," *Public Culture* 14.1 (Fall 2002): 259. Kwadwo Opoku-Agyemang, "A Crisis of Balance: The (Mis)-Representation of Colonial History and the Slave Experience as Themes in Modern African Literature," *Nationalism vs. Internationalism: (Inter)National Dimensions of Literatures in English*, ed. Wolfgang Zach and Ken L. Goodwin (Tubingen: Stauffenburg Verlag, 1996), 219.

18. Mbembe, "African Modes of Self-Writing," 259; Opoku-Agyemang, "Crisis of Balance," 219. In competing ideologies filtered through different lenses, Haile Gerima's 1993 film *Sankofa*, Rachid Bouchareb's 2001 film *Little Senegal*, and Mohammed ben Abdallah's award-winning 2005 play *The Slaves Revisited* stage the nuanced stories that slave-recovery projects dispense.

19. Martin Kilson, *Key Issues in the Afro-American Experience* (New York: Harcourt, 1971).

20. Lisa Woolfork, *Embodying American Slavery in Contemporary Culture* (Urbana: U of Illinois P, 2009), 99.

21. Kwesi Brew, *African Panorama and Other Poems* (New York: Greenfield Review Press, 1981). While at the House of Slaves, I met a mother and son who absurdly claimed to have constructed a makeshift raft in an attempt to simulate the journey made by slaves across the Atlantic to somewhere on the East Coast of the United States. The raft broke up after only a few miles, but the young man vowed to repeat the effort until he succeeded.

22. See A. W. Lawrence, *Trade Castles and Forts of West Africa* (Stanford: Stanford UP, 1964), 29. See also Kwadwo Opoku-Agyemang, *The Transatlantic Slave Trade: Landmarks, Legacies, Expectations: Proceedings of the International Conference on Historic Slave Route Held at Accra, Ghana* (30 August–2 September 2004), ed. Jamed Kwesi Anquandah (Accra: Sub-Saharan, 2007), 24. A. W. Lawrence singles out the uniqueness and the incomparable consequences that have resulted from the ubiquitous slave forts like Ghana's Cape Coast Castle over time: "Nowhere else have small and transitory communities of traders so changed the life of the alien peoples who surrounded them and indirectly of a vast region beyond." The slave fort is so omnipresent in Ghanaian history and geography that its image is emblazoned on the coat of arms of the Republic of Ghana. More than sixty forts were built over a three-hundred-year period along a coastline of three hundred miles.

23. Carol J. Mooney, "Debating the History of Slavery on Senegal's Gorée Island," *Chronicle of Higher Education* 23 May 1997.

24. See Savannah Unit, "Georgia Writers' Project, Work Projects Administration," *Drums and Shadows: Survival Studies among the Georgia Coastal Negroes* (1940; reprint, Athens: U of Georgia P, 1986). See also Michael A. Gomez, *Exchanging Our Country Marks: The Transformation of African Identities in the Colonial and Antebellum South* (Chapel Hill: U of North Carolina P, 1998).

25. Pierre Nora, "Between Memory and History: Les Lieux de Memoire," trans. Mark Poudebus, *Representations* 26 (Spring 1989): 8.

26. Debra Boyd, producer, *Griot of Gorée: Joseph N'diaye*, a film documentary, from *Genius of the Sahel*, 2005, trans. from French to English by Debra Boyd.

27. Boyd, *Griot of Gorée*.

28. Boyd, *Griot of Gorée*.

29. Boyd, *Griot of Gorée*.

30. Boyd, *Griot of Gorée*.

31. For an excellent study of slavery in Senegal, see James F. Searing, *West African Slavery and Atlantic Commerce: The Senegal River Valley, 1700–1860* (New York: Cambridge UP, 1993).

32. Andy Walton, CNN Interactive Writer, "Tiny Island Weathers Storm of Controversy" 26 March 1998.

33. See Mooney, "Debating the History of Slavery." See also Stephan Palmie, "Slavery, Historicism, and the Poverty of Memorialization," *Memory: Histories, Theories, Debates*, ed. Susannah Radstone and Bill Schwarz (New York: Fordham UP, 2010), 363–75.

34. Mooney, "Debating the History of Slavery."

35. Henry Louis Gates Jr., "Ending the Slavery Blame-Game," *New York Times* 23 April 2010, Web, 12 January 2012.

36. In competing ideologies about the slave past filtered through different lenses, for example, Haile Gerima's 1993 film *Sankofa*, Rachid Bouchareb's 2001 film *Little Senegal*, and Mohammed ben Abdallah's award-winning 2005 play *The Slaves Revisited* stage the nuanced stories that slave-recovery projects dispense. Suffice it to say that in a symbolic application of the slave fort, these works highlight discordance among Africans or between diaspora slave-descendant Africans and the indigenous African population in the context of slavery, and each asserts that the slave past resurfaces in the present, albeit in different form.

37. Maurice Halbwachs, in *The Collective Memory*, trans. from the French by Francis J. Ditter Jr. and Vida Yzdi Ditter (New York: Harper & Row), 54. See also Maurice Halbwachs, "The Social Frameworks of Memory," in *On Collective Memory* (Chicago: U of Chicago P, 1992, originally published 1951), 37–189.

I am reminded of South African writer Ivan Vladislavic's short story "The Whites Only Bench," in *Propaganda by Monuments and Other Stories* (1996), which was inspired by an incident in which Mrs. Coretta Scott King asked to sit on an "Apartheid" bench and pose for photographs. The bench was highlighted in the press as one formerly used under Apartheid, but because that bench could not be found or no longer existed, a substitution was manufactured for the auspicious occasion. For Vladislavic, the irony proved too suggestive to pass up.

38. Paul E. Lovejoy expressed skepticism toward Carretta's claims that Equiano faked an African birth and Middle Passage journey in *Interesting Narrative*. See Paul E. Lovejoy, "Autobiography and Memory: Gustavus Vassa, alias Olaudah Equiano, the African," *Slavery and Abolition* 27.3 (December 2006): 317–47. See also Vincent Carretta, "Olaudah Equiano or Gustavus Vassa? New Light on an Eighteenth-Century Question of Identity," *Slavery and Abolition* 20.3 (1999): 96–105; and "Preface" and "Equiano's Africa," in Vincent Carretta, *Equiano, the African: Biography of a Self-Made Man* (Athens: U of Georgia P, 2005).

39. See Arjun Appadurai, *The Social Life of Things: Commodities in Cultural Perspective* (Cambridge: Cambridge UP, 1986), 6. This aspect of authenticity follows Bourdieu's idea of the politics of taste.

40. The museums and slave sites that I have visited have all but ignored or discounted Carretta's compelling but unproven allegations based on circumstantial evidence that Olaudah Equiano was born in South Carolina rather than Africa, as he claims in *The Interesting Narrative of Olaudah Equiano, or Gustavus Vassa, the African* (1789). Nowhere was this observation more clearly evident than at the Birmingham Museum in the United Kingdom, where a special exhibition of Olaudah Equiano was on display in 2007.

41. Chris Harty, director, with Debbie Allen and Steven Spielberg, *Ships of Slaves: The Middle Passage*, A&E, and the History Channel.

42. See Celeste-Marie Bernier and Judie Newman, "Public Art, Artefacts and Atlantic Slavery: Introduction," *Slavery and Abolition* 29.2 (June 2008): 145–47.

43. See Andy Green, "Birmingham, Equiano, and the Transatlantic Slave Trade," *Equiano: Enslavement, Resistance and Abolition*, ed. Arthur Torrington et al. (Birmingham: Birmingham Museums & Art Gallery, 29 September 2007–13 January 2008), 42–49.

44. In the interest of full disclosure, this author wrote a letter in support of the Olaudah Equiano exhibition at Birmingham, with great enthusiasm for its role in educating the general public, as well as students, about Equiano and the *Interesting Narrative*. I also viewed the exhibit at Birmingham and participated in panels organized as part of the 2007 commemoration of the ending of the slave trade in the UK.

45. Tony Bennett, *The Birth of the Museum: History, Theory, Politics* (London: Routledge, 1995).

46. Andreas Huyssen, "Escape from Amnesia," in *Twilight Memories: Marking Time in a Culture of Amnesia* (New York: Routledge, 1995), 14.

47. Huyssen, "Escape from Amnesia," 14.

48. Helena Woodard, "Why Olaudah Equiano Won't Go Away," unpublished paper, conference organized by Brycchan Carey, "Olaudah Equiano: Representation and Reality," 22 March 2003, Kingston University, United Kingdom.

Chapter 2. "Talking Bones" at the African Burial Ground in New York

1. Helena Zhu, "African Burial Ground: Bodies under Buildings," *Epoch Times*, podcast, created 14 September 2009. See John Noble Wilford, "At Burial Site, Teeth Tell Tale of Slavery," *New York Times* 31 January 2006, 1–2, Web, 12 June 2010.
See also Jason Whitely, "Slave Cemetery Revealed by Texas Drought," in WFAA.com. Dallas/Fort Worth WFAA-TV, 3 August 2011, Web, 30 August 2011.

2. Andreas Huyssen, "Escape from Amnesia," in *Twilight Memories: Marking Time in a Culture of Amnesia* (New York: Routledge, 1995), 15.

3. Mary Louise Pratt, *Imperial Eyes: Travel Writing and Transculturation* (New York: Routledge 1992), 64.

4. Suzan-Lori Parks, "Possession," in "*The America Play" and Other Works* (New York: Theatre Communications Group, 1995), 4.

5. Adam Clayton Powell IV, New York state senator, in *The African Burial Ground: An American Discovery* (video recording), executive producer J. Peter Glaws III, director David Kutz, Kutz Television (Springfield, VA: National Audiovisual Center distributor, 1994).

6. "GSA and NPS Civic Engagement," in *GSA Final Report* III, 19. In Visitor Experience Workshops, the GSA gathered select round table comments made by concerned citizens at town meetings held at Medgar Evers College, May 25, 2004, and in Harlem at the Schomburg Center for Research in Black Culture, May 26, 2004. The burial site, bounded by Broadway and Duane, Reade, and Elk Streets, served as a cemetery for slaves and free blacks before city officials closed it because it had been filled. See Sherrill D. Wilson, *African Burial Ground Project: Chronology*, 1–8, Office of Public Education & Interpretation of the African Burial Ground, US Customs House, New York.

7. "GSA and NPS Civic Engagement," in *GSA Final Report* III, 20–21.

8. Trinity Church Vestry Minutes, 25 October 1697, in Warren R. Perry, Jean Howson, and Barbara A. Bianco, eds., *New York African Burial Ground: Archaeology Final Report* (Washington, DC, 2006), I:42. See also Gwynedd Cannan, "Unearthing Our Past," *Trinity News*, February 13, 2004, *Trinity Church Wall Street*, Web, posted on February 13, 2004, https://www.trinitywallstreet.org/blogs/news/unearthing-our-past. Built by slave labor in 1696, Trinity existed at a time when slaves were being interred at the African Burial Ground.

9. See Terrence W. Epperson, "The Contested Commons: Archaeologies of Race, Repression, and Resistance in New York City," *Historical Archaeologies of Capitalism* (1999): 81–97 (Epperson citing Epperson, 1996; Epperson citing LaRoche and Blakey 1997: 11). HTML version of the file, http://www.tcnj.edu/library/Epperson/documents/ContestedCommons.pdf., Web, 12 July 2010.

10. See Jerome S. Handler, "An African-Type Burial, Newton Plantation Barbados," *African-American Archaeology, Newsletter of the African-American Archaeology Network* 15 (Fall 1995): 1–2.

See also Jerome S. Handler, "An African-Type Healer/Diviner and His Grave Goods: A Burial from a Plantation Slave Cemetery in Barbados, West Indies," *International Journal of Historical Archaeology* 1.2 (June 1997): 91–130. Burial #72 was unique not only to Newton but also to early African cemetery sites in the Americas. He had been buried with "a unique and elaborate necklace with obvious, but generalized, African characteristics."

See also Cheryl J. LaRoche, "Beads from the African Burial Ground, New York City: A Preliminary Assessment," *Beads* 6 (1994): 3–20.

11. While no definitive proof of the decedents' class status was determined, the archaeology team led by T. Douglas Price of the University of Wisconsin combined historical records with scientific data and concluded that "these individuals are likely to be among the earliest representatives of the African diaspora in the Americas, substantially earlier than the subsequent, intensive slave trade in the eighteenth century." For a detailed study of the remains in Campeche, Mexico, see T. Douglas Price et al., "Early African Diaspora in Colonial Campeche, Mexico: Strontium Isotopic Evidence," *American Journal of Physical Anthropology* 130.4 (2006): 489, 485–490.

12. Andrew Pearson, Ben Jeffs, Annsofie Witkin, and Helen MacQuarrie, "Infernal Traffic: Excavation of a Liberated African Graveyard in Rupert's Valley, St. Helena," *CBA Research Report* (2011): 169, *British Archaeology*, Web, 2 April 2012. See also *British Archaeology* 123 (March/April 2012): 28–33.

13. See also Terrence W. Epperson, "'The Politics of 'Race' and Cultural Identity at the African Burial Ground Excavations, New York City," *World Archaeological Bulletin* 7 (1996): 108–17.

14. Mark E. Mack, M. Cassandra Hill, and Michael L. Blakey, "Preliminary Analysis Results of the New York African Burial Ground Skeletal Population," paper presented at the 94th Annual Meeting of the American Anthropological Association, Washington, DC, 1995. See also Warren R. Perry, Jean Howson, and Barbara A. Inco, eds., "Archaeology Report, Volume 1," in *The New York African Burial Ground Final Report*, prepared by Howard University, Washington, DC, for the United States General Services Administration, Northeastern and Caribbean Region, February 2006.

15. Saidiya Hartman, *Scenes of Subjection: Terror, Slavery, and Self-Making in Nineteenth-Century America* (New York: Oxford UP, 1997).

16. Ira Berlin and Leslie M. Harris, eds., *Slavery in New York* (New York: published in conjunction with the New-York Historical Society, 2005), 79, 85. See also Ira Berlin, *Many Thousands Gone: The First Two Centuries of Slavery in North America* (Cambridge: Belknap Press of Harvard UP, 1998); and Leslie M. Harris, *In the Shadow of Slavery: African Americans in New York City, 1626–1863* (Chicago: U of Chicago P, 2003).

17. Burial #101, Catalog #843, "New York African Burial Ground Archaeology," *GSA Final Report* (February 2006). The identification of the symbol on the man's coffin as a Sankofa was buttressed by Kwaku Ofori-Ansa, a scholar of African art, who concluded that the heart-shaped image was a Sankofa such as that which he associated with the Akan people of Ghana. See Kwaku Ofori-Ansa, "Identification and Validation of the Sankofa Symbol," *Update: Newsletter of the African Burial Ground and Five Points Archaeological Projects* 1.8 (Summer 1995): 3.

18. See Kofi Anyidoho and James Gibbs, eds, *FonTomFrom: Contemporary Ghanaian Literature, Theater and Film* (Rodopi, B.V. 2000), 5.

19. Erik R. Seeman, "Reassessing the 'Sankofa Symbol' in New York's African Burial Ground," *William and Mary Quarterly* 67.1 (January 2010): 101–22. Seeman writes that some historians "have too readily attributed cultural practices to African antecedents without convincing documentary or archaeological evidence, especially in the study of African American deathways" (102). He further attributes the "poorly substantiated claims about the African origins of African American deathways" to "scant material evidence to corroborate or contradict biased European observations," and "the incomplete state of historical archaeology in West and West-Central Africa" (102).

20. Seeman, "Reassessing the 'Sankofa Symbol' in New York's African Burial Ground," 108.

21. Seeman, "Reassessing the 'Sankofa Symbol' in New York's African Burial Ground," 122.

22. See Nancy J. Peterson, *Against Amnesia: Contemporary Women Writers and the Crises of Historical Memory* (Philadelphia: University of Pennsylvania P, 2001), 2.

23. Joyce Hansen and Gary McGowan, *Breaking Ground, Breaking Silence: The Story of New York's African Burial Ground* (New York: Henry Holt, 1998). Hansen and McGowan

write: "Many of the skeletal remains from the African Burial Ground show signs of deep trauma to the bone, such as lipping on the spine. This is a condition where the vertebrae of the spine start to grow additional bone along the edges and start to lip or curl, eventually causing severely painful arthritis" (77–78). See also Mark E. Mack, "Recent Research Findings concerning the African Burial Ground Population," *Newsletter of the African Burial Ground* 1.9 (1995): 3–4.

24. GSA Report quoted in *New York Amsterdam News* (7 October 2005–5 March 2006): 3.

25. Mack et al., "Preliminary Analysis Results," 8, 10.

26. Burials #335 and 336, Catalog #1616 and #1751, "New York African Burial Ground Archaeology," *GSA Final Report* (February 2006). See also Burial #25, Series I, Catalog #358, "New York African Burial Ground Archaeology," *GSA Final Report* (February 2006).

27. Burial #340, Catalog #1651, United States General Services Administration (GSA), "Draft Management Recommendations for the African Burial Ground," in *The New York African Burial Ground Final Reports, Archaeology, History, and Skeletal Biology*, Department of the Interior (Washington, DC, 2006). Nearly all of the burial ground decedents were buried with their heads tilted to the west, a practice associated with an African cosmology tradition that some scholars dispute. See endnote #23. All subsequent references made to a forensic analysis of the decedents at 290 Broadway are taken from this text, also known as *GSA Final Reports*, and cited by chapter and page number (when provided) in the manuscript.

28. In a eulogy for Sara Baartman, then-president Thabo Mbeki cited past atrocities committed against her, and he vowed to prevent a return of similar incidents in the future: "The changing times tell us that she did not suffer and die in vain. Our presence at her grave site demands that we act to ensure that what happened should never be repeated." See Andreas Huyssen, "Escape from Amnesia: The Museum as Mass Medium," in *Twilight Memories: Marking Time in a Culture of Amnesia* (New York: Routledge, 1995), 6.

29. See Rodney Leon, AARRIS Architects, "Memorial," *The African Burial Ground*, in *U.S. General Services Final Report*, http://www.africanburialground.gov/memorial/ABG_Memo rialDesign_RodneyLeon.htm, Web, 8 July 2010.

30. See Paul Connerton, *How Societies Remember* (Cambridge: Cambridge UP, 1989), 35, quoted in Barbie Zelizer, "Reading against the Grain: The Shape of Memory Studies," *Critical Studies in Mass Communication* 12 (1995): 219.

31. Leon, "Memorial."

32. Chapter 3, "GSA and NPS Civic Engagement," *GSA Final Report*, 22.

Chapter 3. Founding Fathers, Chimeras, and "American Africanisms" at Presidential Estates

1. Barnum, who acknowledged that his sorrow over Heth's death stemmed from loss of revenue from her exhibition, arranged for a noted anatomist to perform an autopsy.

2. "Dissection of Joice Heth—Precious Humbug Exposed," *New York Sun* 26 February 1836, quoted in Benjamin Reiss, *The Showman and the Slave: Race, Death, and Memory in Barnum's America* (Cambridge: Harvard UP), 1001.

3. Reiss, *Showman and the Slave*, 1001. See also Benjamin Reiss, "P. T. Barnum, Joice Heth and Antebellum Spectacles of Race," *American Quarterly* 51.1 (March 1999). See Bluford Adams, *E Pluribus Barnum: The Great Showman and the Making of U.S. Popular Culture* (U of Minnesota P, 1997). Eric Lott aptly historicizes the minstrelsy tradition in *Love and Theft: Black Face Minstrelsy and the American Working Class* (New York: Oxford UP, 1993).

4. Reiss, *Showman and the Slave*, 46.

5. William Morris, ed., *The American Heritage Dictionary of the English Language*, (Boston: Houghton Mifflin, 1969), 234. See also Aaron T. Norton and Ozzie Zehner, "Which Half Is Mommy? Tetragametric Chimerism and Trans-Subjectivity," *Women's Studies Quarterly* 36, no. 3&4 (Fall/Winter 2008): 106–25.

6. See Mary Wollstonecraft Shelley, *Frankenstein, Or the Modern Prometheus*, 1818, 2nd ed., ed. D. L. Macdonald and Kathleen Scherf (Petersborough: Broadview Literary Texts, 1999), 76.

7. Shelley, *Frankenstein, Or the Modern Prometheus*, 95.

8. Rachel L. Sharns, *American Tapestry: The Story of the Black, White and Multiracial Ancestors of Michelle Obama* (New York: Amistad, 2012).

9. Toni Morrison, *Beloved*, 1st ed. (New York: Knopf, 1987), 143–44. Edward Ball, who broaches the subject of "slaves in the family" in a 1998 book by the same title, is among the first to write publicly about the ironic implications of miscegenation in the present day. Ball places the issue front and center from the perspective of a descendant of wealthy slave owners from South Carolina, and he chastises an enslaving society that flouted the unsavoriness of race mixing by banning the practice while still mixing up the races through miscegenation.

10. See Henry Wiencek, *An Imperfect God: George Washington, His Slaves, and the Creation of America* (New York: Farrar, Straus and Giroux, 2003). See also Linda Bryant, *I Cannot Tell a Lie: The True Story of George Washington's African American Descendants* (np: University Star, 2004).

11. See Frederick Douglass, "Expression of Gratitude for Freedom," in *Building the Myth: Selected Speeches Memorializing Abraham Lincoln*, ed. Waldo W. Braden (Urbana: U of Illinois P, 1990), 95.

12. See William Seale, *The President's House: A History*, 2 vols., 2nd ed. (Baltimore: Johns Hopkins University Press, 2008); Robert J. Kapsch, "Building Liberty's Capital," *American Visions* (February/March 1995): 8–10; press release, 29 December 2000, "National Archives to Display Pay Stubs of Slaves Used to Build U.S. Capitol and White House," Washington, DC; William Reed, "Slaves Helped Build White House and Capitol," *Final Call* 13 August 2002, Web.

13. Jennifer Eichstedt and Stephen Small, *Representations of Slavery: Race and Ideology in Southern Plantation Museums* (Washington, DC: Smithsonian Institution Press, 2002). Eichstedt and Small focus on the plantation slavery and the absence of any acknowledgment or discussion of slavery and enslaved African Americans. Furthermore, they write that docents commonly referred to "slaves" and "slavery" euphemistically, as "servants" and "servitude" respectively (107).

14. See *All American History TV*, *C-Span 3*. Broadcast 25 July 2010.

15. The Mount Vernon Ladies Association of the Union, *George Washington's Mount Vernon: Official Guidebook* (Mount Vernon, Virginia). For information about Washington's enslaved laborers, see the following works: Peter R. Henriques, "The Slaves of Mount Vernon," public lecture, Gadsby's Tavern Museum, Alexandria, Virginia, Gretchen Bulova, director, *American History TV on C-Span 3* 16 February 2011. See also Evelyn B. Gerson, "A Thirst for Complete Freedom: Why Fugitive Slave Ona Judge Staines Never Returned to Her Master, President George Washington," master's thesis, Extension Studies, Harvard University, June 2000.

Henry Wiencek, *An Imperfect God: George Washington, His Slaves, and the Creation of America* (New York: Farrar, Straus and Giroux, 2003), 311–34. Ironically, those slaves highly favored by the Washingtons and deemed most valuable were among those most likely to escape and to rebel against their plight.

16. See "Louisiana, Land of Perpetual Romance," *National Geographic Magazine* 57.4 (April 1930): 393–482. See also Danelli Faccone, "The Good Darky Is Gone," *Natchitoches Times* 26 September 1968, Web.

17. Ann Spencer's poem "The Sevignes" is reprinted in J. Lee Greene, *Time's Unfading Garden: Ann Spencer's Life* (Baton Rouge: Louisiana State UP, 1977), 191. See also Greene's commentary on the poem, 135–38.

18. Spencer, "Sevignes," 191.

19. Judith Saunders-Burton, "Slave Memorial at Mount Vernon: Faith, Hope, and Love," in *History in Motion*, Spring 1996 edition. Gum Springs Historical Society, 1997. See also Melissa Wood, "Mount Vernon Presents Special Activities in Honor of Black History Month," press release, 20 December 2005, Mount Vernon Ladies' Association, 2008.

20. Eichstedt and Small, *Representations of Slavery: Race and Ideology in Southern Plantation Museums.* When Jennifer Eichstedt and Stephen Small's team of researchers toured Mount Vernon, they reported being taken by the docent to buildings that guides identified as slave quarters. The reconstructed brick building that they entered was a barracks that probably housed slave laborers and multiple or extended slave families. The docent for the researchers described the building as among the most "architecturally complete" and "superior" of slave quarters, because it was made of brick and contained windows (19).

21. Chuck Hagee, "Slave Cabin Dedicated at Mount Vernon," *Mount Vernon Gazette* 26 September 2007.

22. Hagee, "Slave Cabin Dedicated at Mount Vernon." See also Laura Bly, *USA Today* 23 May 2008.

23. Barbie Zelizer, quoting D. Lowenthal, *The Past Is a Foreign Country* (Cambridge: Cambridge UP, 1985), 307.

24. See Bryant, *I Cannot Tell a Lie*; Wiencek, *Imperfect God*.

25. See Mary V. Thompson, "And Procure for Themselves a Few Amenities: The Private Life of George Washington's Slaves," *Virginia Cavalcade* 48.4 (Autumn 1999): 183. See also Wiencek, *Imperfect God*, 112–31; and Bryant, *I Cannot Tell a Lie*.

26. Michel-Rolph Trouillot, *Silencing the Past: Power and the Production of History* (Boston: Beacon Press, 1995).

27. When I raised questions that alerted a tour guide to my interest in researching slavery at Mount Vernon during a visit there in August 2011, he suddenly shifted discussion

from the physical layout of the estate to Washington's relationship with his slaves, including the president's efforts to circumvent laws that permitted slaves to obtain freedom while in Philadelphia. Rebecca Yamin, *Digging in the City of Brotherly Love: Stories from Philadelphia Archaeology* (New Haven: Yale UP, 2008). See also Stephan Salisbury, "Funeral Ceremony Celebrates the Legacy of Washington's Slaves," *Inquirer* 4 July 2007, *Philly.com*, Web, 13 December 2013. Salisbury writes that in the summer of 2002, a US House of Representatives Appropriation Committee authorized the National Park Services "'to appropriately commemorate" the slaves and the President's House in which they lived (page 2 of 4). See Edward Rothstein, "Reopening a House That's Still Divided," *New York Times*, Art & Design, Museum Review, 14 December 2010, Web, 8 December 2013.

28. *The Papers of George Washington*, W. W. Abbots, Dorothy Twohig, Philander D. Chase, et al., eds. Retirement Series 4 (Charlottesville: UP of Virginia, 1980–), 4:479. Quoted in Wiencek, *Imperfect God*, 4. See also *George Washington's Mount Vernon: Official Guidebook*.

29. Wiencek, *Imperfect God*, 73–74.

30. See Farah Stockman, "Monticello Is Done Avoiding Jefferson's Relationship with Sally Hemings," *New York Times* 26 June 2018.

31. See Maria Franklin, *Black Feminist Archaeology* (Walnut Creek, California: Left Coast Press, 2011). Archaeologist Maria Franklin's excavations around Williamsburg reveal that slaves and enslavers alike ate all portions of the hog until class-conscious planters, seeking to emulate the British, hierarchized food choices, thereby designating certain parts of the hog for slaves and members of the lower class.

See also Whitney Lutricia Battle, "A Yard to Sweep: Race, Gender, and the Enslaved Landscape," Ph.D. thesis, Austin, University of Texas, 2004.

32. Catherine Kerrison, *Jefferson's Daughters: Three Sisters, White and Black, in a Young America* (New York: Ballantine Books, 2018).

33. See Melville Herskovits, *The Myth of the Negro Past* (Boston: Beacon Press, reprint ed., 1990; originally published 1941). Herskovits wrote that slavery in the US did not erase blacks' knowledge of cultural practices rooted in the African past. Edward Franklin Frazier, *The Negro Family in the United States* (Notre Dame, Indiana: University of Notre Dame Press, reprint ed., 1939), argued that for slaves in America, horrific slavery traumas resulted in a loss of West African cultural survival forms.

34. Rick Bragg, "Tour Guides at Monticello Field New Questions about Jefferson," *New York Times* 6 November 1998.

35. William Kelso, *Archaeology at Monticello*, 1st ed. (Charlottesville: U of Virginia P, 2002), 68.

36. "Thomas Jefferson's Home Unveils Rebuilt Slave Quarters to Tell Fuller Tale of Past," *Guardian* 2 May 2015, 1–2, Web, 20 August 2016.

37. DNA tests determined that Jefferson likely fathered at least one child by Sally Hemings. When combined with additional compelling circumstantial evidence, the likelihood is that he fathered all of Hemings's children. Yet perhaps few know of similar claims in oral culture that both George Washington and Andrew Jackson may also have fathered children by enslaved black women.

38. Edward Rothstein, "Life, Liberty and the Fact of Slavery," *New York Times* 25 January 2012, Web, 29 January 2012.

39. *Monticello Newsletter* 12.2 (Winter 2001).

40. Pat Cummins, "A Story of Native American Graves & The Graves of Slaves," the Hermitage Springs Site—Nashville, Tennessee, from an article originally published on *Native-Nashville.com* in February 2012: 1–6, *Native History Association*, Web, 7 September 2013.

41. Cummins, "Story of Native American Graves & the Graves of Slaves," 2.

42. Cummins, "Story of Native American Graves & the Graves of Slaves," 4.

43. See "The Hermitage Selects Union's Benson to Sculpt Slave Memorial," *Union University News*, http://www.uu.edu/news/release.cfm?ID=1491, Web, 14 June 2010.

44. Brian W. Thomas, "Power and Community: The Archaeology of Slavery at the Hermitage Plantation," *American Antiquity* 63.4 (October 1998): 547.

45. "Articulations," Weekly Chat from "About Archaeology," moderated by Pat Garrow and K. Kris Hirst, transcript, 22 April 2001, speaker Larry McKee. *About.com Archaeology*. http://archaeology.about.com/library/chat/n_mckee.htm, Web, 28 June 2010.

46. See Thomas, "Power and Community," 531–51. Thomas writes that artifacts such as a disproportionate number of surviving "good luck" blue beads, pendants, etc. point to community cohesion in religious and/or cultural practices preservation that were independent of the planters' control. He also writes that foodstuffs, such as domestic and wild game, pork torso as opposed to extremities, did not favor a hierarchical or class structure that was based on domestic slaves and field slaves.

47. See Nicholas Wade, "Descendants of Slave's Son Contend That His Father Was George Washington," *New York Times* 7 July 1999; Papers of GW, Confederation Series, vol. 3, John Augustine Washington to GW, 17 July 1785, Papers of GW, Confederation series, vol. 2, John Augustine Washington to GW, July 1784, cited in Wiencek, *Imperfect God*, 304–5.

48. Solomon Northup, *Twelve Years a Slave*, Henry Louis Gates Jr., ed. (New York: Penguin Books, 2012; first published in the US by Derby and Miller, 1853), 128. See Kathleen Deagan, "Rethinking Modern History," *Archaeology* 51.5 (September/October 1998): np. Deagan describes this idea as a first-time "two-sided version of cultural contact, plantation economy, and slavery" that revises certain previous assumptions about the institution. This could also refer to a slave economy and culture supported through items that slave families secreted in subfloor pits and other private spaces. www.archaeolgy.org/9809/abstracts/deagan.html.

Chapter 4. The "Neo Middle Passenger" and the Traveling Slave Ship Exhibition

1. In 1781 slave ship merchant Luke Collingwood ordered crew members to throw 133 enslaved Africans overboard from an eighteenth-century rigger known as the *Zong* so that the ship's owners could file an insurance claim for their commercial value. Because many of the slaves had fallen ill, Collingwood calculated that recovering their value in insurance would greatly exceed the price in the marketplace. He reasoned that if the remaining sick slaves were thrown overboard while still alive, based on the assumption that their illness would threaten healthy slaves, then insurers would be required by law to compensate the slave ship investors for their loss of profit. In the subsequent case known

as *Gregson versus Gilbert* (1783), the court ordered insurance underwriters to pay £30 per slave to the ship's owners.

2. For accounts of the *Zong* replica's exhibition, see "Slave Ship Comes to London," *Ethnicnow online*, 29 March 2007, www.royalnavy.mod.uk.

3. See "Visiting *Amistad* Slave Ship," *Jet Magazine* 113.14 (14 April 2008): 37.

4. Shoshana Felman and Dori Laub, *Testimony: Crises of Witnessing in Literature, Psychoanalysis, and History* (New York: Routledge, 1992); cited in Nancy J. Peterson, *Against Amnesia: Contemporary Women Writers and the Crises of Historical Memory* (Philadelphia: U of Pennsylvania P, 2001), 7. In solidarity with Felman and Laub's ideas about literature bearing witness to history, Peterson adds that literature permits "the narrative flexibility and the willing suspension of disbelief" that essentially functions as history (7). But I do not agree with Dean Franco, who suggests too narrowly that Petersen and others would endow the novelist with the power to heal the wounds of history. See Dean Franco, "What We Talk about When We Talk about *Beloved*," *Modern Fiction Studies* 52.2 (2006): 418.

5. Anita Rupprecht, "'A Limited Sort of Property': History, Memory and the Slave Ship *Zong*," in *Slavery and Abolition* 29.2 (2008): 266. I am inspired by—and indebted to—Rupprecht for her observations about contrasts in the *Zong* exhibition that marked the end of Atlantic slavery while still contending with its lingering effects in the present day. See also Franco, "What We Talk about When We Talk about *Beloved*," 428.

6. See Maurice Halbwachs, "The Social Frameworks of Memory," in *On Collective Memory*, ed. and trans. Lewis A. Coser (Chicago: U of Chicago P, 1992). He writes, "Since social memory erodes at the edges as individual members, especially older ones, become isolated or die, it is constantly transformed among the group itself" (82).

7. See Barry Unsworth, *Sacred Hunger* (New York: W. W. Norton, reprint ed., 1993); and Marcus Rediker, *The Slave Ship: A Human History* (New York: Penguin Books, reprint ed., 2008), who discuss how the Middle Passage obscures slavery horrors, as well as the slave's humanity, through such abstractions as slave ship ledgers and other data. Formerly enslaved African Olaudah Equiano, in his 1789 autobiography, *Interesting Narrative of Olaudah Equiano, or Gustavus Vassa, the African*, referred to the slave ship as a huge hollow vessel filled with cannibals, upon his first encounter with it in West Africa.

8. See "Services of Reconciliation and Commitment," *Free at Last: The History and Legacy of the European Slave Trade*, http://www.free-at-last.org/1kit/Events/ServiesofReconciliationCommitment/tabid/3801/language/en-GB/Default.aspx, Web, 2 September 2011. A gallery of photographs of the *Zong* exhibition in London is displayed at this site.

9. Quoted in an interview that Marika Preziuso conducted with Marlene Nourbese Philip, Marika Preziuso, "M. Nourbese Philip—*Zong!*" 2–3, http://latineos.com/en/articles/literature/item/46-m-nourbese-philip-zong.html.

10. Rupprecht, "'Limited Sort of Property,'" 266. See also Franco, "What We Talk about When We Talk about *Beloved*," 428.

11. Rupprecht, "Limited Sort of Property," 266.

12. See Katherine McKittrick, *Demonic Grounds: Black Women and the Cartographies of Struggle* (Minneapolis: U of Minnesota P, 2006). I am indebted to Katherine McKittrick for this concept. In reference to Paul Gilroy's *The Black Atlantic: Modernity and Double Consciousness* (Cambridge: Harvard UP, 1993), McKittrick concedes that if anchored with

material sites connected with slavery, Gilroy's work "clarifies that there are genealogical connections between dispossession, transparent space, and black subjectivities" (xxi). However,
as shown in chapter 2, I find the term "genealogical dispossession" useful when applied
not only to historical gaps and silences in archival records for slavery but also to ruptures,
breaks, and cold trails in the circuitry of the slave family's ancestral roots.

13. Ian Baucom, *Specters of the Atlantic: Finance Capital, Slavery, and the Philosophy of
History* (Durham: Duke UP, 2005), 293–94. See also Saidiya Hartman, "Venus in Two Acts,"
in *Small Axe* 12.2 (June 2008). Hartman addresses the impossibility of representing the
unknowable (as meta histories are wont to do) and chooses, instead, to perform "the limits
of writing history through the act of narration" (13).

14. Katherine McKittrick sees the Black Atlantic as transcending mere metaphors about
the slave ship and Middle Passage as sites of displacement by marking such physical geog-
raphies as the Atlantic Ocean in order to situate political struggles with experiences in the
lives of blacks in the present day (ix).

15. See the *Freedom Schooner Amistad* website at www.amistadamerica.org.

16. Bo Petersen, "Embodying the Soul of a Sailor," *Post and Courier* 13 May 2008, Web, 20
August 2011.

17. See Cheryl Finley, "Schematics of Memory," in *Small Axe* 15.2 (July 2011): 96–116.

18. See "Join the Voyage," *Freedom Schooner Amistad*, www.amistadamerica.org.

19. Sam Helfrich, "Getting into and out of History," *Amistad* opera playbill, 36.

20. Helfrich, "Getting into and out of History," 36.

21. Helfrich, "Getting into and out of History," 36.

22. For information about the *Freedom Schooner Amistad*'s visit to Cuba, I consulted
Elizabeth Ellis, "Historic Homecoming for *Amistad* Replica," *Soundings online*, posted
1 July 2010, http://www.soundingsonline.com/news/home-waters/100-long-island/260072
-historic-homecoming-for-amistad-replica. See also "*Amistad* Replica Visits Cuba to Commemorate Victims of Slavery," *Latin American Tribune*, http://www.laht.com/article.asp?Ca
tegoryId=14510&ArticleId=354426, Web, 5 August 2011; "*Amistad* Replica Visits Cuba," *Truth
Seekers News* 24 March 2010, http://truthseekersvideo.com/news/8086_amistad-replica
-visits-cuba.html, Web, 5 August 2011.

23. Will Weissert, Associated Press writer, "Cuban Slave Ship Amistad: U.S. Replica Sails
into Havana Harbor," 25 March 2010.

24. "Amistad Replica Visits Cuba."

25. George C. Wolfe, *The Colored Museum* (New York: Grove Press, 1985).

26. Winnie Hu, "Relics of Slavery, Up from the Ocean's Depths," New York Report, *New
York Times* 24 December 2001.

27. Michael Paul Williams, "Unshackling History: Revisiting Slavery's Middle Passage:
Should We Go There?" *Richmond Times-Dispatch* 10 August 1997, #222.

28. Williams, "Unshackling History."

29. Pierre Bourdieu, *The Field of Cultural Production* (New York: Columbia UP), 110.

30. Vamik Volkan, "Chosen Trauma: Unresolved Mourning," in *Bloodlines: From Ethnic
Pride to Ethnic Terrorism*, 37–49 (Boulder, Colorado: Westview Press, 1997), 48.

31. Mike Toner, "Relics from a Shameful Past," *Atlanta Journal-Constitution* 11 January
1998.

32. Andrea Ford, *Los Angeles Times* 11 August 1996.

33. Andrea Ford, "Slave Trade Ship Exhibition Stirs Waves of Emotion," *Los Angeles Times* 11 August 1996, sec. B.

34. Shannon Buggs, "Reminder of Past Horrors," *Raleigh News & Observer* 19 February 1997.

35. Interview with the author.

36. Ricardo Gandara, "Shedding Light on a Grim Era in History," *Austin American Statesman* 11 February 2006, B1, B4.

37. Gilroy, *Black Atlantic*, 4.

38. Paul Tiyambe Zeleza, "Rewriting the African Diaspora: Beyond the Black Atlantic," *African Affairs* 104.414 (2005): 37, cited in Laura Murphy, *Metaphors and the Slave Trade in West African Literature* (Athens: Ohio UP, 2012), 41. Zeleza sees *The Black Atlantic* as "a monument to America's self-referential conceit and myopia in its obsession with the cultural inventions of the African American diaspora," 37. See also Houston Baker, *The Journey Back* (Chicago: U of Chicago P, 1980); Joan Dyan, "Paul Gilroy's Slaves, Ships, and Routes: The Middle Passage as Metaphor," *Research in African Literatures* 27.4 (Winter 1996): 7–14.

39. Eric Gable makes this point in "Maintaining Boundaries, or 'Mainstreaming' Black History in a White Museum," in *The New History in an Old Museum: Creating the Past at Colonial Williamsburg*, ed. Richard Handler and Eric Gable (Durham: Duke UP, 1997). See also Tony Bennett, *The Birth of the Museum: History, Theory, Politics* (London: Routledge, 1965). For Bennett, the museum, curator, and spectator share relational components—and hence, claims to power—similar to literary text, author, and reader. Hence, an analysis of museum theory poses little difference than literary or other textual theory but for its cultural and/or aesthetic components.

40. George Fredrickson, "The Skeleton in the Closet," *New York Review of Books* 47.17 (2000): 61, quoted in Ron Eyerman, *Cultural Trauma: Slavery and the Formation of African American Identity* (Cambridge: Cambridge UP, 2001), 18.

41. Charisse Jones, "Bringing Slavery's Long Shadow to Light," *New York Times* 2 April 1995), late ed.

Chapter 5. The Bench by the Road Slave Memorial at Sullivan's Island

1. Toni Morrison, "A Bench by the Road," Unitarian Universalist Association *World Magazine* (January–February, 1989), 1, Web, 17 August 2016, http://www.uuworld.org/articles/a-bench-by-road. This article originally appeared in *World: Journal of the Unitarian Universalist Association* 3.1 (January–February 1989): 4–5, 37–41.

2. An estimated twelve million Africans were brought to the US as part of the Atlantic slave trade. In 1860 some 57 percent of South Carolina residents were enslaved blacks. Of the fifteen people who owned more than five hundred slaves, eight were South Carolinians. After the domestic slave trade was outlawed in the United States in 1808, some 250,000 Africans were shipped illegally.

3. See Stephen Greenblatt, "Resonance and Wonder," *Bulletin of the American Academy of Arts and Sciences* 43.4 (January 1990): 11–34.

4. William Morris, ed., *The American Heritage Dictionary of the English Language*, new college ed. (Boston: Houghton Mifflin, 1969), 75.

5. Andreas Huyssen, "Escape from Amnesia," *Marking Time in a Culture of Amnesia* (New York: Routledge, 1995), 21.

6. J. Lee Greene, *The Diasporan Self: Unbreaking the Circle in Western Black Novels* (Charlottesville: U of Virginia P, 2008), 58.

7. Lisa Woolfork, *Embodying American Slavery in Contemporary Culture* (Urbana: U of Illinois P, 2009), 173–74. Woolfork interprets Rex Ellis's experience in a reenactment of a slavery scene at Williamsburg, Virginia, as putting on the skin or living in the skin of an enslaved individual. See also Rex Ellis, "Re:living History: Bringing History into Play," in *American Visions* 7.6 (1992): 22–25.

8. Toni Morrison, "Bench by the Road."

9. Brian Hefferman, "Toni Morrison Bench Helps Hilton Head, Mitchelville Remember Its Past," 16 April 2013, Web, 13 August 2016.

10. Artist Juan Logan says that the "foundation of American Society was built upon the backs of slaves and sharecroppers." (The sculpture is permanently housed at the University of North Carolina at Chapel Hill, where Logan teaches studio art.) He entered his artwork at Charleston's Gibbes Museum in the summer of 2008 as part of a special exhibition titled *Landscape of Slavery: The Plantation in American Art*, which consisted entirely of paintings and artifacts about plantation slavery. See Angela D. Mack and Stephen G. Hoffius, eds., *Landscape of Slavery: The Plantation in American Art* (Columbia: U of South Carolina P, published in cooperation with the Gibbes Museum of Art, 2008).

11. See the official website of the Toni Morrison Society for a full accounting of the twenty Bench by the Road memorial placement sites, www.tonimorrisonsociety.org/bench .html.

12. *Toni Morrison Society* website.

13. Toni Morrison, "Bench by the Road," Toni Morrison Society, Paris, France, podcast streamer, November 2010.

14. Dottie Ashley, *Charleston, South Carolina, Post and Courier* 27 July 2008, 1B. See also Kyle Stock, "Selling Slavery," *Charleston, South Carolina, Post and Courier* 27 July 2008, 1A and 4A.

15. Stock, "Selling Slavery," 4A.

16. See Bruce Smith, "South Carolina Slave Cabins Housed Family through '60s," *Grio*, 03 June 2009, http://www.thegrio.com/news/south-carolina-slave-cabins-housed-family -through-60s.php, Web, 10 November 2011. See also "From Slavery to Freedom: The Magnolia Cabin Project," *Magnolia Plantation & Gardens*, http://www.magnoliaplantation.com/ slaverytofreedom.html, Web, 10 November 2011.

17. See John G. Beech, "The Marketing of Slavery Heritage in the United Kingdom," *International Journal of Hospitality and Tourism Administration* 2.3/4: 85–105. See also Graham M. H. Dann and A. V. Seaton, eds., *Slavery, Contested Heritage and Thanatourism* (Binghamton: Haworth Hospitality Press), 2002.

18. Huyssen, "Escape from Amnesia," 22.

19. Adi Gordon and Amos Goldberg, "An Interview with Professor James E. Young," English and Judaic Studies at the University of Massachusetts at Amherst, Shoah Resource

Center, the International School for Holocaust Studies, Yad Vashem, Jerusalem (24 May 1998), 5.

20. Felicia R. Lee, "Bench of Memory at Slavery's Gateway," *New York Times* 28 July, 2008, E1, https://www.nytimes.com/2008/07/28/arts/design/28/bench/html.

21. Lee, "Bench of Memory at Slavery's Gateway," 1.

22. See Maurice Halbwachs, "The Social Frameworks of Memory," in *On Collective Memory* (Chicago: U of Chicago P, 1992), 54, originally published 1951. James G. Gibbs and Karen Lee Davis, "History Exhibits and Theories of Material Culture," *Journal of American Culture*, 12.2 (Summer 1989): 27, Web, 7 June 2004. Gibbs and Davis note that "scholars primarily rely on archival data," such as written documents, while museum curators tend to "interpret the past with artifacts" (27).

23. Morrison, "Bench by the Road," 8.

24. Kristall Brent Zook, "Black Girl Wonder," *Essence Magazine* 46.5 (September 2015): 1–2, Web, 9 August 2016.

25. Zook, "Black Girl Wonder," 1.

26. See Rachel Kaadzi Ghansah's Pulitzer Prize–winning article, "A Most American Terrorist: The Making of Dylann Roof," *GQ: Gentleman's Quarterly Magazine*, 21 August 2017.

27. Lucy Perkins et al., "The Victims: 9 Were Slain at Charleston's Emanuel AME Church," *NPR* 18 June 2015, 1–4, Web, 9 October 2016.

28. See "Emanuel A.M.E. Church," *Charleston's Historic Religious & Community Buildings*, 3, *National Park Service*, www.nps.gov./nr/travel/Charleston/ema.htm, Web, 12 August 2016.

29. Christina Elmore, "Thousands Witness the End of an Era as Confederate Flag Comes Down in South Carolina," *Charleston, South Carolina, Post and Courier* 10 July 2015, 2, Web, 10 August 2016.

30. Stephanie McCrummen and Elahe Izadi, "Confederate Flag Comes Down on South Carolina's Statehouse Grounds," *Washington Post* 10 July 2015, 1, Web.

31. Jessica Taylor, "The Complicated Political History of the Confederate Flag," 22 June 2015, NPR webarchive.

32. *Today*, quoted by Stephanie McCrummen and Elahe Izadi in "Confederate Flag Comes Down on South Carolina's Statehouse Grounds," *Washington Post* 10 July 2015, 3, Web.

33. Mark Berman, "'I Forgive You.' Relatives of Charleston Church Shooting Victims Address Dylann Roof," *Washington Post* 19 June 2015, Web, 9 October 16.

34. *Today*, quoted by McCrummen and Izadi in "Confederate Flag Comes Down," 1.

35. See Hannah Alani, "It's Official: Charleston Apologizes for Its Role in Slavery," *Charleston, South Carolina, Post and Courier* 19 June 2018, updated 21 June 2018.

Epilogue: Opening the Smithsonian National Museum of African American History and Culture

1. President Barack Obama, keynote address, the National African American Museum of History and Culture, 24 September 2016.

2. Eric Foner, interview with Vinson Cunningham several months before the museum's opening, quoted in *New Yorker* 11 March 2015, 10.

3. Foner, interview with Vinson Cunningham, 9.

4. Vinson Cunningham, "Making a Home for Black History," *New Yorker* 2 August 2016, 1–13, Web, 8 October 2016. See also Amy Goodman, interview with Eric Foner, "Civil War Historian Eric Foner on the Radical Possibilities of Reconstruction," 11 March 2015, *Democracy Now*, Web, 8 October 16.

5. Foner, *New Yorker*, 9.

6. Speculation for the failure of the proposed museum at Fredericksburg has ranged from its close proximity to the Smithsonian's more substantially funded National Museum of African American History and Culture to opposition to and/or lack of interest in a museum wholly devoted to slavery. Museum director Douglas Wilder has not commented publicly on the museum's difficulties. Nonpayment of real estate taxes to the City of Fredericksburg and other fees by museum organizers led to the setting of a public auction for October 31, 2013, according to the *Washington Post*. "Fredericksburg Site of Proposed US Slavery Museum Heads to Auction Oct. 31," *Washington Post* 11 October 2013, local ed.: 1–4, Web, 14 October 2014. See also Susan Svrluga, "Former Va. Gov. L. Douglas Wilder's Slavery Museum Project Stalled in Fredericksburg," *Washington Post* 18 September 2010, 1–4, Web, 7 March 2013.

7. Lonnie G. Bunch III, "Race, Memory, and the Museum," lecture, the Bob Bullock Museum at Austin, Texas (22 February 2006); Lonnie Bunch, keynote address, "The Challenge of Interpreting Slavery in American Museums," Slavery & Public History: An International Symposium, the Gilder Lehrman Center's Eighth Annual International Conference, Yale University (3 November 2006).

8. See Edward T. Linenthal, *Preserving Memory: The Struggle to Create America's Holocaust Museum* (New York: Viking, 1995), 68.

9. See Patricia Pierce Erikson, "Decolonizing the 'Nation's Attic': The National Museum of the American Indian and the Politics of Knowledge-Making in a National Space," in *The National Museum of the American Indian: Critical Conversations*, ed. Amy Lonetree and Amanda J. Cobb (Lincoln: U of Nebraska P, 2008), 77.

10. Bunch, "Race, Memory, and the Museum."

11. Pierre Nora, "Between Memory and History: Les Lieux de Mémoire," trans. Mark Roudebus, *Representations* 26 (Spring 1989): 7.

12. See Kate Taylor, "The Thorny Path to a National Black Museum," *New York Times* 23 January 2011: 1–9, Web, 10 March 2013.

13. Bunch, "Race, Memory, and the Museum."

SELECTED BIBLIOGRAPHY

The African Burial Ground [video recording]: An American Discovery. Executive producer, J. Peter Glaws. Producer/director/editor, David Kutz. Associate producer/writer, Christopher More. Photography, John Hanlon and Ronald Gray. Kutz Television, Inc. for United States General Services Administration. Springfield, VA: National Audiovisual Center [distributor], 1994.

Apel, Dora. *Memory Effects: The Holocaust and the Art of Secondary Witnessing.* New Brunswick: Rutgers UP, 2002.

Appadurai, Arjun, ed. *The Social Life of Things: Commodities in Cultural Perspective.* Cambridge: Cambridge UP, 1986.

Battle, Whitney Lutricia. "A Yard to Sweep: Race, Gender, and the Enslaved Landscape." Dissertation. Austin: U of Texas Libraries, 2004.

Beaulieu, Elizabeth Ann. *Black Women Writers and the American Neo-Slave Narrative: Femininity Unfettered.* Westport: Greenwood Press, 1999.

Ben-Abdallah, Mohammed. *"The Slaves" in The Fall of Kumbi and Other Plays.* Accra: Woeli, 1989.

Benjamin, Walter. "Theses on the Philosophy of History." *Illuminations.* Ed. Hannah Arendt. Trans. Harry Zohn. New York: Schocken Books, 1968: 253–65.

Bennett, Tony. *The Birth of the Museum: History, Theory, Politics.* London: Routledge, 1995.

Berlin, Ira, and Leslie M. Harris, Eds. *Slavery in New York.* New York: New Press and the New-York Historical Society, 2005.

Bernier, Celeste-Marie, and Judie Newman. "Public Art, Artefacts and Atlantic Slavery: Introduction." *Slavery and Abolition.* 29.2 (June 2008): 135–50.

Blackmon, Douglas A. *Slavery by Another Name: The Re-enslavement of Black People in America from the Civil War to World War II.* New York: Doubleday, 2008.

Bourdieu, Pierre. *The Field of Cultural Production.* New York: Columbia UP, 1993.

Cantwell, Anne-Marie E. *Unearthing Gotham: The Archaeology of New York City.* New Haven: Yale UP, 2001.

Captive Passage: The Transatlantic Slave Trade and the Making of the Americas. Washington, D.C.: Smithsonian Institution Press, 2002.

Carroll, Orville W. *Historic American Buildings Survey.* Washington: Library of Congress, 1960: VA-605.

Caruth, Cathy, ed. *Trauma: Exploration in Memory.* Baltimore: Johns Hopkins UP, 1995.

Christensen, Matthew J. *Rebellious Histories: The Amistad Slave Revolt and the Cultures of Late Twentieth-Century Black Transnationalism.* Albany: State U of New York P, 2012.

Coates, Ta-Nehisi. "The Case for Reparations." *Atlantic* (June 2014): 54–71.

Connerton, Paul. *How Societies Remember*. Cambridge: Cambridge UP, 1989.

Derrida, Jacques. *Archive Fever: A Freudian Impression*. Trans. Eric Prenowitz. Chicago: U of Chicago P, 1995.

Eckstein, Lars. *Re-Membering the Black Atlantic: On the Poetics and Politics of Literary Memory*. Amsterdam: Rodopi, 2006.

Eichstedt, Jennifer L., and Stephen Small. *Representations of Slavery: Race and Ideology in Southern Plantation Museums*. Washington: Smithsonian Institution Press, 2002.

Ellison, Ralph. *Invisible Man*. New York: Random House, 1952.

Eyerman, Ron. *Cultural Trauma: Slavery and the Formation of African American Identity*. Cambridge: Cambridge UP, 2001.

Felman, Shoshana. *Testimony: Crises of Witnessing in Literature, Psychoanalysis, and History*. New York: Routledge, 1992.

Fretwell, Jacqueline K. *Kingsley Beatty Gibbs and His Journal of 1840–1843*. St. Augustine: St. Augustine Historical Society, 1984. General Services Administration.

George Washington's Mount Vernon: Official Guidebook. The Mount Vernon Ladies Association of the Union. Mount Vernon, Virginia, nd. www.mountvernon.org.

Ghansah, Rachel Kaadzi. "A Most American Terrorist: The Making of Dylann Roof. *GQ Gentleman's Quarterly Magazine* 21 August 2017.

Gilroy, Paul. *Against Race: Imagining Political Culture beyond the Color Line*. Cambridge: Harvard UP, 2000.

Gilroy, Paul. *The Black Atlantic: Modernity and Double Consciousness*. Cambridge: Harvard UP, 1993.

Gordon, Adi, and Amos Goldberg. "An Interview with Professor James E. Young." English and Judaic Studies at the University of Massachusetts at Amherst, Yad Vashem, Jerusalem (24 May 1998). Shoah Resource Center, International School for Holocaust Studies.

Gordon-Reed, Annette. *The Hemingses of Monticello*. New York: W. W. Norton, 2008.

Greenblatt, Stephen. *Marvelous Possessions: The Wonder of the New World*. Chicago: U of Chicago P, 1991.

Greene, J. Lee. *The Diasporan Self: Unbreaking the Circle in Western Black Novels*. Charlottesville: U of Virginia P, 2008.

Greene, J. Lee. *Time's Unfading Garden: Anne Spencer's Life and Poetry*. Baton Rouge: Louisiana State UP, 1977.

Grimes, William. *Life of William Grimes, the Runaway Slave*. New York: W. Grimes, 1825.

Halbwachs, Maurice. *The Collective Memory*. Trans. Francis J. Ditter Jr. and Yazdi Ditter. New York: Harper and Row.

Halbwachs, Maurice. "The Social Frameworks of Memory." *On Collective Memory*. Ed. and trans. Lewis A. Coser. Chicago: U of Chicago P, 1992.

Halloran, Vivian Nun. *Exhibiting Slavery: The Caribbean Postmodern Novel as Museum*. Charlottesville: U of Virginia P, 2009.

Handler, Jerome S. "An African-Type Healer/Diviner and His Grave Goods: A Burial from a Plantation Slave Cemetery in Barbados, West Indies." *International Journal of Historical Archaeology* 1.2 (1997): 91–130.

Handler, Jerome S., and Eric Gable. *The New History in an Old Museum: Creating the Past at Colonial Williamsburg*. Durham: Duke UP, 1997.

Handler, Jerome S., and Frederick W. Lange. *Plantation Slavery in Barbados: An Archaeological and Historical Investigation*. Cambridge: Harvard UP, 1978.

Hansen, Joyce, and Gary McGowan. *Breaking Ground, Breaking Silence: The Story of New York's African Burial Ground*. New York: Henry Holt, 1998.

Hartman, Saidiya. *Lose Your Mother: A Journey along the Atlantic Slave Route*. New York: Farrar, Straus and Giroux, 2007.

Hartman, Saidiya. *Scenes of Subjection: Terror, Slavery, and Self-Making in Nineteenth-Century America*. New York: Oxford UP, 1997.

Hartman, Saidiya. "Venus in Two Acts," *Small Axe*, Number 26, 12.2 (June, 2008): 1–14.

Hirsch, Marianne, and Nancy K. Miller, eds. *Rites of Return: Diaspora Poetics and the Politics of Memory*. New York: Columbia U Press, 2011.

Hobsbawm, Eric, and Terence Ranger, eds. *The Invention of Tradition*. Cambridge: Cambridge UP, 1983.

Hoelscher, Steven. "Making Place, Making Race: Performances of Whiteness in the Jim Crow South." *Annals of the Association of American Geographers*. 93.3 (2003): 657–86.

Holsey, Bayo. *Routes of Remembrance: Refashioning the Slave Trade in Ghana*. Chicago: U of Chicago P, 2008.

Howard, Peter, Ian Thompson, and Emma Waterton, eds. *The Routledge Companion to Landscape Studies*. London, New York: Routledge, 2013.

Hutcheon, Linda, and Michael Hutcheon. *Opera: The Art of Dying*. Cambridge: Harvard UP, 2004.

Hutchisson, James. "Race, Identity, & Art." *Charleston* 22.6 (May 2008): 177–189.

Hutton, Patrick H. *History as an Art of Memory*. Hanover and London: U of Vermont P, 1993.

Hutton, Patrick H. "Recent Scholarship on Memory and History." *History Teacher* 33.4 (August 2000): 533–48.

Huyssen, Andreas. *Twilight Memories: Marking Time in a Culture of Amnesia*. New York: Routledge, 1995.

Johnson, Richard, et al., eds. *Making Histories: Studies in History, Writing, and Politics*. London: Centre for Contemporary Cultural Studies, U of Birmingham, 1982.

Kroger, Larry. *Black Slaveowners: Free Black Slave Masters in South Carolina, 1790–1860*. Columbia: U of South Carolina P, 1985.

LaCapra, Dominick. *Writing History, Writing Trauma*. Baltimore: Johns Hopkins UP, 2001.

Landsberg, Alison. *Prosthetic Memory: The Transformation of American Remembrance in the Age of Mass Culture*. New York: Columbia UP, 2004.

Linenthal, Edward. *Preserving Memory: The Struggle to Create America's Holocaust Museum*. New York: Viking Penguin, 1995.

Lipsitz, George. *Time Passages: Collective Memory and American Popular Culture*. Minneapolis: U of Minnesota P, 1990.

Littler, Dawn, ed. *Guide to the Records of Merseyside Maritime Museum*. Volume II. St. Johns: International Maritime Economic History Association, 1999.

Lonetree, Amy, and Amanda J. Cobb. *The National Museum of the American Indian: Critical Conversations*. Lincoln: U of Nebraska P, 2008.

MacDonald, Sharon, and Gordon Fyfe, eds. *Theorizing Museums*. Oxford: Blackwell, 1996.

Mack, Angela D., and Stephen G. Hoffius, eds. *Landscape of Slavery: The Plantation in American Art*. Columbia: U of South Carolina P, 2008.

Malkin, Jeanette R. *Memory-Theater and Postmodern Drama*. Ann Arbor: U of Michigan P, 1999.

McKittrick, Katherine. *Demonic Grounds: Black Women and the Cartographies of Struggle*. Minneapolis: U of Minnesota P, 2006.

Meacham, Jon. *American Lion: Andrew Jackson in the White House*. New York: Random House, 2008.

Michaels, Walter Benn. "'You Who Never Was There': Slavery and the New Historicism, Deconstruction and the Holocaust." *Narrative* 4.1 (January 1996): 1–16.

Morrison, Toni. *Playing in the Dark: Whiteness and the Literary Imagination*. New York: Vintage Books, 1990.

Murphy, Laura T. *Metaphor and the Slave Trade in West African Literature*. Athens: Ohio UP, 2012.

Napier, Winston, Ed. *African American Literary Theory: A Reader*. New York: New York UP, 2000.

Nora, Pierre. "Between Memory and History: Les Lieux de Mémoire." Trans. Mark Roudebus. *Representations* 26 (Spring 1989): 1–18.

Northup, Solomon. *Twelve Years a Slave*. Ed. Henry Louis Gates Jr. First published in the United States by Derby and Miller in 1853 (New York: Penguin Books, 2012).

Osman, Jena. *The Network*. New York: Fence Books, 2011.

Parks, Suzan-Lori. "*The America Play*" *and Other Works*. New York: Theatre Communications Group, 1995.

Parks, Suzan-Lori. "Possession." "*The America Play*" *and Other Works*. New York: Theatre Communications Group, 1995.

Patterson, Orlando. *Rituals of Blood: Consequences of Slavery in Two American Centuries*. New York: Basic Civitas Books, 1998.

Perry, Warren R., Jean Howson, and Barbara A. Bianco, eds. *New York African Burial Ground: Archaeology Final Report*, Volume I. Washington, DC: Howard University, 2006.

Peterson, Nancy J. *Against Amnesia: Contemporary Women Writers and the Crises of Historical Memory*. Philadelphia: U of Pennsylvania P, 2001.

Philip, Marlene Nourbese. *ZONG! As Told to the Author by Setaey Adamu Boateng*. Middletown: Wesleyan UP, 2008.

Pratt, Mary Louise. *Imperial Eyes: Travel Writing and Transculturation*. London: Routledge, 1992.

Price, David W. *History Made, History Imagined: Contemporary Literature, Poiesis, and the Past*. Urbana and Chicago: U of Illinois P, 1999.

Price, T. Douglas, Vera Tiesler, and James H. Burton. "Early African Diaspora in Colonial Campeche, Mexico: Strontium Isotopic Evidence." *American Journal of Physical Anthropology* 130 (2006): 485–90.

Radstone, Susannah, and Bill Schwarz, eds. *Memory: Histories, Theories, Debates.* New York: Fordham UP, 2010.

Redford, Dorothy Spruill, with Michael D'Orso. *Somerset Homecoming: Recovering a Lost Heritage.* Chapel Hill: U of North Carolina P, 1998.

Rediker, Marcus. *The Slave Ship: A Human History.* New York: Viking, 2007.

Reiss, Benjamin. *The Showman and the Slave.* Cambridge: Harvard UP, 2001.

Richards, Sandra L. "Notes from the Road: Cultural Tourism to Slave Sites." *BTNEWS* 9.2&3 (Winter/Spring 2002): 10–14.

Rushdy, Ashraf H. A. *Neo-slave Narratives: Studies in the Social Logic of a Literary Form.* New York: Oxford UP, 1999.

Ryan, Katy. "'No Less Human': Making History in Suzan-Lori Parks' *The America Play.*" *Journal of Dramatic Theory & Criticism.* 13.2 (1999): 81–94.

Sankofa. Haile Gerima. Negod-Gwad Productions; in co-production with the Ghana National Commission on Culture, Diproci of Burkina Faso, NDR/WDR Television, Mypheduh Films, 2003. Videorecording.

Schafer, Daniel L. *Anna Madgigine Jai Kingsley: African Princess, Florida Slave, Plantation Slaveowner.* Gainesville: UP of Florida, 2003.

Seeman, Erik R. *Death in the New World: Cross-Cultural Encounters, 1492–1800.* Philadelphia: U of Pennsylvania P, 2010.

Seeman, Erik R. "Reassessing the 'Sankofa Symbol' in New York's African Burial Ground." *William and Mary Quarterly* 67.1 (January 2010): 101–22.

Shelley, Mary. *Frankenstein.* The original 1818 text. 2nd ed. Ed. D. L. MacDonald and Kathleen Scherf. Ontario: Broadview, 1999.

A Slave Ship Speaks: The Wreck of the Henrietta Marie; A Docent Guide. Key West: Mel Fisher Maritime Heritage Society, 1995.

Smallwood, Stephanie E. *Saltwater Slavery: A Middle Passage from Africa to American Diaspora.* Cambridge: Harvard UP, 2007.

Solomon, Alisa. "Signifying on the Signifyin': The Plays of Suzan-Lori Parks." *Theater* 21.3 (1990): 73–80.

Stanton, Lucia. *"Those Who Labor for My Happiness": Slavery at Thomas Jefferson's Monticello.* Charlottesville: U of Virginia P, 2012.

Stowell, Daniel W., and Kathy Tilford. *Kingsley Plantation: A History of the Fort George Plantation.* Jacksonville: Eastern National, 1998.

Sturkin, Marita. *Tourists of History: Memory, Kitsch, and Consumerism from Oklahoma City to Ground Zero.* Durham: Duke UP, 2007.

Sturkin, Marita, and Lisa Cartwright. *Practices of Looking: An Introduction to Visual Culture.* 2nd ed. New York: Oxford University Press, 2009.

Swarns, Rachel L. *American Tapestry: The Story of the Black, White, and Multiracial Ancestors of Michelle Obama.* New York: Amistad, 2012.

Tillet, Salamishah. *Sites of Slavery: Citizenship and Racial Democracy in the Post–Civil Rights Imagination.* Durham: Duke UP, 2012.

US General Services Administration. *Draft Management Recommendations for the African Burial Ground.* National Park Service. Washington, DC, 2006.

Volkan, Vamik. "Chosen Trauma: Unresolved Mourning. *Bloodlines: From Ethnic Pride to Ethnic Terrorism*, 37–49 (Boulder, Colorado: Westview Press, 1997).

Wallace, Elizabeth Kowaleski. *The British Slave Trade & Public Memory*. New York: Columbia UP, 2006.

Walvin, James. *The Zong: A Massacre, the Law, & the End of Slavery*. New Haven: Yale UP, 2011.

Wideman, John Edgar. *The Cattle Killing*. Boston: Houghton Mifflin, 1996.

Wiencek, Henry. *An Imperfect God: George Washington, His Slaves, and the Creation of America*. New York: Farrar, Straus and Giroux, 2003.

Wiencek, Henry. *Master of the Mountain: Thomas Jefferson and His Slaves*. New York: Farrar, Straus and Giroux, 2012.

Wilkerson, Isabel. *The Warmth of Other Suns: The Epic Story of America's Great Migration*. New York: Vintage Books, 2010.

Wilkie, Laurie A. *Creating Freedom: Material Culture and African American Identity at Oakley Plantation, Louisiana, 1840–1950*. Baton Rouge: Louisiana State UP, 2000.

Wilson, August. *The Piano Lesson*. New York: Penguin, 1990.

Wolfe, George C. *The Colored Museum*. New York: Grove Press, 1985.

Wood, Marcus. "Atlantic Slavery and Traumatic Representation in Museums: The National Great Blacks in Wax Museum as a Test Case." *Slavery and Abolition* 29.2 (June 2008): 151–71.

Wood, Marcus. *Blind Memory: Visual Representations of Slavery in England and America, 1780–1865*. Manchester: Manchester UP, 2003.

Woodard, Helena. *African-British Writings in the Eighteenth Century: The Politics of Race and Reason*. Westport: Greenwood Press, 1999.

Woolfork, Lisa. *Embodying American Slavery in Contemporary Culture*. Urbana: U of Illinois P, 2009.

Yamin, Rebecca. *Digging in the City of Brotherly Love: Stories from Philadelphia Archaeology*. New Haven: Yale UP, 1998.

Zelizer, Barbie. "Reading against the Grain: The Shape of Memory Studies." *Critical Studies in Mass Communication* 12 (1995): 214–39.

INDEX

References to illustrations appear in **bold**.

ABOUT THE AUTHOR

Helena Woodard is associate professor of English at the University of Texas at Austin. She is author of *African-British Writings in the Eighteenth Century: The Politics of Race and Reason*. Her work has appeared in *Tennessee Studies in Literature* and *Margaret Garner: The Premiere Performances of Toni Morrison's Libretto* (ed. La Vinia Jennings).